China and North Africa

China and North Africa

Between Economics, Politics, and Security

Edited by
Adel Abdel Ghafar

I.B. TAURIS
LONDON • NEW YORK • OXFORD • NEW DELHI • SYDNEY

I.B. TAURIS
Bloomsbury Publishing Plc
50 Bedford Square, London, WC1B 3DP, UK
1385 Broadway, New York, NY 10018, USA
29 Earlsfort Terrace, Dublin 2, Ireland

BLOOMSBURY, I.B. TAURIS and the I.B. Tauris logo are trademarks
of Bloomsbury Publishing Plc

First published in Great Britain 2022
This paperback edition published 2023

Copyright © Adel Abdel Ghafar, 2022

Adel Abdl Ghafar and contributors have asserted their right under the Copyright, Designs and Patents Act, 1988, to be identified as Author of this work.

Copyright Individual Chapters © 2021 Adel Abdel Ghafar, Anna L. Jacobs, Nael Shama, Tarek Magresi, Sarah Yerkes, Yahia H. Zoubir, Anouar Boukhars

For legal purposes the Acknowledgements on p. viii constitute
an extension of this copyright page.

Series design by Adriana Brioso
Cover image: Chinese President Xi Jinping with Egyptian President Abdel-Fattah
El-Sisi, Cairo, Egypt, 2016. (© Pool Photo/Alamy Stock Photo)

All rights reserved. No part of this publication may be reproduced or transmitted in any form or by any means, electronic or mechanical, including photocopying, recording, or any information storage or retrieval system, without prior permission in writing from the publishers.

Bloomsbury Publishing Plc does not have any control over, or responsibility for, any third-party websites referred to or in this book. All internet addresses given in this book were correct at the time of going to press. The author and publisher regret any inconvenience caused if addresses have changed or sites have ceased to exist, but can accept no responsibility for any such changes.

A catalogue record for this book is available from the British Library.

A catalog record for this book is available from the Library of Congress.

ISBN:	HB:	978-0-7556-4183-3
	PB:	978-0-7556-4187-1
	ePDF:	978-0-7556-4184-0
	eBook:	978-0-7556-4185-7

Typeset by Integra Software Services Pvt. Ltd.

To find out more about our authors and books visit www.bloomsbury.com
and sign up for our newsletters.

To Lina

Contents

Acknowledgements		viii
Contributors		ix
1	Introduction *Adel Abdel Ghafar & Anna L. Jacobs*	1
2	Beyond Economics: Sino-Egyptian Relations under El-Sisi *Nael Shama*	27
3	Libya & China: A Tale of Two Eras *Tarek Megerisi*	65
4	The Burgeoning China–Tunisia Relationship: Short-Term Reward, Long-Term Risk *Sarah Yerkes*	93
5	China's Relations with Algeria: From Revolutionary Friendship to Comprehensive Strategic Partnership *Yahia H. Zoubir*	125
6	Sino-Moroccan Relations: A Partnership Seeking to Reach Its Full Potential *Anouar Boukhars*	167
Conclusion		199
Bibliography		208
Index		248

Acknowledgements

This project was made possible with support from the Brookings Doha Center (BDC) where I have been based since 2015. Both the Center's Director Tarik Yousef and its Managing Director Nadine Masri have supported the project from inception to completion, for which I am very grateful. I am also indebted to Anna Jacobs, BDC's previous Senior Research Assistant and my co-author for the introduction chapter, for all her support not only for this volume, but also for all her work and our collaboration over the years.

I am also indebted to the world-class contributors to this volume, Nael Shama, Tarek Megerisi, Sarah Yerkes, Yahia Zoubir, and Anouar Boukhars all of whom are valued colleagues and friends. The team at I.B Tauris led by Senior Editor Sophie Rudland have also been fantastic to collaborate with, and I hope this project is the first of many that we work on together. I would like to also thank the anonymous reviewers whose comments helped sharpen and strengthen the volume.

This volume was completed as COVID-19 raged across the world, and I would not have been able to complete it without the support of my family and my wife Jane, as we dealt with the personal and professional ramifications and challenges of the pandemic. During the project, Jane and I were blessed with our first newborn Lina, to whom this volume is dedicated. She has brought so much joy into our lives, for which we are eternally grateful.

Contributors

Adel Abdel Ghafar is a Fellow in the Foreign Policy program at Brookings and at the Brookings Doha Center, where he was previously Director of Research. He is also Adjunct Professor at Georgetown University's School of Foreign Service in Qatar. He specializes in political economy, and his research interests include state–society relations, socioeconomic development, and foreign policy in the MENA region. He is the author, editor and co-editor of several volumes and reports, including *Egyptians in Revolt: The Political Economy of Labor and Student Mobilizations 1919–2011* (Routledge, 2017), "A Stable Egypt for a Stable Region" (European Parliament, 2018), *The European Union and North Africa: Prospects and Challenges* (Brookings Institution Press, 2019), *The European Union and the GCC: Towards a New Path* (Palgrave Macmillan, 2021), and *The Middle East: Revolution or Reform?* (Melbourne University Press, 2014). He has prepared studies and consulted for various international and intergovernmental organizations and government agencies, including the European Union, the UK Foreign, Commonwealth and Development Office, and the Australian Department of Foreign Affairs and Trade.

Anna L. Jacobs is a Nonresident Fellow at the Arab Gulf States Institute in Washington, USA, and a contributor to the North Africa Policy Initiative. She is a Doha-based political scientist focusing on foreign policy in the Middle East and North Africa. She specializes in the politics of North Africa, global and regional power competition, US–China relations, and US foreign policy. Previously, she was Senior Research Assistant at the Brookings Doha Center, where she managed the center's research and publications. Her own work focused on Chinese and US foreign policy in the Middle East and North Africa as well as governance and political economy in the Maghreb countries. Prior to moving to Doha she was Adjunct Professor at the Ecole de Gouvernance et d'Economie in Rabat, Morocco, where she taught courses on media and political economy in the Middle East. Her work has been published by the Brookings Institution, *The Washington Post*, *Al Jazeera English*, *The National Interest*,

Jadaliyya, Muftah Magazine, and other outlets. She is also a contributor to the edited volume *The European Union and North Africa: Prospects and Challenges* (Brookings Institution Press, 2019).

Anouar Boukhars is a professor of Countering Violent Extremism (CVE) and Counter-Terrorism (CT) at the Africa Center for Strategic Studies (ACSS), National Defense University, Washington, DC and a nonresident fellow in Carnegie's Middle East Program. He is also an associate professor of international relations at McDaniel College in Westminster, Maryland.

Nael M. Shama is an independent political researcher and writer. His research focuses on the international relations and comparative politics of the Middle East. He is the author of *Egyptian Foreign Policy from Mubarak to Morsi* (Routledge, 2013).

Sarah Yerkes is a Senior Fellow in Carnegie's Middle East Program, USA, where her research focuses on Tunisia's political, economic, and security developments as well as state–society relations in the Middle East and North Africa. She has been Visiting Fellow at the Brookings Institution and a Council on Foreign Relations international affairs fellow and has taught in the Security Studies Program at Georgetown University, USA, and at the Elliott School of International Affairs at the George Washington University, USA. Yerkes is a former member of the State Department's policy planning staff, where she focused on North Africa. Previously, she was Foreign Affairs Officer in the State's Department's Office of Israel and Palestinian affairs. Yerkes also served as Geopolitical Research Analyst for the US military's Joint Staff Strategic Plans and Policy Directorate (J5) at the Pentagon, advising the Joint Staff leadership on foreign policy and national security issues.

Tarek Megerisi is a Policy Fellow with the North Africa and Middle East program at the European Council on Foreign Relations. He is a political analyst and researcher who specializes in Libyan affairs and more generally politics, governance, and development in the Arab world. Megerisi started his career in Tripoli, Libya, with the Sadeq Institute and various INGOs providing diverse research and democratization assistance to Libya's post-revolutionary authorities between 2012 and 2014. Megerisi returned to London in 2014 and has since been working freelance as an analyst and researcher, advising on Libya policy to a range of international missions to Libya, commentating on Libyan developments for publications like *Foreign Policy*, and co-authoring policy briefs or assisting with the Libya programming of a variety of think tanks. He has also authored commissioned papers for organizations such as WPF and the Legatum Institute and contributed to wider publications for journals like *ISPI*.

Yahia H. Zoubir is a Senior Professor of International Studies and Director of Research in Geopolitics at KEDGE Business School, France, and was previously a nonresident fellow at the Brookings Doha Center. Prior to joining KEDGE in 2005, he taught at multiple universities in the United States, and was a visiting faculty member at various universities in China, Europe, the United States, India, Indonesia, South Korea, and the Middle East and North Africa. His numerous publications include many books, such as *Algerian Politics: Domestic Issues & International Relations* (Routledge 2020), *North African Politics: Change and Continuity* (2016); *Building a New Silk Road: China & the Middle East in the 21st* (2014); *Global Security Watch—The Maghreb: Algeria, Libya, Morocco, and Tunisia* (2013); *North Africa: Politics, Region, and the Limits of Transformation* (Routledge, 2008). His scholarly articles were published in academic journals, such as *Foreign Affairs, Third World Quarterly, Mediterranean Politics, International Affairs, Africa Spectrum, Journal of North African Studies, Middle East Journal, Journal of Contemporary China, Arab Studies Quarterly, Africa Today, Middle East Policy*, etc. He has also contributed to many book chapters and various entries in encyclopedias. He has recently completed a major study, "Civil Strife, Politics, and Religion in Algeria," for the Oxford Research Encyclopedia of Politics & Religion (2019).

1

Introduction

Adel Abdel Ghafar & Anna L. Jacobs

As the United States slowly disengages from the Middle East, and as Europe faces internal challenges, a new actor is quietly exerting greater influence across North Africa. China has been strategically ramping up engagement with such countries as Egypt, Algeria, and Morocco, which lie at the intersection of three key regions: the Middle East, Africa, and the Mediterranean.[1] Beijing's growing footprint in these countries encompasses, but is not limited to, trade, infrastructure development, ports, shipping, financial cooperation, tourism, and manufacturing.

Through this engagement, China is setting up North Africa to play an integral role in connecting Asia, Africa, and Europe—a key aim of President Xi Jinping's Belt and Road Initiative (BRI). While the current BRI map only officially includes Egypt, BRI Memorandums of Understanding (MoUs) have been signed between China and every state in North Africa, demonstrating that it is expanding its foothold in the region.

China is expanding its cooperation with North African countries, not only in the economic and cultural spheres, but also those of diplomacy and defense. Furthermore, it is showcasing a development model that seeks to combine authoritarianism with economic growth—a model that has an eager audience among regimes across the Middle East and North Africa (MENA) region. As such, China's growing role in North Africa is likely to have far-reaching economic and geopolitical consequences for countries in the region and around the world.

Sino-Arab Relations: A Historical Background

Historically, Sino-Arab relations date back to the first days of Islam, where extensive trade relations began with the Tang dynasty and deepened through the historical Silk Road from the seventh till the seventeenth centuries.[2] Political and socioeconomic changes in both China and the Arab World, and the rise of European colonialism, paused the relationship during the eighteenth and nineteenth centuries. Following China's own liberation from Western powers and Japan, and the consolidation of power under Chairman Mao, the relationship with the Arab World would resume through the various national liberation movements that would take hold across the Arab world.

During the anticolonial struggle, China's relationship with the Arab world was grounded in ideological support for national liberation movements. In North Africa, China was the first non-Arab country to recognize Algeria and provided political and military support for its revolutionary struggle. In the wake of the 1955 Bandung Conference, China deepened its relationship with the Egyptian government and President Gamal Abdel Nasser, and supported Egypt during the 1956 Suez Crisis.[3] China also supported the liberation movement in Palestine, including military training cadres of the PLO and PFLP.[4] Arab states also sought to support China diplomatically, voting with African states in 1971 in favor of restoring the People's Republic of China's seat in the United Nations Security Council.[5]

With the beginning of the Deng Xiaoping era in 1978, the basis of China's relationship with the Arab world shifted away from "revolutionary romanticism," and toward economic and strategic concerns, at the end of the twentieth century.[6] Under Deng, China would accelerate its development and become the "workshop of the world."[7] This workshop would need energy resources, and thus the relationship with Arab states in the Gulf would become increasingly important. China established diplomatic relations with the UAE in 1984, followed by Qatar in 1988, and Bahrain in 1989. Saudi Arabia was the last country of the Gulf Cooperation Council (GCC) to establish diplomatic relations with China in 1990.[8]

Since the Hu Jintao era, China has pursued a dual diplomatic strategy with the Arab world. First based on direct bilateral ties, and secondly through multilateral forums, such as the China-Arab States Cooperation Forum (CASCF) established in 2004. Since its inception, CASCF would be the main vehicle for China's engagement with the Arab world with continued head of state- and ministerial-level meetings.

In terms of bilateral engagement, China engages in five categories of "partnership diplomacy." The two highest levels of classifications are strategic partnerships (SPs) and comprehensive strategic partnerships (CSPs).[9] Almost all of China's bilateral relations with MENA countries are categorized in the top two tiers of the country's partnership diplomacy.

Relations between partner countries under an SP have the following four characteristics:

1. They go beyond typical diplomatic relations, involving consistent meetings between government officials and agencies to develop communication and trust.
2. They do not fall within the confines of treaty-based alliances or coalitions.
3. They are more "goal driven" than "threat driven," typically focusing on areas of mutual cooperation in economics, culture, security, and technology.
4. They are characterized by an emphasis on behavior and institutional processes.[10]

In comparison with SPs, CSPs involve a higher level of institutional communication, including regular high-level meetings between top leadership members of both partner countries. Strüver notes that "three conditions have to be met before an agreement on a ... [CSP] can be achieved, i.e. political trust, dense economic ties, cultural exchanges, and good relations in other sectors."[11]

Lower-level classifications include the Comprehensive Cooperative Partnership, Cooperative Partnership, and Friendly Cooperative Partnerships, which represent varying phases of bilateral cooperation on issues of common interest. These are most often used for countries with which China is developing growing ties in trade and investment. Goldstein argues that China's strategic partnership diplomacy is rooted in four key areas of focus: (1) developing bilateral ties that do not threaten a third state, (2) increasing economic ties, (3) prioritizing areas of mutual cooperation with no focus on domestic affairs, and (4) standardizing official visits and security cooperation/military exchanges.[12]

The Arab world would take on increasing importance for Chinese policy makers after the launch of the BRI, the principal mammoth project of the Xi Jinping era. Launched in 2013, according to some estimates it is set to cost around $1 trillion and will include over eighty countries, which are responsible for around 36 percent of global GDP and 41 percent of global trade.[13] South Asia has so far received the majority of BRI projects, but the initiative's expansion west, toward Europe and the MENA region, is well underway. While China's economic presence in Africa and Asia has been the subject of much study and scrutiny, the relationship between China and North Africa deserves more attention. This developing relationship reveals key trends and sheds light on China's strategic priorities, as well as on how countries like Morocco, Algeria, Tunisia, Libya, and Egypt are increasing cooperation with new foreign partners.

Contemporary Relationship with North Africa

In the wake of the 2008 recession and the Eurozone crisis, North African states, which have historically relied on trade with and investment from Europe and the United States, worked to diversify their markets and economic partners.[14] During the same period, China's economy maintained impressive momentum, boasting a 9.5 percent GDP growth rate in 2011.[15] Despite slower economic growth in recent years,[16] China has promoted its economic and soft power with the region.

As the table below illustrates, China has established CSP with Algeria and Egypt and an SP with Morocco. These include dozens of MoUs and promises for major infrastructure and development projects. It is worth noting that, while China has signed BRI MoUs with Libya and Tunisia, it has yet to establish an official strategic partnership with either North African state.[17]

China's Partner Countries in the MENA region[18]

Country	Year	Partnership
Algeria	2014	CSP
Egypt	2014	CSP
Iran	2016	CSP
Iraq	2015	SP

Jordan	2015	SP
Kuwait	2018	SP
Morocco	2016	SP
Oman	2018	SP
Qatar	2014	SP
Saudi Arabia	2016	CSP
United Arab Emirates	2018	CSP

These partnerships demonstrate how China and North African states have strengthened their diplomatic, economic, and cultural relations in recent years, especially since the BRI was launched. Across the region, Chinese Cultural Centers and Confucius Institutes have opened, while visa restrictions and travel advisories for Chinese tourists have been lifted, causing tourism to expand rapidly. Chinese diplomats at both the Rabat and Cairo embassies said that these strengthened relations reflect the key BRI aim of promoting connectivity and economic development in five priority areas: policy coordination, infrastructure connectivity, increased trade, financial integration, and people-to-people exchanges.[19]

Senior fellows of the China Institute for International Studies, Ruan Zongze and Zeng Aiping, argued that China's contribution to the MENA is to demonstrate how BRI can be a dividend for these countries and help them achieve higher levels of economic development. For them, BRI is an inclusive economic initiative that helps frame China's foreign policy in MENA, which they describe as consistent, balanced, pragmatic, and low profile. They also point out that BRI is not charity and that Chinese investors do care about profits and returns on their investments—this is why the concept of mutually beneficial economic dividends is so crucial to BRI partnerships.[20] China's establishment of CSPs with both Egypt and Algeria reflects the major role these states play in the MENA region, as well as the fact that these are its two key bilateral relationships in the region in terms of trade, arms sales, and infrastructure projects. In turn, China has become the top trading partner for both Egypt and Algeria.[21]

While China's relations with Egypt and Algeria are characterized by a robust diplomatic and security partnership, its growing presence in countries like Morocco and Tunisia remains primarily economic and cultural. In Libya, Chinese firms have ceased operations due to ongoing instability, though the previous prime minister of the internationally recognized Government of National Accord (GNA), Fayez Serraj, has said that they are welcome to return.[22] Before 2011, Chinese business interests in Libya were extensive. They operated seventy-five companies, had more than $18 billion of business interests, and employed 36,000 Chinese workers constructing over fifty projects in infrastructure, energy, and telecommunications.[23]

At the beginning of the Libyan conflict, China broke with its long-standing tradition of noninterference and voted in favor of Resolution 1970 that referred Gaddafi and other leaders to the International Criminal Court for treatment of protesters (as Douglas H. Paal argued, not unlike China's treatment of protesters in Tiananmen Square in 1989). China also decided to not veto Resolution 1973, which authorized the use of force against Gaddafi and led to the beginning of a multi-state NATO-led intervention in Libya.[24] It has since shifted back toward noninterference, neutrality, and quiet diplomacy. It is seeking to not take sides so as not to block any future diplomatic and commercial ties, especially in the post-conflict reconstruction era. However, China officially supports the UN-backed, Tripoli-based GNA, which still controls the Central Bank of Libya, thus making it a viable partner for Beijing and Chinese companies looking to sign contracts.

However, they have also kept their options open with Haftar forces in eastern Libya. As Frederic Wehry and Sandy Alkoutami argue, "Chinese state-owned companies' agreement to fund eastern-based Prime Minister Abdullah al-Thinni's development projects in 2016 reflects Beijing's inclination to adapt to changing realities on the ground. Unlike Russia, which has provided substantial, frontline military aid to the Haftar camp, China's direct relationship with the east is strictly economic."[25]

The deputy director of the Bureau of West Asia and North Africa at the International Department of the Central Committee of the Communist Party of China (CCP), Zhu Lihan, also highlighted China's interests in security and stability in North Africa. The CCP is especially concerned about terrorism and jihadist groups across North Africa and the Sahel, as well as the impact of ongoing conflicts like the war in Libya. Zhu argued for the importance of international efforts, multilateral engagement, and national reconciliation for countries in conflict, without foreign interference. For him, there is no military solution to Libya's conflict, only a political one.²⁶

Soft Power: Economic and Cultural Pillars

Chinese policy in North Africa combines both soft power and hard power elements, but soft power has been particularly prominent in Chinese discourse.²⁷ While many types of economic power are understood to be forms of hard power, China engages in a softer form of economic influence, using economic diplomacy "more as carrots than as sticks."²⁸ The CCP claims to prioritize mutually beneficial economic development above all else. Their diplomacy is consequently more goal oriented than threat oriented. China also still considers itself a developing country seeking to ensure its own economic objectives related to economic development, energy security, and global connectivity through the BRI. CCP officials emphasize the importance of a peaceful global environment and the benefits of having strong relations with all countries.²⁹ The commercial side of Chinese influence in North Africa is directly related to the growing legitimacy of the Chinese development model, which emphasizes economic development and noninterference in political affairs, in contrast to the traditional Western emphasis on advocating for liberal and democratic norms. In line with these observations, this paper defines soft power to include economic and commercial relations, based on an understanding of how China uses trade, investment, and finance as noncoercive tools in its relations with North African countries.

Currently, most BRI engagement in North Africa is tied to economic and commercial relations, giving the involved countries the opportunity to increase trade volumes, foreign investments, tourism revenues, and the number of manufacturing bases. Ruan Zongze, underlined how China is especially aiming to work with North African countries on infrastructure projects through the BRI. Zeng Aiping, echoed the importance of infrastructure projects, adding that the region's expanding economic zones and tourism are contributing to China–North Africa connectivity and mutual development. These BRI priorities, they believe, are contributing to a positive image of China across the MENA.[30] This has also had the effect of encouraging competition among traditional Western partners, such as the European Union,[31] as well as China and Russia. Chinese diplomats stress that North African countries are especially attractive prospects for economic cooperation due to their proximity to European, African, and Asian markets, a high number of industrial zones, and high levels of investment in infrastructure development.[32]

Trade

From Morocco to Egypt, China is increasingly trading with and investing in North African countries. China has become a top source of imports for every North African economy, but there is a significant balance of trade deficit. China's economic strategies differ from country to country, with Egypt, Morocco, and Algeria representing its highest priorities. According to the Chinese Ministry of Commerce, in 2019, the trade volume between China and Egypt reached $13.2 billion, while the value of Egypt's imports from China was $12.2 billion, the highest in North Africa.[33] This makes China Egypt's number one source of imports. China's trade with Morocco is more modest, but is expanding every year; trade volume in 2018 reached $4.3 billion, an increase of 14.7 percent, behind only those from France and Spain.[34]

Algeria, meanwhile, is one of China's oldest and largest economic partners in North Africa. China became Algeria's top trade partner in 2013, overtaking France. However, there is a significant trade deficit. While China has become Algeria's primary source for imports, which were valued at $7.65 billion in 2019,[35] Algeria's exports to China remain relatively insignificant compared to its exports to European countries, and are almost entirely from the hydrocarbon sector. However, its exports to China are rising, having jumped 60-fold between 2000 and 2017.[36]

Trade has also risen between China and Tunisia, with the latter's imports from the former valued at $2.04 billion in 2019, ranking third behind France and Italy.[37] However, one Chinese diplomat argued that China still views the country as an investment risk and is skeptical of its democratic transition and economic challenges.[38] Ruan Zongze argues that the landscape in North Africa changed drastically with the 2011 Arab Spring, causing substantial regional instability and economic downturns. Since then, governments in the region have attempted to reassert political stability and national reconciliations to improve these country's economic woes. Since 2013, China engaged these countries primarily through the BRI framework with the aim of expanding trade, investment, and infrastructure development. This strategy seems to be working, as evidenced by the rapid increase in trade volume with China since the Arab Spring.[39]

After civil war broke out in Libya in 2011, China and many other countries were forced to evacuate their citizens and pull out of major projects and investments. However, Libya's oil exports to China have more than doubled since 2017,[40] and China is eyeing post-reconstruction opportunities. In July 2018, GNA foreign minister Mohamed Sayala signed an MoU with his Chinese counterpart, paving the way for Libya to join the BRI. Unlike other regional powers, the Chinese have not taken sides in the Libyan conflict because of their commitment to political noninterference. This puts them in a strong position to make deals with whichever government takes the lead of Libya in the future.

Investment and Infrastructure

In Algeria, Chinese companies are primarily interested in the construction, housing, and energy sectors. Major Chinese-funded and/or -built construction projects, such as the Algiers Opera House, the Sheraton Hotel, the Great Mosque of Algiers, and the East-West Highway, mark the landscape, as do the thousands of Chinese workers who have established a "Chinatown" in a suburb of Algiers.

The Chinese presence in Morocco and Egypt, meanwhile, is concentrated in industrial zones, free trade zones, and financial centers. In Morocco, these include the Atlantic Free Zone in Kenitra, Casablanca Finance City (CFC), and the Tanger Med Port Complex. At the latter port complex, Chinese companies, including telecommunications giant Huawei, are planning to establish regional logistics centers.[41]

In March 2017, King Mohammed VI announced plans for the new "Mohammed VI Tangier Tech City," which is expected to become the largest Chinese investment project in North Africa[42] and to feature several industrial zones. After China's Haite Group pulled out of the project, the China Communications Construction Company (CCCC) and its subsidiary, the

China Road and Bridge Corporation (CRBC), signed an MoU with Morocco's BMCE Bank.[43] Construction on the "Tech City" had already begun as of July 2019.[44] Following the announcement of the "Tech City" project, Chinese auto manufacturing companies, including BYD, Citic Dicastal, and Aotecar New Energy Technology, signed agreements with the Moroccan government to build various plants.[45]

In Egypt, the Chinese are demonstrating increasing interest in building and financing projects in the New Administrative Capital, the Suez Canal Economic Zone, and various other industrial zones across the country, even though many of these projects are still in the planning phase. Even as Egypt faces challenges in attracting foreign investment,[46] Chinese construction projects are on the rise. In some cases, negotiations between the Egyptian government and Chinese firms have fallen through. One major example of this was when talks between Egypt and the China Fortune Land Development Company (CFLD) over a $20 billion project in the New Administrative Capital came to a halt in December 2018 over discrepancies in revenue sharing.[47] However, Chinese diplomats also mentioned the success story of the fiber production workshop run by the Egyptian branch of Chinese fiberglass company Jushi in the Suez Canal Economic Zone, which has allowed Egypt to become one of the leading producers of fiberglass in the world.[48]

In our discussions with the China Railway Construction Corporation (CRCC), "the pace-setter of China's construction industry," the vice-president in charge of production, Li Chongyang, described their rapid expansion of infrastructure construction across the world. They have projects in over 100 countries. In North Africa, Li focused on projects in Algeria, highlighting the East-West Highway, as well as military housing and infrastructure. Regarding hiring practices, they said that half of their workers in Algeria are local hires, arguing for the importance of hiring local workers and supporting local employment. The CRCC are also eyeing infrastructure investment in Libya's future reconstruction efforts.[49]

People-to-People Exchanges

According to Chinese diplomats, "people-to-people exchanges" are a key element of the BRI, with infrastructure projects, ports, and shipping routes meant to facilitate not only trade and investment, but also the movement of people. They emphasize how the BRI should be understood as a means to give the ancient concept of the "Silk Road" a place in modern society, with one diplomat saying: "The picture we have in mind is communication among different civilizations ... when we say the Silk Road, it's the road of peace."[50]

The BRI has been evidently successful in facilitating the desired movement of people. Algeria hosts more than 50,000 Chinese workers, who comprise one of the largest Chinese communities in Africa.[51] Likewise, Chinese restaurants and markets continue to pop up in Casablanca, Morocco's business hub, and Rabat, its administrative capital, as Chinese communities there expand; 4,000 Chinese residents live in the Casablanca business district of Derb Omar alone.[52] In addition to these new residents, Chinese tourism to countries like Morocco and Egypt has skyrocketed as visa restrictions and travel warnings have been lifted. According to a Chinese diplomat, 400,000 Chinese tourists visited Egypt in 2017, up from 125,000 in 2015.[53] Meanwhile, Morocco hosted 140,000 Chinese tourists in 2019.[54]

Another element of "people-to-people" exchanges has been the expansion of Chinese cultural institutions in North Africa. Tunisia's first Confucius Institute opened in November 2018,[55] while the China Culture Center in Rabat was inaugurated in December 2018.[56] Meanwhile, Egypt is home to two Confucius Institutes, located at Cairo University and the Suez Canal University, as well as to a Chinese cultural center. These cultural institutions organize classes on Chinese language and culture, as well as festivals. Overall, the rising numbers of Chinese residents, tourists, and cultural institutions in North Africa indicate that China's soft power initiative in the region has been effective and will continue to expand.

Hard Power: Diplomacy and Defense

Diplomacy and Geopolitics

Tensions between North African states and their traditional Western partners have pushed the former to explore the possibility of economic, diplomatic, and security partnerships with other great powers, such as China and Russia. For example, when tensions rose between Morocco and the European Union in 2016 over the application of the agricultural and fishing agreement, which involved the disputed Western Sahara territory, Morocco broke off contact with the EU delegation, greatly straining their relationship.[57]

Meanwhile, high-level state visits between North African and Chinese government officials have increased in the past five to ten years. During the September 2018 Beijing Summit of the Forum on China-Africa Cooperation (FOCAC), President Xi met with Moroccan prime minister Saadeddine El Othmani,[58] former Algerian prime minister Ahmed Ouyahia,[59] Tunisian prime minister Youssef Chahed,[60] and Egyptian president Abdel-Fattah al-Sissi. Meetings between al-Sissi and Xi have been especially common, with the most recent taking place in April 2019 during the second Belt and Road Forum for International Cooperation.[61] Chinese diplomats have met with Libya's GNA officials nine times between 2016 and 2020.[62]

China's official policy of noninterference represents an attractive alternative to the normative engagement that often marks cooperation with Western countries. As Zoubir argues:

> Many MENA … countries have observed that they have been the losers under the West's hegemonic order, regardless of their respective alignments with Western powers … China never colonized MENA countries or interfered in their domestic affairs. The country's regional and international expansion is natural and inevitable due to its economic weight. Its policy of noninterference certainly appeals to MENA states. Those factors partly explain the region's acceptance of the BRI and China's larger role in the global arena.[63]

However, it is important to keep in mind that noninterference and neutrality may not always be options for China; the larger China's role in the region becomes, the greater the pressure will be for it to become more actively involved in resolving regional disputes. China has avoided playing a more direct role in the Libyan conflict, in contrast to countries like Russia, the United Arab Emirates, Turkey, and Egypt. China has generally followed its policy of strategic noninterference since the fall of Gaddafi in 2011. As Wehry and Alkoutami highlight:

> While China's nonalignment in Libya was motivated by an attempt to protect interests in 2011, China's hesitation to take sides in 2020 points instead to a

desire to maximize its diplomatic and economic gains no matter the conflict's outcome. Part of China's strategy in Libya has remained consistent: When balancing competing interests, the path of least resistance is most appealing and fruitful—and, often, this is the path of neutrality.[64]

In Morocco, the Western Sahara is considered to be Moroccan, and supporting its self-determination is considered to be crossing a red line. Morocco's sovereignty over the disputed territory is a national cause and constitutes one of the country's fundamental policy priorities. However, when Chinese diplomats discuss this issue, they say that they respect the UN mandate on the question.[65] This position has been tenable so far, but the regional conflict directly and indirectly involves major Chinese partners, such as Algeria, South Africa, Angola, Nigeria, and the GCC.[66] This could lead to tension between China and some key allies in the future. In addition to its policy of noninterference, China is hoping to avoid questions of self-determination because of its own challenges in dealing with separatism, such as in the cases of Taiwan, Xinjiang, Tibet, and Inner Mongolia.[67]

As such, China continues to take a back seat with respect to major regional conflicts. However, even though it currently engages with North African countries through a primarily bilateral framework,[68] it is attempting to engage in more regional diplomacy through multilateral mechanisms, such as the FOCAC and the CASCF.

Ekman argues that this diplomatic effort relates the principle of *xinxing daguo guanxi*, or "a new type of major power relations," whereby China seeks to engage with smaller countries once they have been grouped into major regional forums.[69] Only then are they considered to be powerful enough for high-level cooperation. In other words, balance of power constitutes a core component of China's vision for a pragmatic and productive global order.

Zhu Lihan affirmed China's commitment to international engagement and multilateralism, as well as the primacy of UN peace processes. He hailed the Joint Comprehensive Plan of Action as "a victory for multilateralism" as well as the benefits of China's "independent and peaceful" foreign policy. They seek to promote political negotiations and international cooperation to ensure greater global stability, something they see as essential to economic development. The fact that China enjoys good relations with countries often at odds, such as both

Saudi Arabia and Iran, and UAE and Qatar, is a strength according to Zhu. They aim to practice and promote peaceful development, arguing that this can only be done through multilateral institutions and international engagement.[70]

For Zhu, China seeks to play a more constructive role in the region than the United States. US policy under the Trump administration, he contended, was fomenting conflict in the Middle East instead of mitigating it. For example, Trump's maximum pressure policy against Iran, he posited, has augmented regional tensions and the threat of military confrontation. The CCP views this as a US policy promoting regime change, and instead prefers to use quiet diplomacy to support international cooperation through multilateral institutions and to maintain a strict commitment to noninterference in the domestic affairs of other countries.[71]

Security and Defense Cooperation

China's security and defense cooperation in North Africa is expanding along with its economic presence. Maritime projects, and especially the production of submarine cables, are a particularly crucial element of China's focus on telecommunications connectivity. China's Huawei Marine Networks delivered the "Hannibal" cable, linking Tunisia to Italy, in 2009, as well as another major cable linking Libya to Greece, in 2010. This has led to concerns about Chinese commercial investments being used for noncommercial activities, such as intelligence gathering and naval/military cooperation in the Mediterranean.[72] These concerns stem from the precedent set by BRI projects in South Asia, such as the Hambantota port in Sri Lanka, where Sri Lankan officials claimed that the Chinese insisted on an intelligence-gathering component that would monitor all traffic through the port.[73]

China's first significant military action in the region took place in Libya in 2011, when the People's Liberation Army Navy (PLAN) helped to evacuate nearly 40,000 Chinese workers from the country before NATO airstrikes began. Subsequently, in 2015, a joint Chinese–Russian military exercise took place in the Mediterranean and in 2017, China opened its first overseas military base in Djibouti. In January 2018, two warships from the 27th Chinese naval escort stopped by Algiers for a four-day friendly visit as part of a four-month tour.[74] Furthermore, the two major North African military powerhouses—Egypt and Algeria—are among the top buyers of Chinese weapons. According to CSIS's

China Power project, "Northern African countries are the primary destination of Chinese weapons [in Africa], constituting 42 percent of Chinese exports to the continent."[75]

Structure of the Book

To delve deeper and analyze many of the issues highlighted in this introduction, five experts have written country-specific chapters on Egypt, Libya, Tunisia, Algeria, and Morocco that are collated in this volume. When it comes to China's relationship with North African countries, there are some parallels, but there are also unique dynamics for each country. Each chapter offers important background about China's relationship with the individual countries, an evaluation of the costs and benefits of current bilateral relations, and some projections about what the future may hold in a context of declining Western engagement in the MENA regions and the rise of Great Power Competition.

Egypt

Nael Shama lays out the long history of Sino-Chinese relations and subsequently focuses his chapter on the ways in which this relationship changed around the 2011 Arab Spring protests, and especially after El-Sisi came to power in 2014. His analysis seeks to elucidate the significant increase in China–Egypt bilateral ties, how these ties fit into broader Egyptian and Chinese foreign policy, and the future impact of this relationship—especially the potential consequences on Egypt's Western allies. He argues, perhaps more directly than our other authors, that China could equal or even overtake the United States as Egypt's key international partner.

Along the same lines as China's relationship with other North African states, there is an array of both positive and negative aspects to deepening ties in the case of Egypt. Trade has skyrocketed between the two countries, but as is the case with other states, there is a major trade imbalance. Furthermore, while FDI is steadily rising, Shama highlights the fact that China investment is still relatively low, compared to both overall Chinese FDI and total FDI within Egypt. Shama insists that Egypt needs to do more to benefit from its ties with China; the country needs to focus on attracting more Chinese investment and tourists. Another important shift is that Egypt has become a significant client for both Chinese and Russian arms, challenging the traditional dominance of the United States, the United Kingdom, and other European countries in the weapons industry. Shama concludes with a message of caution. He describes the growing concerns about the trade imbalance and the negative impact of an increasing number of Chinese imports on Egypt's local manufacturing. He raises concerns about neocolonialism and how the Chinese "development" model is often not so mutually beneficial. He argues that the economic superpower is promoting its own exports and looking to extract natural resources to benefit its own economic growth. This could hurt many developing countries and their own economic growth.

Libya

Tarek Megerisi examines the unique case of China–Libya relations, arguing that due to the ongoing civil war this North African country represents a particularly distinctive case that is difficult to frame. He analyzes this relationship through two eras, before and after the 2011 revolution. Relations with the mercurial Qaddafi leading up to 2011 experienced characteristic highs and lows, given China's growing interest in Libya and Qaddafi's ever-changing foreign policy vis-à-vis Western countries. China's vast projects in Libya were put at risk in 2011, and the superpower was forced to execute a major evacuation of its citizens in February 2011. He analyzes how both countries are at a pivotal moment; Libya is attempting to end a violent conflict and implement some level of national reconciliation, while China is on its way to becoming the preeminent global economic superpower.

Megerisi argues that China is interested in a stable Libya that could become a major partner in energy, infrastructure, and trade, but is weary of the heightened global competition over Libya's vast oil wealth and lucrative construction contracts. Overall, Megerisi emphasizes that there is ample potential for this bilateral relationship to expand given the mutual benefits for both parties; China would be able to increase its influence in the Mediterranean and in Europe's neighborhood, while also security energy resources and construction contract; Libya could secure much-needed infrastructure investment and revenues from a revamped hydrocarbon sector.

Tunisia

In her thoughtful examination of China–Tunisia ties, Sarah Yerkes analyzes an overlooked, but very strategic, bilateral relationship. It is defined by growing diplomatic engagement, educational and cultural exchanges, and economic ties (albeit to a lesser extent than some of its neighbors). Similar to other North African states, the trade relationship reflects a significant imbalance that needs to be addressed. Yerkes describes how Tunisia and China are increasing cooperation in tourism, agricultural products (and especially olive oil), and aerospace. China is also expanding much-needed infrastructure investment, which Yerkes recommends using to help address Tunisia's struggle with job creation. She highlights that, as the only burgeoning democracy in the MENA region, Tunisia has more in common with the values of liberal democracy promoted by its main economic partners: Europe and the United States.

However, she underlines that Tunisia could benefit from its economic relationship with China. At the same time, she advises that strengthening ties with China comes with the risk of alienating Western allies. Tunisia needs both greater economic aid and infrastructure investment, which Western countries are perhaps unable (or unwilling) to offer, Yerkes says. China can provide this. Yet, she advises caution about the security implication of China's growing footprint in the Tunisian economy and critical infrastructure. She warns of threats related to sensitive sectors, such as telecommunications, and cites the well-known concerns about Huawei's potential to access mass data. Overall, she recommends that Tunisia focus on attracting Chinese tourists and infrastructure investment for job creation. She concludes that the United States and Europe must play a greater role in balancing China's influence through cultivating deeper trade relations and providing more economic aid.

Algeria

In his analysis of China–Algeria ties, Yahia Zoubir describes the transition from a relationship built on revolutionary friendship to a practical, more economically oriented dynamic. He emphasizes that China's relationship with Algeria is one of the longest and strongest in the entire MENA region. The history of ideological ties between the CCP and Algeria's National Liberation Front makes this case an especially interesting one. Furthermore, Algeria has immense hydrocarbon wealth and acts as a major security actor in North Africa and the Sahel region. Similar to its ties with other states in the MENA, China's ties with Algeria have expanded in the last two decades thanks to China's "Going Global" strategy and its unprecedented economic growth. The launching of Xi Jinping's BRI in 2013 further consolidated Chinese interest in African markets. Algeria became one of the most important countries for China, as evidenced by the establishment of a CSP in 2014. China has also supplanted France as Algeria's number one source of imports.

The current commercial relationship is focused on trade, infrastructure investment, and construction projects, and there is much room for growth in the energy, manufacturing, health care, and tourism sectors. Algeria's priority is both economic and political reforms: the country needs to diversify its economic model away from hydrocarbon rents toward other critical industries, and China could be essential in supporting economic reform, but will likely maintain its policy of noninterference in the question of political reform, unlike Algeria's Western partners. Zoubir, similar to Boukhars' assessment of great power competition in Morocco, contends that the Chinese threat to Western interests is exaggerated. Europe (and especially France) and the United States will likely remain Algeria's two key foreign partners, even though it is also seeking to diversify its alliance base and has traditionally avoided positioning itself too solidly in the West's sphere of influence. Zoubir concludes that Algeria's relationship with China is unique in that it encompasses more than commercial interests—it is rooted in economic, diplomatic, and security ties.

Morocco

In the final chapter of the volume, focused on Sino-Moroccan relations, Anouar Boukhars describes the contours of a partnership seeking to reach its full potential. In many ways, China has come to view Morocco as an essential element to its Africa strategy, especially after the king's state visit to China in 2016. After this point, relations began to deepen, primarily in the economic and cultural realms. Morocco formally joined the BRI in 2017 and benefits from greater political stability and ease of doing business than many of its neighbors. For the Chinese, Morocco offers one of the best climates in terms of finance, investment, and manufacturing, especially in the automotive industry, renewable energy, aeronautics, and agriculture. Morocco also benefits from especially close proximity to the European market and hosts the largest port in Africa, Tanger-Med. For this reason, the flagship BRI project in the country will be the Tangier Tech Industrial City. The strategic partnership between Morocco and China is a budding one.

However, Boukhars argues, it suffers from language and cultural differences that sometimes hinder business. There is also a substantial trade imbalance between the two countries. Morocco needs to better incorporate the Chinese market into its industrial strategy, notably to increase its exports. In his view, the agricultural sector offers the most potential for this. The tourism industry also holds much potential, as "people-to-people exchanges" continue to constitute a core pillar of BRI. Boukhars concludes that Europe and the United States will remain Morocco's primary economic and political partners, even as the kingdom seeks to diversify its alliances with other great powers such as China and Russia. This could cause friction between Morocco and its traditional Western allies in the future. The Morocco dossier also includes the Western Sahara conflict and thorny relations with its neighbor, Algeria. Thus far, China has managed to remain on the sidelines of these issues and cultivate strong bilateral ties with these two regional powers.

Notes

1   This chapter was previously published, in part, as the authors paper titled *Beijing Calling: Assessing China's Growing Footprint in North Africa*, Brookings Doha Center Policy Briefing, September 2019.
2   See for example, Morris Rossabi (Ed.), *China among Equals: The Middle Kingdom and Its Neighbors, 10th–14th Centuries* (Berkeley: University of California Press, 1983). Schafer and Edward H, *The Golden Peaches of Samarkand: A Study of T'ang Exotics* (Berkeley: University of California Press, 1985).
3   Kyle Haddad-Fonda, "The Domestic Significance of China's Policy toward Egypt, 1955–1957," *The Chinese Historical Review* 21, no. 1 (2014), pp. 45–64.
4   Lillian Craig Harris, "China's Relations with the PLO," *Journal of Palestine Studies* 7, no. 1 (1977), pp. 123–54.
5   Bruce D. Larkin, *China and Africa 1949–1970: The Foreign Policy of the People's Republic of China*. No. 5. (Berkeley: University of California Press, 1973).

6   David H. Shinn and Joshua Eisenman, *China and Africa: A Century of Engagement* (Philadelphia: University of Pennsylvania Press, 2012), 228; Thierry Pairault, "La Chine au Maghreb: de l'esprit de Bandung à l'esprit du capitalisme" [China in the Maghreb: From the Spirit of Bandung to the Spirit of Capitalism], Revue de la régulation 21, first semester (Spring 2017), https://journals.openedition.org/regulation/12230

7   Story, Jonathan, "China: Workshop of the World?" *Journal of Chinese Economic and Business Studies* 3, no. 2 (2005), pp. 95–109.

8   Imad Mansour, "A GCC-China Security 'Strategic Partnership': Its Potential and Contours," in *The Arab States of the Gulf and BRICS: New Strategic Partnerships in Politics and Economics,* edited by Tim Niblock, Degang Sun, and Alejandra Galindo (Frankfurt: Gerlach Press, 2016).

9   George Strüver, "China's Partnership Diplomacy: International Alignment Based on Interests or Ideology," *The Chinese Journal of International Politics* 10, no. 1 (Spring 2017), p. 33, https://doi.org/10.1093/cjip/pow015

10 Ibid., pp. 36–7.

11 Ibid., p. 45.

12 Jonathan Fulton, "Friends with Benefits: China's Partnership Diplomacy in the Gulf," 2019, *POMEPS Studies 34: Shifting Global Politics and the Middle East,* 34, https://www.academia.edu/38580068/Friends_with_Benefits_Chinas_Partnership_Diplomacy_in_the_Gulf

13 "China's Belt and Road Initiative: 5 Years Later," posted by Bloomberg Markets and Finance, February 3, 2019, https://www.youtube.com/watch?v=Z0iMgoFPnDw

14 Riccardo Fabiani, "Morocco's Difficult Path to ECOWAS Membership," Carnegie Endowment for International Peace, *Sada Journal*, March 28, 2018, https://carnegieendowment.org/sada/75926; Nasser Saidi and Aathira Prasad, "Trends in Trade and Investment Policies in the MENA Region," *Organisation for EconomicCo-operation and Development*, Background Note, November 2018,http://www.oecd.org/mena/competitiveness/WGTI2018-Trends-Trade-Investment-Policies-MENA-Nasser-Saidi.pdf

15 Statista, "China: Growth Rate of Real Gross Domestic Product (GDP) from 2011 to 2024," February 21, 2019, https://www.statista.com/statistics/263616/gross-domestic-product-gdp-growth-rate-in-china/

16 Betty Wang, "China's Economic Growth Hits a 30 Year Low," *Australian Broadcasting Company*, January 21, 2019, https://www.abc.net.au/radionational/programs/drive/chinas-economic-growth-hits-a-30-year-low/10733492

17 Xinhua, "China and Another Two Arab Countries Sign MOUs on the Belt and Road Initiative," *Belt and Road Portal*, July 12, 2018, https://eng.yidaiyilu.gov.cn/home/rolling/59886.htm
18 Strüver, "China's Partnership Diplomacy," 62–5. See also, Jonathan Fulton, "Friends with Benefits: China's Partnership Diplomacy in the Gulf," 2019, *POMEPS Studies 34: Shifting Global Politics and the Middle East*, https://www.academia.edu/38580068/Friends_with_Benefits_Chinas_Partnership_Diplomacy_in_the_Gulf
19 Rolland, *China's Eurasian Century?*; "Belt and Road Initiative (BRI)," *European Bank for Reconstruction and Development*, August 14, 2019; Chinese diplomats, interviews with the authors, Rabat, Morocco and Cairo, Egypt, January 2019.
20 Ruan Zongze and Zeng Aiping, Senior Fellows at China Institute for International Studies (interviews with the authors, September 2019), Beijing, China.
21 See "Egypt-China Trade Hits $7.5 bln in 7 Months: Chinese Customs," *Ahram Online*, August 26, 2018, http://english.ahram.org.eg/NewsContent/3/12/310274/Business/Economy/EgyptChina-trade-hits—bln-in–months-Chinese-cus.aspx: "The trade volume between the two countries reached $7.5 billion, while China's exports to Egypt were estimated at $6.5 billion, a 22.6 percent increase year-on-year. Egypt's exports to the Asian giant jumped 34.1 percent to $1 billion." See also Lamine Ghanmi, "Algeria Draws Europe's Ire by Cutting Imports, Boosting Trade with China," *The Arab Weekly*, April 22, 2018, https://thearabweekly.com/algeria-draws-europes-ire-cutting-imports-boosting-trade-china: "China has emerged as Algeria's main import market, sending $8.3 billion worth of goods to the North African country in 2017."
22 Xinhua, "Libya Welcomes Return of Chinese Companies, PM Says ahead of FOCAC Beijing Summit," *China Daily*, September 1, 2018, http://www.chinadaily.com.cn/a/201809/01/WS5b8a2b1aa310add14f389061.html
23 Frederic Wehry and Sandy Alkoutami, "China's Balancing Act in Libya," *Carnegie Endowment for International Peace*, May 10, 2020, https:// carnegieendowment.org/2020/05/10/china-s-balancing-act-in-libyapub-81757
24 Douglas H. Paal, "China: Mugged by Reality in Libya, Again," *Carnegie Endowment for International Peace*, April 11, 2011, https://carnegieendowment.org/2011/04/11/china-mugged-by-reality-in-libya-again-pub-43554
25 Frederic Wehry and Sandy Alkoutami, "China's Balancing Act in Libya," *Carnegie Endowment for International Peace*, May 10, 2020, https://carnegieendowment.org/2020/05/10/china-s-balancing-act-in-libyapub-81757

26 Zhu Lihan, Deputy Director of the Bureau of West Asia and North Africa, International Department of the Central Committee, Communist Party of China (interview with the authors, September 2019), Beijing, China.
27 Joseph Nye coined the term "soft power" in the aftermath of the Cold War to better describe how countries exert power beyond the traditional coercive means known as "hard power," such as military might and aggressive economic and diplomatic strategies. Nye argues that soft power involves noncoercive means "to do things and control others," encompassing cultural, ideological, and institutional elements. Chinese officials have often referred to the BRI as a "vehicle for soft power." See Eleanor Albert, "China's Big Bet on Soft Power," Council on Foreign Relations, Backgrounder, February 9, 2018, https://www.cfr.org/backgrounder/chinas-big-bet-soft-power
28 John Wong, "China's Rising Economic Soft Power," *Asia Dialogue*, March 25, 2016, https://theasiadialogue.com/2016/03/25/chinas-rising-economic-soft-power/
29 Zhu Lihan, Deputy Director of the Bureau of West Asia and North Africa, International Department of the Central Committee, Communist Party of China (interview with the authors, September 2019), Beijing, China.
30 Ruan Zongze and Zeng Aiping, Senior Fellows at China Institute for International Studies (interviews with the authors, September 2019), Beijing.
31 Thierry Pairault, "Economic Relations between China and Maghreb Countries," in *China, the European Union and the Developing World: A Triangular Relationship*, edited by Jan Wouters, Jean-Christophe Defraigne, and Matthieu Burnay (Cheltenham: Edward Elgar Publishing, 2015), p. 312.
32 Chinese diplomats, interviews with the authors, Cairo, Egypt and Rabat, Morocco, January 2019; Nadège Rolland, *China's Eurasian Century? Political and Strategic Implications of the Belt and Road Initiative* (Seattle and Washington, DC: The National Bureau of Asian Research, 2017), p. 3.
33 "Trade Exchange between Egypt, China Hits $13.2bn in 2019," *Egypt Today*, May 8, 2020, https://www.egypttoday.com/Article/3/86546/Trade-exchange-between-Egypt-China-hits-13-2bn-in-2019
34 "Maroc-Chine. De la culture pour faire du business," LesEchos.ma., January 17, 2020, https://leseco.ma/maroc-chine-de-la-culture-pour-faire-du-business/
35 Algerie Presse Service, "Commerce extérieur: un déficit de plus de 6 milliards de dollars en 2019," February 15, 2020, http://www.aps.dz/economie/101654-commerce-exterieur-un-deficit-de-plus-de-6-milliards-de-dollars-en-2019

36 Guy Burton, "What Protests in Algeria and Sudan Mean for China," *The Diplomat*, March 8, 2019, https://thediplomat.com/2019/03/what-protests-in-algeria-and-sudan-mean-for-china/

37 "Tunisia Imports from China, 2019," *Trading Economics*, last updated November 2020, https://tradingeconomics.com/tunisia/imports/china

38 Chinese diplomat, interview with the authors, Cairo, Egypt, January 2019.

39 Ruan Zongze, Senior Fellow at the China Institute for International Studies (interviews with the authors, September 2019), Beijing.

40 "Libya's Oil Exports to China More than Double in 2018—NOC," *Reuters*, November 30, 2018, https://www.reuters.com/article/libya-china-oil/libyas-oil-exports-to-china-more-than-double-in-2018-noc-idUSL8N1Y46TN

41 "Huawei to Set up Regional Logistics Centre in Tanger Med Port," *PortSEurope*, September 7, 2018, https://www.portseurope.com/huawei-to-set-up-regional-logistics-centre-in-tanger-med-port/

42 "Tangier: King Mohammed VI Launches $1 Billion Chinese Investment Project," *Morocco World News*, March 20, 2017, https://www.moroccoworldnews.com/2017/03/211612/tangier-king-mohammed-vi-launch-largest-chinese-investment-project-north-africa/

43 Linus Kemboi, "Morocco Begins Construction of New Tech City in Tangier," *Construction Review Online*, July 9, 2019, https://constructionreviewonline.com/2019/07/morocco-begins-construction-of-new-tech-city-in-tangier/

44 Ibid.

45 Xinhua, "Morocco, China Give New Impetus to Bilateral Partnership in 2017", *Global Times*, December 31, 2017, http://www.globaltimes.cn/content/1082762.shtml

46 According to the central bank, "FDI dropped $200 million to $7.7 billion in the 2017–2018 fiscal year ... " See Mirette Magdy, "Emaar's Talks with Egypt over New Capital City Project Stall," *Bloomberg*, December 30, 2018, https://www.bloomberg.com/news/articles/2018-12-30/emaar-s-talks-with-egypt-over-new-capital-city-project-stall

47 Mirette Magdy, "China's $20 Billion New Egypt Capital Project Talks Fall Through," *Bloomberg*, December 16, 2018, https://www.bloomberg.com/news/articles/2018-12-16/china-s-20-billion-new-egypt-capital-project-talks-fall-through

48 Xinhua, "China's Jushi Firm Celebrates Largest Fiberglass Production in Egypt," *Xinhuanet*, August 29, 2018, http://www.xinhuanet.com/english/2018-08/29/c_137426120.htm

49 China Railway Construction Corporation, Vice-President in charge of production, Li Chongyang (interview with the authors), September 2019, Beijing.
50 Chinese diplomat, interview with the authors, Cairo, Egypt, January 2019.
51 John Calabrese, "Sino-Algerian Relations: On a Path to Realizing Their Full Potential?" *Middle East Institute,* "All about China" Series Essay, October 31, 2017, https://www.mei.edu/publications/sino-algerian-relations-path-realizing-their-full-potential
52 Hasnae Belmekki, "Derb Omar, Stronghold of the Chinese Traders of Casablanca," University of the Witwatersrand Africa-China Reporting Project, Francophone Africa and China Series, May 4, 2018, http://africachinareporting.co.za/2018/05/derb-omar-stronghold-of-the-chinese-traders-of-casablanca-francophone-africa-china-series/
53 Chinese diplomat, interview with the authors, Cairo, Egypt, January 2019.
54 "Maroc-Chine. De la culture pour faire du business," *LesEchos.ma.*, January 17, 2020, https://leseco.ma/maroc-chine-de-la-culture-pour-faire-du-business/
55 Xinhua, "Confucius Institute Opens Classroom in Tunisia," *Xinhuanet,* November 13, 2018, http://www.xinhuanet.com/english/2018-11/13/c_129992290_2.htm
56 Xinhua, "Feature: China Cultural Center in Morocco's Rabat launched," *Xinhuanet,* December 18, 2018, http://www.xinhuanet.com/english/2018-12/18/c_137682999.htm
57 Aziz El Yaakoubi, "Morocco Suspends Contacts with EU Delegation over Trade Row," *Reuters,* January 28, 2016, https://www.reuters.com/article/uk-morocco-eu-westernsahara/morocco-suspends-contacts-with-eu-delegation-over-trade-row-idUKKCN0V6294
58 "Xi Meets Morocco's Prime Minister," Ministry of Foreign Affairs of the People's Republic of China, August 15, 2019, https://www.fmprc.gov.cn/mfa_eng/zxxx_662805/t1592950.shtml
59 Xinhua, "Xi Meets Algerian Prime Minister," *Xinhuanet,* September 5, 2018, http://www.xinhuanet.com/english/2018-09/05/c_137447518.htm
60 Xinhua, "Xi Meets Tunisian Prime Minister," *Xinhuanet,* September 5, 2018, http://www.xinhuanet.com/english/2018-09/05/c_137447045.htm
61 Xinhua, "Xi Meets Egyptian President," *Xinhuanet,* April 25, 2019, http://www.xinhuanet.com/english/2019-04/25/c_138009830.htm
62 Frederic Wehry and Sandy Alkoutami, "China's Balancing Act in Libya," *Carnegie Endowment for International Peace,* May 10, 2020, https://carnegieendowment.org/2020/05/10/china-s-balancing-act-in-libyapub-81757

63 Yahia Zoubir, "The Welcome Multilateralization of Global Power," in *Belt and Road Initiative: Toward Greater Cooperation Between China and the Middle East*, Brookings Doha Center, Event Proceedings, January 13–14, 2018, 4, https://www.brookings.edu/wp-content/uploads/2018/01/English_BDC_SASS_Event_Proceedings.pdf

64 Frederic Wehry and Sandy Alkoutami, "China's Balancing Act in Libya," *Carnegie Endowment for International Peace*, May 10, 2020, https://carnegieendowment.org/2020/05/10/china-s-balancing-act-in-libya-pub-81757

65 See United Nations Security Council, "Resolution 2468 (2019)," April 30, 2019, https://www.securitycouncilreport.org/atf/cf/%7B65BFCF9B-6D27-4E9C-8CD3-CF6E4FF96FF9%7D/S_res_2468.pdf

66 Samir Bennis, "Moroccan Pragmatism: A New Chapter for Western Sahara," *Aljazeera English*, February 13, 2017, https://www.aljazeera.com/indepth/opinion/2017/02/moroccan-pragmatism-chapter-western-sahara-170213074116469.html

67 See June Teufel Dreyer, "China's Vulnerability to Minority Separatism," *Asian Affairs: An American Review* 32, no. 2 (Summer 2005), pp. 69–85, https://www.jstor.org/stable/30172869

68 See Pairault, "Economic Relations between China and Maghreb Countries," 316, in which he argues: "It must also be observed that Sino-Maghreb economic relations do not appear to be the fruit of a specific China strategy towards the Maghreb but rather expressions specific to each of the Maghreb countries in an approach that is the mere reflection of an overall strategy with regard to developing countries. Actually, if one takes account of the de facto autonomy enjoyed by the Chinese enterprises, and more specifically by the central enterprises that achieve 80 percent of Chinese investment abroad, it is quite obvious that there is not one Chinese strategy but a plurality of strategies (as much as actors)."

69 Alice Ekman, "China's Regional Forum Diplomacy," *European Union Institute for Security Studies (EUISS)*, November 2016, 1, https://www.iss.europa.eu/sites/default/files/EUISSFiles/Alert_44_China_diplomacy.pdf

70 Zhu Lihan, Deputy Director of the Bureau of West Asia and North Africa, International Department of the Central Committee, Communist Party of China (interview with the authors, September 2019), Beijing, China.

71 Ibid.

72 Ibid., p. 16.

73 "Gateway to the Globe: China Has a Vastly Ambitious Plan to Connect the World," *The Economist*, July 26, 2018, https://www.economist.com/briefing/2018/07/26/china-has-a-vastly-ambitious-plan-to-connect-the-world

74 "Chinese Naval Ships Visit Algeria," *China Military Online*, January 9, 2018, http://eng.chinamil.com.cn/view/2018-01/09/content_7901306.htm

75 "How Dominant Is China in the Global Arms Trade?" *Center for Strategic and International Studies, China Power Project*, April 26, 2018, March 6, 2019, https://chinapower.csis.org/china-global-arms-trade/

2

Beyond Economics: Sino-Egyptian Relations under El-Sisi

Nael Shama

In all avenues, Chinese-Egyptian relations have deepened and widened over the past few years. Levels of bilateral trade have increased exponentially, Chinese investments in Egypt have grown and become more diversified, closer military ties have been fostered, and a special place for Egypt in China's ambitious "Belt and Road" plan is envisaged. In tandem, cultural relations have also seen a qualitative development. All that gave rise to speculation that the two countries have become important strategic partners for each other, and that if bilateral relations continue to grow, Beijing may parallel, or even outbid, Washington as Egypt's major international partner.

This chapter looks into recent developments in Sino-Egyptian relations, strategically, politically, and economically, in an attempt to answer a number of central questions. Chief among them is: What explains the sharp political and economic upswing in Sino-Egyptian relations in recent years? How can these relations be situated within the overall structure of Egypt's foreign relations? Also, what is the view in Beijing? What motivated Chinese leaders to pursue closer ties with Cairo? And finally, what does the present picture tell us about the likely future trajectory of Chinese-Egyptian relations and its potential impact on Egypt's current set of international alliances?

The chapter is divided into a number of sections. The first provides a brief historical glimpse of Sino-Egyptian relations in modern times. The following section explores at some length the various facets of Chinese-Egyptian relations, particularly since Abdel-Fattah El-Sisi became president of Egypt in 2014. These include political relations, the different aspects of economic collaboration (trade, investment, and tourism), cultural relations, and military ties.

Then, a lengthy discussion about Egypt's foreign policy post-2011 is provided followed by concluding remarks and future outlook.

Historical Background

Although Egypt's famed Prime Minister Mostafa El-Nahas decided in 1936 to establish an Egyptian consulate in Shanghai, direct exchanges between the two countries were in the 1930s and 1940s limited to Chinese Muslims studying in Cairo at Al-Azhar, the celebrated 1,000-year-old university and center of learning.[1] Yet, soon after the Free Officer's takeover of power in July 1952, the new regime sent a commercial representative to Beijing in 1953 to manage Egyptian exports to China, consisting mainly of cotton.[2]

The turning point in bilateral relations came in April 1955 when former Egyptian president Gamal Abdel-Nasser engaged in a deep dialogue with China's historic leader Zhou Enlai on the sidelines of the milestone Afro-Asian Conference in Bandung, Indonesia. Both leaders found common ground in combatting colonialism and buttressing the cause of the newly independent countries in Africa and Asia. A year later, Egypt became the first Arab and African country to establish direct diplomatic relations with the People's Republic of China (PRC). In the same year, Beijing provided Egypt with a modest and inconsequential, but highly symbolic, grant of 20 million Swiss Francs (then around US $4.6 million), making Egypt the first country in the Arab world and Africa to receive Chinese foreign aid.[3] Thereafter, in response to the Suez crisis, China expressed its full political support for Egypt's sovereignty and independence, and, more importantly, threatened to send thousands of volunteers to fight the invading troops.[4] Chinese authorities also incited demonstrations in large cities in support of Egypt, including an orchestrated one in Beijing that involved more than 400,000 demonstrators.[5]

In the 1950s and 1960s, China's desire to break out of its stifling isolation and to gain a footing in the developing world made Egypt the center of its foreign policy efforts in the Middle East. In line with these efforts, Zhou Enlai paid a historic visit to Cairo in 1963. This was then a natural choice given the meteoric rise of Egypt's international political influence, boosted by Nasser's active championing of liberation movements across the Third World and his embrace of the principle of nonalignment in international affairs. On his part, Nasser "emphatically" called for China's admission to the United Nations in his address to the UN's National Assembly in September 1960.[6] Also, when the Sino-Indian war erupted in 1962, Egypt reportedly attempted to mediate between the two Asian giants.[7] Despite Beijing's deliberate mitigation of its communist rhetoric in its dealings with Cairo, bilateral relations were frequently marred by Nasser's crackdown on communists in Egypt and in Syria (during its brief amalgamation with Egypt, 1958–61),[8] and, generally, by Cairo's unmistakable leaning toward the Soviet Union, then at deep political and ideological loggerheads with China. Overall, Nasser took a dim view of Mao's radical socialist vision,[9] and he perceived China to be a "non-actor in the Middle East."[10]

Due to the indoctrination and reeducation purposes of the Cultural Revolution (1966–76), China recalled its ambassadors to Arab countries, except for its ambassador to Cairo, a sign of Egypt's centrality to Beijing's interests in the Arab world and Africa. China's political support of Egypt in its wars against Israel comes, therefore, as no surprise. In 1967, it unequivocally condemned Israel's aggression against the Arab world, and throughout the 1973 crisis, the Chinese press "expressed jubilation" at Egyptian and Syrian military advances and the oil embargo imposed by oil-producing Arab states on Western countries.[11]

Egypt and China turned a new leaf in their history by restructuring their socioeconomic outlooks in the second half of the 1970s. Indeed, China's economic reform program, launched by Deng Xiaoping in 1978, came on the heels of the launch of Egypt's economic open-door policy and the subsequent shift in its foreign relations from the use of nationalist platitudes to economic pragmatism, from geopolitics to geo-economics.[12] Still, President Anwar Sadat (1970–81) harbored deep anti-communist feelings and his foreign policy after 1973 was preoccupied with the two issues of rapprochement with the West and peace with Israel. And so it was only after Sadat's assassination, the rise of his vice-president Hosni Mubarak to power in 1981, and China's transformation into a global economic powerhouse catching the eyes of the world that Egypt's leadership became interested in developing closer ties with China. In 1983, Mubarak paid an official visit to Beijing, the first ever of an Egyptian president to the PRC. The visit was reciprocated in 1986 by the Chinese president Li

Xiannian. Over his thirty years at the helm of Egyptian politics (1981–2011), Mubarak visited China six times,[13] including a landmark visit in 1999, which witnessed the signing of a "strategic cooperation" agreement between the two countries. On the other hand, Chinese presidents Shangkun and Zemin visited Egypt in 1989 and 1996, respectively.

In sum, Sino-Egyptian relations were quintessentially political in nature under Nasser and Sadat, underpinned by both countries' active support of developing countries against imperialism. Bilateral relations then became economic to the core under the three-decade rule of Mubarak. The following sections discuss the various facets of Sino-Egyptian relations under the leadership of President Abdel-Fattah El-Sisi.

Sino-Egyptian Political Relations

Cairo's keenness on boosting its relations with China was unmistakably clear from President El-Sisi's first months in power. El-Sisi visited China six times in five years (in December 2014, September 2015, September 2016, September 2017, September 2018, and April 2019). On his part, the Chinese president Xi Jinping visited Egypt during his charm offensive tour in the Arab world in January 2016, marking the first visit of a Chinese president to Egypt since 2004. Commenting on the frequent meetings between the two presidents, a Chinese diplomat said: "This has not been the pattern before."[14] Indeed, to put this volume of diplomatic activity into perspective, one has to contrast it with the fact that President Mubarak, the longest-serving Egyptian president in more than a century, visited China only six times during his thirty long years of rule (i.e., an average of one visit every five years), while, in the same period, he visited France forty-six times, the United States twenty-three times, and Germany twenty-four times.[15] Another sign of political closeness came in 2014 when the two countries signed a Comprehensive Strategic Partnership, the highest in the hierarchy of cooperation schemes adopted by the Chinese government (which also includes "strategic partnerships" and "strategic co-operative partnerships").

Politically, Egypt supported China's endeavors to join the World Trade Organization in 2001. Egypt also supports the PRC's long-standing "One

China" principle, a fundamental bedrock of Chinese diplomacy which ardently emphasizes that there is only one unified and sovereign state under the name "China," as opposed to the fact that another state, Taiwan, also uses the word "China" in its official name. Moreover, cooperation between Egypt and China strengthened in the fields of security and counterterrorism, driven on one hand by Egypt's decades-long experience in warring against terrorism and on the other by China's apprehension of the rise of ISIS and the potential links between Egyptian Islamists and China's Muslim minority living in its Northwestern province of Xinjiang.

Remarkably, praise, even glamorization, of China's economic progress and calls for Egyptian policy makers to learn from its economic successes are conspicuous in the Egyptian press, both state-led and private. Back in 2000, long before the official announcement of the "Belt and Road" initiative (BRI), a leading political scholar opined that, when finalized, the expected effects of the new Silk Road on Egyptian national interests "will be mostly positive."[16] More recently, prominent economic expert (and former chairman of the state-run *Al-Ahram*), Ahmed Al-Naggar, depicted China as the "perfect partner" for Egypt.[17] Another writer went as far as describing Cairo as the "capital of the new Silk Road."[18] In the same vein, a senior columnist for the daily *Al-Ahram* wrote, "I was, and still am fascinated by what I read about China … [which is] establishing a new economic theory as a model for self-development."[19] Another journalist called for teaching Mandarin at Egyptian public schools and building a Chinese Taoist or Buddhist temple in Egypt.[20] A perceptive study that analyzed hundreds of op-ed articles published in leading Egyptian newspapers in the period 2012–17 using content-analysis methods concluded that the "Chinese experience of fast economic growth has been repeatedly romanticized," and that China "is often cavalierly portrayed as a magic-bullet formula" to overcome Egypt's fundamental economic challenges.[21]

Sino-Egyptian Economic Relations

The recent growth in Sino-Egyptian economic relations has been part and parcel of China's economic foray into the Arab world over the past few decades. Suffice it to know that total Arab-Chinese trade stood at a meager $1.5 billion in 1991, then it increased by leaps and bounds, skyrocketing to $33.8 billion in 2005 and then to about $250 billion by 2014 (i.e., a whopping 700 percent increase in less than a decade).[22] In 2016, Chinese exports to the region constituted 7 percent of total Chinese exports.[23] China's energy needs, coupled with its audacious desire to assert itself as a major economic player, made it advance beyond its own shores, methodically carving new zones of influence in Europe, Asia, and Africa. Promulgated in the late 1990s, its "Go Out" policy, involving the need to enter new fertile markets and find new investment opportunities overseas, drove it to foster closer economic ties with several Arab countries, both in West Asia and North Africa. And so by 2010, China has become the main trading partner of the Arab world as a whole, and the main trading partner of nine Arab states.[24] Table 1 shows a list of the Middle East's main trading partners, highlighting China's position on top of that list.

Egypt's economic relations with China are currently vast, deep, and multifaceted. They comprise outstanding levels of trade and investment (albeit involving a trade balance tilting heavily in favor of China), a vigorous joint economic zone in the Suez region, strong cooperation on energy and power, an extensive participation by Chinese construction firms in the building of Egypt's new administrative capital, an upward surge in the number of Chinese tourists visiting Egypt, and a prospective role for Egypt's economy in China's hemisphere-wide BRI, now ostensibly Beijing's main foreign policy plank. The two sides have also signed a substantial number of bilateral economic agreements, memoranda, and protocols in the last few years. In an official sign of greater economic interest in China, the Egyptian government has set up a special committee (headed by its deputy prime minister) to handle its rapidly expanding economic and financial relations with China.

Table 1 Top Trading Partners of the Middle East (2016)

No.	Country	Trade ($ Million)	Partner Share (%)
1	China	58,699	9.79
2	United States	45,765	7.63
3	Germany	33,471	5.63
4	India	27,503	4.59

Source: Anu Sharma, "An Analysis of 'Belt and Road' Initiative and the Middle East," *Asian Journal of Middle Eastern and Islamic Studies* 13, no. 1 (2019), p. 40.

Egyptian and Chinese officials seem to agree that Egypt has a vital role to play in China's BRI, under which China plans to strengthen its trade relations with sixty-five countries, in Asia, Europe, and Africa, hosting more than 4 billion people. In their relentless pursuit of foreign investments and development aid, the Egyptian side can, indeed, boast about Egypt's unique geographic position and its long maritime coasts, which enable her to serve as a pivotal port of entry and access to Europe, Africa, and the Middle East. Egypt is also the most populous country in the Arab world, and the third in Africa. And so for investors and trade partners, it is attractive for being a huge market for consumer products and a source for a relatively cheap labor force. Although hamstrung by an array of chronic socioeconomic challenges, Egypt's economy has managed to grow at decent rates in the past few decades. From 1992 to 2017, for instance, Egypt's GDP rose at an annual average rate of 4 percent.[25] Navigating through treacherous waters, Egypt's economy is expected to grow at a rate of 5.9 percent in the fiscal year 2019–20,[26] and it targets a growth rate of 6.4 percent in the fiscal year 2020–21.[27]

According to the October 2019 estimates of the International Monetary Fund, the Egyptian economy's GDP (based on purchasing power parity calculations) is ranked the nineteenth worldwide.[28] Moreover, it is estimated that Egypt's economy will be ranked the seventh among the world's largest economies by 2030.[29] Meanwhile, the $8 billion expansion of the Suez Canal project, which deepened the waterway and allowed two-lane shipping in 35 kilometers of it, and current efforts to establish an expansive economic zone in the Suez region add to Egypt's connectivity to global markets, increase its economic attractiveness, and upgrade its infrastructure capabilities (currently ranked the second most developed in Africa).[30] Given that Egypt is the largest market in Africa (in terms of GDP) and the largest investment market in the MENA region, South Africa's Rand Merchant Bank picked Egypt as "the best country in Africa for investment in 2019" for the third year in a row.[31]

China has therefore ample reasons to be interested in Egypt. In the overall scheme of China's "Going West" strategy, seemingly a reaction to Obama's "pivot to Asia" policy, Egypt figures prominently. Egypt's population, which has swelled to more than 100 million people (about one quarter of the Arab world's population), constitutes a huge market and an abundant source of cheap labor. In addition, China is currently the largest user of the Suez Canal.[32] Chinese companies can also benefit from the many free trade deals Egypt had struck with economic blocs in Africa, Europe, and the Middle East.[33] Conversely, China is a leading member of the BRICS economic bloc (which also includes Brazil, Russia, India, and South Africa), a group of economic tigers with which Egypt would, undoubtedly, want to develop more formidable ties.[34]

On the face of it, these mutual benefits explain why the presidents of the two countries, El-Sisi and Jinping, see eye-to-eye on promoting Egypt's participation in the BRI. In 2017, President El-Sisi stated: "We need to synergize the development strategies and take advantage of the building of infrastructures and cooperation on capacity to make Egypt a supporting country along the 'Belt and Road,'"[35] while President Jinping stressed that "Egypt will be the point of connection for China and the Arab world."[36] In the same vein, Egypt's former minister of investment Sahar Nasr praised China's BRI, saying that it is "the cornerstone of the world's growth and development."[37] Moreover, in his speech before the second Belt and Road Forum for International Cooperation, held in April 2019, El-Sisi emphasized that China's initiative is congruent with Egypt's own Vision 2030, a long-term economic and social vision which aims to place Egypt by 2030 among the top thirty countries worldwide in terms of economic size, market competitiveness, human development, fighting corruption, and the quality of life.[38] To highlight Egypt's centrality in the African continent, he also made reference to the Cape to Cairo Highway (a proposed road project that would stretch the length of Africa from Cape Town to Cairo) and the Lake Victoria–Mediterranean Sea navigation line (an Egyptian initiative for enhancing transport on the Nile River whose feasibility studies are currently in the works).[39]

Trade, Investment, and Tourism

Although the first trade agreement between Egypt and China was signed in 1955, and was followed by dozens of bilateral agreements and protocols covering the domains of trade, scientific, and technical cooperation, economic ties between the two countries remained quite limited in the 1950s, 1960s, and 1970s. It was only in the 1990s that bilateral trade began to show clear signs of improvement. A veritable milestone on the road to fostering closer economic ties was President Mubarak's visit to Beijing in April 1999, which witnessed the signing of a "strategic cooperation" agreement between the two countries. The agreement comprised numerous areas of cooperation, including politics, the economy, tourism, and culture. One palpable consequence of the deal is that bilateral economic relations were upgraded from their traditional form (i.e., primarily trade-based) to encompass other activities, such as investment, joint ventures, and the establishment of an economic zone in Egypt's north–west Suez Gulf region. And so by 2005, Chinese investors had established thirty-five projects in Egypt in diverse sectors and industries, including infrastructure, construction and chemical materials, oil, maritime, textiles, and food.[40] Consequently, the National Bank of Egypt, the country's flagship state-owned bank, opened in 2008 a branch in Shanghai, becoming the first Arab and African bank to have a presence in China.

Figures show that the volume of trade between China and Egypt rose exponentially between the late 1980s and the second decade of the twenty-first century. From a meager US$135 million in 1987 and $452 million in 1995, trade leapfrogged to $750.2 million, $2.14 billion, $5.8 billion, $8.8 billion, and $11.6 billion in the years 1999, 2005, 2009, 2011, and 2014, respectively.[41] By 2017, trade increased further to around US$10.8 billion, and then in 2018 it reached a record high of $13.8 billion.[42] To put things into perspective, China has since 2012 become Egypt's main trading partner, providing in 2017 around 13 percent of the total value of Egypt's imports (almost double that delivered by Germany, the second-highest exporter to Egypt).[43] Table 2

Table 2 Volume of Sino-Egyptian Trade, 2001–12 (in US$ Millions)

Year	Trade Volume	Year	Trade Volume
2012	9,544.73	2006	3,192.27
2011	8,801.58	2005	2,145.18
2010	6,958.9	2004	1,576.37
2009	5,845.02	2003	1,089.58
2008	6,303.2	2002	944.77
2007	4,672.53	2001	953.21

Source: Muhamad Olimat, *China and North Africa since World War II: A Bilateral Approach* (London: Lexington Books, 2014), p. 59.

Original Source: For the years 2001–10: China 2010 Statistical Yearbook, National Bureau of Statistics of China, 238. For the years 2011 and 2012: China 2013 Statistical Yearbook, National Bureau of Statistics of China, 232.

highlights the steady increase in the volume of bilateral trade in the years from 2001 to 2012.

Chinese exports to Egypt constitute the bulk of bilateral trade. Figures amounted to around US$8 billion in 2017 and $12 billion in 2018.[44] The percentage of Chinese imports to total Egyptian imports increased from around 4 percent in 2000 to 10.5 percent in 2013, making China the top exporting country to Egypt.[45] China's exports include a wide range of products, such as machinery, electronic equipment, steel, chemicals, plastics, textiles, vehicles, and various manufactured goods. While Chinese-Egyptian bilateral trade has always tilted in favor of China, Egyptian exports to China have gone a long way, rising from an insignificant US$10.6 million in 1994 to $342.5 million in 2008.[46] A decade later, in 2018, Egyptian exports to China hit, according to some estimates, a record of US$1.8 billion.[47] Concomitantly, while in 1983, China imported 0.9 percent of total Egyptian exports, and was ranked the twentieth among Egypt's export markets, that percentage increased to 2 percent in 2013, making China the fifteenth market in that rank.[48] Today, around 70–80 percent of Egypt's marble are exported to China. Egypt also exports a wide range of industrial products to China, including carpets, linen, ceramic, distillation products, sanitary wares, crystal, and glass, in addition to agricultural commodities, such as cotton and oranges.[49] In fact, Egypt became the third largest exporter of oranges to China in 2017.[50] Figure 1 demonstrates the rise in the volume of Egyptian exports to China in the period 1993–2018, and Table 3 underscores the conspicuous rise in China's share in Egypt's overall exports and imports in the period from 1994 to 2008.

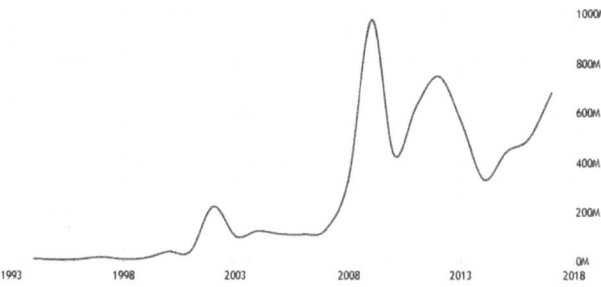

Figure 1 Egyptian Exports to China, 1993–2018

Source: Emmanuel Matambo, "Sino-Egyptian Industrial and Infrastructure Cooperation: Determinants and Outcomes," *UJ Centre for Africa-China Studies*, May 2019 (http://confucius-institute.joburg/wp-content/uploads/2019/06/Belt-Road-Policy-Brief-No-1-desktop.pdf), p. 13.

Original Source: Comtrade

Cumulative Chinese investments in Egypt surged in parallel with the growth in bilateral trade. Highlighting how economic relations are closely tied to political considerations, a Chinese official noted in October 2018 that more than 80 percent of these investments were made in the last four years (i.e., shortly after El-Sisi's ascendance to the heights of power in June 2014).[51] Significantly, these investments are diversified among a number of vital sectors, including energy, manufacturing, construction, and transport.

To begin with, it is worth noting that Egypt has since the aughts hosted a Chinese special economic zone (SEZ), one of only five zones China set up in Africa. In a US$1.5 billion joint venture with the Egyptian government, the Tianjin Economic-Technological Development Area (TEDA), officially launched in 2008 in the Suez region, is a trade and economic zone which hosts Chinese and Egyptian firms that wish to set up manufacturing and trading

Table 3 China's Share in Egyptian Exports and Imports, 1994–2008

Year	China's Share in Egypt's Exports	China's Share in Egypt's Imports
1994	0.3	2.0
1995	0.2	2.5
1996	0.2	2.2
1997	0.4	2.2
1998	0.3	2.5
1999	0.4	3.9
2000	0.8	4.6
2001	1.0	4.0
2002	4.7	4.5
2003	1.6	5.0
2004	1.6	5.01
2005	1.0	4.6
2006	0.8	5.8
2007	0.88	6.0
2008	1.3	8.4

Source: Assem Abu Hatab, Nada Shoumann and Huo Xuexi, "Exploring Egypt-China Bilateral Trade: Dynamics and Prospects," *Journal of Economic Studies* 39, no. 3 (2012), p. 318.

Original Source: United Nations Comtrade Database SITC Revision III (www.unstats.org/unsd/comtrade).

operations. While Egypt's interest lay in attracting Chinese investments, especially into sectors such as information and communication technology, manufacturing and renewable energy, the zone for China has acted as a gateway for Chinese companies into the markets of Europe, Africa, and the Middle East, especially countries with which Egypt has existing preferential trade agreements.[52] The flagship venture of Egyptian-Chinese economic collaboration under Mubarak, which covers an area of 7.3 million square meters, has succeeded in attracting sixty enterprises with a total investment of around US$1 billion.[53] The TEDA Suez zone currently hosts the Jushi Group, Asia's largest manufacturer of fiberglass, the light truck manufacturer Dayun, the manufacturer of electrical equipment XD, the producer of X-ray components IMD, and the manufacturing giant Muyang.[54] In 2016, the two countries agreed to expand the zone by approximately six square kilometers at an estimated investment of US$230 million.[55] Moreover, inspired by the success story of the Suez SEZ, the Egyptian government signed in 2018 a memorandum of understanding with the state-owned Chinese company CGCOC to plan and develop another industrial zone in the Mediterranean city of New Alamein.[56]

Remarkably, after El-Sisi became president, China has indulged in a number of huge investments in different sectors of Egypt's economy. In transportation, the Egyptian government and the Aviation Corporation of China (AVIC) signed in 2017 a US$1.2 billion deal to establish a 70-kilometer light electrical train that will link Cairo to the tenth of Ramadan City over eleven stations.[57] China also signed another thirteen-year contract worth US$110 million for the maintenance of the project.[58] Furthermore, an alliance of Chinese companies and banks signed a framework agreement in 2017 with Egypt's Suez Canal Economic Zone to take part in the development of the Ain Sokhna Port (Egypt's third-largest port), crucial for its proximity to the Suez Canal and Cairo.[59] In the following year, the Beijing-based China Harbour Engineering Company, the world's second-largest dredging company, won a tender to build a container terminal at the port with a contract value of US$118 million.[60] Signaling a special Chinese interest in ports, the Hong Kong-based Hutchison Port Holdings (HPH) bought in 2016 a 30.3 percent stake in Alexandria International Container Terminal, which owns and operates two terminals in Egypt.[61] HPH also operates the Egyptian ports of Alexandria and El-Dekheila, located on the Mediterranean Sea.

China has also got a sizeable share in the construction of Egypt's administrative capital, a three-phase megaproject launched in 2015, whose construction is estimated to cost an exorbitant sum of money, roughly $58 billion.[62] The Chinese State Construction Engineering Corporation (CSCEC) is building the city's business district, which includes twenty towers scattered over a vast area of 1.7 million meters, including a giant eighty-floor tower that, once completed, will be the tallest building in Africa.[63] The wide Chinese involvement in the construction of the new city also includes providing the Egyptian government with a $3 billion loan to design and build the business zone.[64] Earlier, Egypt was in talks with China Fortune Land Development for a whopping $20 billion investment project in the city, but the two-year negotiations faltered in 2018 due to a disagreement over revenue sharing.[65]

China has also committed billions of dollars-worth to numerous other economic fields. Chinese companies made their appearance in the energy sector, with CSCEC signing a $6.1 billion deal with Egypt's Eastern Oil and Gas Company to build an oil refinery in the Suez region.[66] In the field of renewable energy, China took part in the construction of the Benban solar plant in Aswan, slated to be the world's largest solar plant, building three solar stations in the complex with a total investment of about $180 million.[67] In electricity, the two countries signed a deal in 2018 to build the largest coal-fired power plant in the Middle East in the Red Sea port of Hamrawein. A consortium of China's Shanghai Electric, Dongfang Electric Cooperation, and Egypt's Hassan Allam Construction will construct the plant with investments worth a hefty $4.4 billion.[68] In the same year, China's state-owned Sinohydro reached an agreement with the Egyptian government to build an electricity storage station in the mountain of Ataka to the tune of $2.6 billion.[69] Chinese companies also made inroads into the agricultural market. The agribusiness giant New Hope established three animal feed-producing factories in Egypt. The third of these factories, located in El-Behera province, was established in 2016 at an investment of $15.8 million.[70] Further, the China Development Bank, China's largest bank for foreign investment and financial cooperation, offered in 2017 a $100 million loan to two Egyptian banks (Banque Misr, Egypt's second-largest state bank, and SaiBank) to finance small and medium-sized projects.[71]

Chinese tourism to Egypt has also flourished in the past few years. The number of Chinese tourists visiting Egypt more than doubled in 2017 to 300,000 up from some 130,000 in the previous year. Furthermore, around

400,000 Chinese tourists visited Egypt in 2018, according to the estimates of the counselor for economic affairs at China's embassy in Cairo.[72] In fact, Egypt was ranked in 2017 as the fourteenth popular destination for Chinese tourists traveling on the occasion of the Chinese New Year holiday (surpassing all countries located outside the Asia-Pacific area).[73] To absorb this increase, there are now fourteen charter flights a week operating from Chinese cities to Egyptian airports.[74] Consequently, the number of Chinese-speaking Egyptian tour guides reached 1,000 by 2016.[75] As a result of these burgeoning relations, the Chinese community in Egypt expanded to reach, according to one estimate, 35,000 in 2011.[76] Some of these might have left the country in the frantic period 2011–13, but it is reasonable to reckon that the upswing in economic and cultural relations after 2013 has attracted others to sojourn in Egypt.

The robustness of Egyptian-Chinese economic relations became evident in the age of COVID-19. When the pandemic hit China, Egypt was one of the earliest countries to send medical supplies to China.[77] Reciprocally, China delivered to Egypt three batches of medical supplies with a total weight of 38 tons in April and May of 2020. These consisted of millions of medical masks, and thousands of protective suits, medical gloves, test kits, and temperature assessment devices.[78] Also, experts from both sides exchanged their expertise and empirical observations on pandemic control and emergency response, agreeing to increase the capacity of the Cairo-based Sino-Egyptian masks factory to 100,000 masks daily.[79] Moreover, Egypt has reached an agreement with the Beijing-based Sinovac Biotech to manufacture its COVID-19 vaccine in Egypt once its production begins. According to an official Egyptian statement, the deal is set to make Egypt "the African hub for manufacturing China's vaccine for COVID-19."[80] Economically, the pandemic seemingly had a limited impact on bilateral trade and investment. Chinese projects in Egypt have not been suspended; Beijing's construction of a business district in Egypt's new capital has continued unabated; and bilateral trade in the first quarter of 2020 hit $3.1 billion, marking a modest increase from the same period in the previous year.[81] However, total bilateral trade in the first seven months of 2020 stood at $5.2 billion,[82] indicating that the total trade volume for the year would be slightly lower than the 2019 figures. Meanwhile, the Egyptian government is accelerating work on large infrastructure projects, including the construction of fourteen "fourth generation cities" which involve a wide participation by Chinese companies.[83] Additionally, a Chinese-led consortium won in September 2020 a $9 billion deal to design, build, and operate a high-speed rail that links the resort cities of Ain Sokhna and Alamein. Connecting the Red Sea with the Mediterranean, the 543-kilometer line is slated to be the longest in the Middle East.[84]

Cultural Relations

Egyptian-Chinese cultural relations and people-to-people exchanges have seen multiple signs of growth in recent years. For example, the University of Ain Shams, Egypt's second-largest university, who had set up a center of Chinese studies in 2004, established in 2019 another research center, the "Center for Studies and Research of the Silk Road," in order to conduct studies on topics of interest to the two countries.[85] In total, there are now fifteen Egyptian universities that have established a major in Chinese language, including the preeminent Al-Azhar University. Students exchange programs have also been expanded. The number of Egyptian students who currently study in China has reached around 1,000 while there are about 2,300 Chinese students studying in Egypt, making Egypt the first among West Asian and North African states to host Chinese students.[86] Additionally, the Egyptian-Chinese University (ECU), the only Chinese university in the Middle East, was founded in Cairo and started its operations in 2018. Established by a presidential decree as a nonprofit organization, the nascent university has four colleges: engineering and technology, economics and international trade, pharmacy, and medical technology and physical therapy. It currently has about 2,500 students.[87] In the same year, the Suez Canal University established an Egyptian-Chinese Applied Technology College, which offers bachelor degrees in the fields of communication, electronic technology, and mechatronic technology.[88] Crowning these various developments on the sixtieth anniversary of establishing diplomatic relations between China and Egypt, Cairo and Beijing inaugurated the Egyptian-Chinese Cultural Year in 2016, during which more than 100 cultural events were held in both countries.[89]

Military Relations

Since 2014, Egypt has taken pains to lessen its dependence on Western arms through diversifying its arms sources. Most of its efforts have focused on Russia, with which Egypt has signed arms deals worth billions of US dollars. Still, Cairo also showed interest in upgrading its military relations with China. To that end, an Egyptian-Chinese joint committee on defense cooperation was set up to augment bilateral security cooperation against terrorism and organized crime, and to boost Chinese arms sales to Egypt. Concomitantly, China's army chief of staff visited Cairo in 2014, and in 2015 Egypt's defense minister and the vice-president of the Central Military Commission (China's highest military authority) vowed to broaden the level of military cooperation between their countries. Military cooperation thereafter widened to include arms sales, joint navy drills, visits by warships, and mutual support in the fight against terrorism.[90]

Signs of bilateral military and security cooperation are abundant. In September 2015, for instance, Egyptian infantry troops participated in the massive military parade held in Beijing to commemorate the seventieth anniversary of the Second World War.[91] In the same month, a Chinese naval fleet consisting of a guided-missile destroyer, a guided-missile frigate, and an integrated supply ship arrived at the Alexandria Harbor, Egypt's biggest port, for a five-day visit.[92] Even more noteworthy, the naval forces of Egypt and China carried out in August 2019 joint military drills off Egypt's Mediterranean coast, involving counter-terrorism and anti-piracy operations.[93]

Additionally, Egypt purchased from China 32 Wing Loong-1D unmanned aerial vehicles, commonly known as armed drones, at a total cost of $64 million.[94] Much like their US counterparts, the Chinese drones could be used for purposes of surveillance, reconnaissance, and target acquisition, but Middle Eastern customers, including Egypt, favor them because they come "with fewer political strings."[95] Other aspects of military cooperation have been shrouded in secrecy, but it was reported that they include negotiations over Egypt's potential purchase of China's fighter jet J-10 (comparable to America's well-known F-16) as well as missile and air defense systems, the joint production in Egypt of China's advanced military training jet K-8, and cooperation in the field of space-based remote sensing technologies.[96] Overall, Egypt is the largest buyer of Chinese weapons in Africa, with a total import bill that exceeds the value of China's arms exports to its two close African allies, Sudan and Zimbabwe, combined.[97]

As a whole, the study of Sino-Egyptian relations has been framed within economic terms, treating economic considerations as the sole driver of Egypt's policy toward China. Yet, given the high pace and intensity of dealings between Egypt and China since 2014, it is profitable to think that political motivations lay behind the upgrade of bilateral relations. Due to the centralized nature of Egypt's political system, and the extent to which economic decisions are hostage to underlying political contexts, it is likely that deliberations and decisions on huge economic contracts and deals involved Egypt's top leadership, including the president. In other words, it could be argued that politics took precedence, and economics merely followed in its footsteps. The following section attempts to explain why, strategically and politically, the Egyptian regime has heavily sought to promote closer relations with China.

Egypt's "Going East" Foreign Policy

Perhaps more than most Middle Eastern countries, regime security considerations in Egypt have invariably had, from Nasser to El-Sisi, a huge impact on the conduct and attitude of foreign policy. Thus, no understanding of this policy in recent years can be complete without taking into account the impact of the Arab Spring on the worldviews and perceptions of its policy makers. The popular revolution that erupted in January 2011 came after three decades of near stagnation. Its potency threw the state into disarray and shook some of the fundamental pillars upon which it had survived for decades. For the first time in recent Egyptian history, political action embarked at the grassroots level and managed to sustain its momentum for eighteen days culminating in a major, hitherto unimaginable, change: the ouster of the president of the state.

On a different but related note, political sociologist Daniel Ritter endeavored to study the relationship between the success of unarmed revolutions in a country and the type of that country's international allies by studying a set of unarmed uprisings in the Middle East, including the stupendous wave of 2011. The main argument he put forward in his outstanding book, *The Iron Cage of Liberalism*, is that the success of unarmed revolutions "can be linked to the respective country's close relations with Western democracies."⁹⁸ This is the case because Western allies are "constrained by an *iron cage of liberalism* that made overt repression of nonviolent demonstrators politically costly" (emphasis in original).⁹⁹ The worldwide diffusion of the human rights discourse, Ritter cogently argues, has undermined the repressive capacities of regimes that are dependent on Western allies, emboldening the opposition in these countries in ways unavailable to their counterparts in countries that are not aligned to the West. This explains why the popular uprisings in Iran (1979), Tunisia (2011), and Egypt (2011) succeeded in toppling their rulers while those in Iran (2009) and Syria (2011) were crushed at ease. For rulers fixated on matters of security and survival, Ritter explains, Western patronage has turned "from benefit to burden."¹⁰⁰

Egypt's senior political elites have in all likelihood not read Ritter's book, but seeing first-hand the curtain come down on Mubarak's era, they have grasped its main proposition. Indeed, hell-bent on slipping out of liberalism's iron cage, El-Sisi has distanced his regime from liberal Western powers and dropped the liberal rhetoric from official discourse (in stark contrast to Mubarak who had stuck to the vocabulary of democracy in pursuit of legitimacy and international acceptance). Reviewing international alliances through the lens of internal security, he seemingly assessed the reliability of Egypt's allies according to their stance in 2011. Like the rest of Egypt's official elites, he was particularly frustrated with the Obama administration, even though it played no direct role in instigating or bolstering up the uprising. A few days into the popular mobilization in 2011, Obama had demanded the immediate launch of a meaningful transition process. This drew the ire of these elites, who expected nothing short of full support from their main foreign patron, only to see that it could switch sides to protesters in the throes of social upheaval. Again, they grew skittish about the Obama administration's response to the tumultuous developments of 2013: the popularly backed sacking of the Islamist president Mohamed Morsi and the subsequent institution of a military-led government in his place. Although Obama and senior US officials equivocated, refraining from blatantly describing what had happened as a coup (to avoid a wholesale suspension of US aid to Egypt in accordance with federal law), still, responding to human rights abuses, the US administration cancelled joint military exercises, froze military assistance, and was reluctant to receive Egypt's new leader, general-turned-president Abdel-Fattah El-Sisi, in the White House.[101] Even when Donald Trump, with whom El-Sisi had developed an amicable relationship, came to the saddle of US foreign policy, the US administration cut $100 million in military and economic aid to Egypt (and delayed the delivery of $200 million in military financing), pending improvements in its human rights record.[102] The incident served notice that unremitting US support is not guaranteed.

In short, Obama's response to the tumultuous events of 2011 and 2013 unnerved Egyptian officials, many of whom are men of the barracks, who, viewing politics primarily through a narrow security prism, innately see peril everywhere. They felt that they had been betrayed by the United States during two existential moments.[103] In an illuminating interview with the *Washington Post* conducted in August 2013, El-Sisi sniped at the US government: "You left the Egyptians. You turned your back on the Egyptians, and they won't forget that."[104] Fueled by this experience, Egypt sought alternative backers and allies, opting for Saudi Arabia and the UAE in quest for much-needed financial support, and Russia and China as sources of weapons and trade partners. Meanwhile, realizing the unreliability of US institutions, especially the Congress, quiet disengagement from the United States ensued after El-Sisi became president in 2014. The objective has not been to rupture Egypt's ties with the United States, something Cairo is ill-prepared to do, but rather to mitigate or loosen that alliance. In brief, the goal has been to diversify Cairo's foreign backers, maintaining its ties with Western capitals and Gulf states while also counterbalancing US influence by incorporating Moscow and Beijing to the list of allies in a bid to acquire a measure of aid and protection. Therefore, Cairo's "Going East" strategy, hailed by some Egyptian commentators and media anchors as a sign of independence, does not denote a bland geographical pivot, but rather, essentially, an alignment with countries that are more authoritarian and whose aid is not attached to any political conditions.

Within this context, China seemed like a perfect partner. Beijing's long-held principles of noninterference in the domestic affairs of other states and respect for states' sovereignty (reiterated in its 2016 China Arab Policy Paper)[105] are particularly relieving for the Egyptian government. Likewise, China's redefinition of human rights as consisting of social and economic rights only fits Cairo's own discourse on human rights, and its all-too-familiar resistance to, and flouting of, Western attempts to widen the margin for external intervention (under the umbrella of concepts like "humanitarian intervention" and "responsibility to protect") is also well-received by Cairo. In practice, both countries have always stressed their opposition to any foreign military intervention in the affairs of any other country under any circumstances.[106] In Cairo's calculations, China's veto power in the UN Security Council could be relied upon in the case of such events. Meanwhile, the Chinese model, commonly referred to as the "Beijing Consensus,"[107] which comprises a mix of strict monopoly of political life, export-oriented economic growth, and state-led development schemes, is immensely attractive for Egyptian statesmen.

More crucially, unlike Washington and major Western capitals, Beijing saw eye-to-eye with Cairo on the Arab Spring, and for the same reasons. Indeed, the massive demonstrations that swept across many cities in the Arab world in 2011 "frightened the Chinese government … [which] faces social and political tensions caused by rising inequality, injustice, and corruption."[108] To nip any potential unrest in the bud, the Chinese state imposed rigid internet monitoring techniques and tightened its grip on public gatherings. Chinese authorities blocked terms like "Egypt," "Tahrir Square," and "Jasmine Revolution" on the internet, and the Chinese press dropped the term "Arab Spring" or any other positive appellation in reference to the Arab uprisings, employing instead descriptions associated with "disorder," "civil war," and "irrationality."[109] *The People's Daily*, for example, described the Arab uprisings as "a movement that sacrifices people's interests," adding that "the 'freedom' finally makes the people threatened by death and humanitarian crisis."[110] Diplomatically, the Chinese government remained silent throughout Egypt's uprising in 2011 and until February 10, one day before Mubarak's resignation, when its foreign minister announced that his country rejected outside interference in Egypt's internal affairs.[111] Also, in the midst of Egypt's cruel turmoil in 2013, China reportedly assured Egypt about its resolve to use its status as a permanent Security Council member to oppose any attempt to politicize or internationalize Egypt's internal affairs.[112]

Reciprocating China's backing of the Egyptian government's oppression of its own dissidents, Cairo not only turned a blind eye to, but also took part in, China's suppression of the Uyghur Muslim minority, a Turkic-speaking ethnic group who live for the most part in northwestern China. Ostensibly obliging a request from the Chinese government, the Egyptian authorities waged a crackdown on Uyghur students living in Cairo in the summer of 2017. According to human rights reports, the wide campaign involved arresting between 90 and 120 Uyghurs, detaining them for months and allowing Chinese officials to interrogate them while in custody.[113] Even worse, there are serious suspicions that some of these Chinese Muslims were secretly extradited to China[114]; if true, a flagrant violation of international treaties Egypt had signed and ratified, particularly the 1987 UN Convention against Torture. A security agreement between China's Ministry of Public Security and Egypt's Interior Ministry, signed a fortnight before the roundup, left little room for doubt as to its real motivations.[115] As an anthropologist whose research focuses on the Uyghur nation observed, "The autonomy with which Chinese authorities were permitted to act in Egypt [was] unprecedented."[116] The grim ordeal reduced the thriving community of Muslim Chinese in Egypt from about 6,000 people to just fifty families.[117]

By not only averting its gaze from the prosecution of Chinese Muslims, but also partaking in it, Egypt in effect sacrificed some of the time-honored tenets of its foreign policy in the Islamic world at the altar of its mounting interests with China. Although identity issues were hardly a core issue to modern Egyptian rulers, from Nasser to Mubarak, and were, more often than not, used as an instrument to score points and undermine opponents, they have never vanished altogether from its foreign policy behavior. Traditionally, if the issue at hand required taking a stand that would undermine national interests, the Egyptian government would not respond in meaningful deeds, but would still resort to face-saving symbolic measures in defense of, and deference to, Islamic populations and values. Two cases from the last years of Mubarak's reign illustrate the point. First, capitalizing on its clout in the Islamic world and international organizations, the Egyptian diplomacy took the initiative in 2006 against the Danish cartoons that had depicted Prophet Mohammed as a terrorist, something which then put it on a collision course with the Danish government.[118] Secondly, Egypt's foreign minister from 2004 to 2011, Ahmed Abu El-Gheit, wrote in his memoirs that he had felt "too much uneasiness" about some of Pope Benedict XVI's public critique of Islam.[119] Albeit a staunch secular, he accordingly attempted to convince the Grand Sheikh of Al-Azhar to cancel a planned visit to the Vatican. The Sheikh, however, showed reluctance to do this, prompting Abu El-Gheit to discuss the matter with President Mubarak, who in turn informed the Sheikh that the visit's "timing is not appropriate."[120]

Doubtless, what the Muslim Chinese community has suffered in the past few years, it has now come to light, is far more serious than a cartoon or remarks made in passing in an esoteric speech. According to credible media and human rights organizations reports, about one million Uyghurs have been subjected to gross human rights abuses, including prolonged detention, psychological torture, and "systematic brainwashing" techniques in a dystopian network of secret high-security concentration camps.[121] While acts of torture and gang rape have also reportedly taken place in these camps,[122] Muslim women whose husbands had been detained were forced to "share beds with male government officials" assigned to keep watch of their behavior in their homes.[123] Nevertheless, the Egyptian government has not joined the call at the UN Human Rights Council (UNHCR) to investigate the abuses. In fact, along with thirty-six other countries, Egypt signed a letter in defense of China's policies that was submitted to the UNHCR and the UN High Commissioner for Human Rights.[124] The letter, which read "like a Chinese propaganda statement,"[125] commended China's "remarkable achievements in the field of human rights" and noted "*with appreciation* that human rights are respected and protected in China in the process of counterterrorism and de-radicalisation" (emphasis mine).[126]

Conclusion

Economic relations between Egypt and China are promising and expected to grow but they are also riddled with challenges. Bilateral trade figures point out to a pattern that has persisted over the decades, namely, a monumental Egyptian trade deficit with China. This deficit amounted to around $7.4 billion and $9.2 billion in 2012 and 2014, respectively.[127] Then, with the constant growth in trade levels, it has exceeded $10 billion in the last few years. From an Egyptian standpoint, therefore, more needs to be done to address this imbalance. Meanwhile, although rising steadily, the annual value of China's investments in Egypt remains limited, not only when compared with the total value of outward Chinese FDI (the third largest source of FDI in the world in 2018),[128] but also in comparison with total foreign investment in Egypt and total Chinese investments in some African states. In 2010, for instance, Egypt received only 2.6 percent of total Chinese investments in Africa, while the share of South Africa and Nigeria amounted to 31.8 percent and 9.3 percent, respectively.[129] Until 2015, China was ranked the fifteenth country in terms of foreign direct investments in Egypt.[130] Then, it became the thirteenth top investing country in Egypt in the fiscal year 2018–19.[131] The same thing could be said about the low volume of Chinese tourism to Egypt when contrasted with the fact that China has recently become the world's largest source of outbound tourism,[132] although, to be fair, this could be attributed to distance and cost considerations.

Truth be known, Egypt can do way more to attract a bigger number of Chinese investors and tourists. Egypt's economy was ranked the 114th (out of 190 countries) in the 2019 index of the Ease of Doing Business produced by the World Bank.[133] Exerting more effort to roll back red tape, enact business-friendly regulations, combat corruption, and enhance good governance are but a few measures that could be employed to increase Egypt's economic attractiveness. Further, Egypt's relations with China have for the most part been based on government-to-government ties. Civil society groups of all stripes can, in fact should, be encouraged to take part in the making of Egypt's relations with China, raising demands, voicing concerns, and providing feedback.

Despite their continual growth, Egypt–China economic ties are no bed of roses. The potential negative impact of Chinese imports on the ability of locally manufactured goods to survive, let alone compete in local and international markets, is a source of worry in Egypt. Furthermore, Chinese investments are encouraged to use more local materials and equipment instead of predominantly relying on Chinese inputs. Also, Egyptians are under-represented in senior positions of Chinese entities based in Egypt, which clearly diminishes the prospects of managerial know-how and skills transfer.[134] There is also concern among Egyptian bureaucrats and economic experts that China is primarily nourishing its fast-growing economy while insidiously harming the backwater economies of developing countries. Indeed, China's mercantilist overseas economic activities, particularly in Africa and Asia, promoting exports and extracting natural resources, give credence to fears that China's motives are not entirely benign. These fears were expressed by the ex-Malaysian prime minister Mahathir Mohamad when he, dropping diplomatic niceties, warned against "a new version of colonialism," alluding to growing unease in Asian states about the rising Chinese influence in their economies.[135] In the same vein, an Egyptian parliamentarian said in wrathful words that "whatever they say, it is a fact that the Chinese come to Africa not just with engineers and scientists—they are coming with farmers. It is neo-colonialism … There are no ethics, no values."[136] Likewise, an Egyptian researcher told me that some Egyptian bureaucrats working for state agencies tend to regard China with a jaundiced eye. "They say things like: The Chinese are fooling us. This is no different from Western colonialism," he said.[137] Moreover, there are widespread misgivings about China's deep pockets being primarily "debt traps" to recipient countries of Sino investments. To be sure, as long as economic cooperation between China and Egypt involves, predominantly, China's import of raw materials and its export of manufactured products, these relations can hardly be described as constituting a form of integration. Solid integration should include more parity, balance, and transparency.

On another crucial front, the specific roles assigned for Egypt in China's overriding BRI foreign policy strategy are still unclear. The Chinese government will have to clarify these roles to Egypt's government, business circles, and public opinion. Egyptians would like to ascertain exactly whether, and in what ways, the plan is going to be mutually beneficial. Two pertinent questions here are: (1) Will the BRI lower the volume of freight passing through the Suez Canal by redirecting it to the Eurasian land route? and (2) Are Egyptian territories seen as transit routes, merely springboards for Chinese manufacturers targeting international markets, or as sites for mutually advantageous manufacturing, infrastructure, technology-transfer, and labor-training operations? On a very general level of analysis, the question is, can Chinese monies help over the long-run in transforming the underdeveloped structure of Egypt's economy? So far, as a savvy scholar observed, Chinese financing has generally not been "directed to changing the economic structure of Middle Eastern economies."[138] Doubtless, in the absence of a comprehensive and well-articulated economic development plan, it is far from clear, as a recent report on Chinese-Egyptian economic relations concluded, whether "the sectors in which China has invested are those that will advance Egypt's long-term strategic economic interests."[139]

Politically, China cannot hope to effectively deal with the complex and jumbled challenges of the Middle East without a blueprint, assertiveness, and allies. To be sure, leadership comes with responsibilities; one cannot assume the former before shouldering the latter. In fact, if China continues to stay above the fray—remaining as Obama put it, "a global free rider"[140]—it will run the risk of being perceived in Egypt, and the entire region, as a self-serving, opportunistic power, reaping economic dividends without incurring political costs. No less importantly, negative perceptions among pro-democracy Arab peoples about China's authoritarian tendencies, undisguised in its antipathy toward the Arab uprisings, its naked support of the worst brands of authoritarian regimes in the region (such as the pitiless Syrian regime) and its suppression of its own Muslims, could become a veritable stumbling block. These actions are not only outrageous, but also potentially damaging to China's interests in Egypt and the Arab world.

Notes

1   Kyle Haddad-Fonda, "The Rhetoric of 'Civilization' in Chinese-Egyptian Relations," *Middle East Institute*, August 1, 2017, https://www.mei.edu/publications/rhetoric-civilization-chinese-egyptian-relations. The first delegation of Chinese students at Al-Azhar University arrived in Cairo in 1931. In the following year, King Fouad issued a decree that established a special section for Chinese students at the university. See "Chinese-Egyptian Relations," *Marefa*, https://www.marefa.org/العلاقات_الصينية_المصرية. For a good source on the Chinese Azharites from the 1930s to the 1950s, see John Chen, "Re-orientation: The Chinese Azharites between Umma and Third World, 1938–55," *Comparative Studies of South Asia, Africa and the Middle East* 34, no. 1 (2014), pp. 24–51.

2   Yasser Gadallah, "An Analysis of the Evolution of Sino-Egyptian Economic Relations," in *Toward Well-Oiled Relations? China's Presence in the Middle East Following the Arab Spring*, edited by Niv Horesh (London: Palgrave Macmillan, 2016), p. 95.

3   Muhamad Olimat, *China and North Africa since World War II: A Bilateral Approach* (London: Lexington Books, 2014), pp. 49 & 58.

4   Kyle Haddad-Fonda, "The Domestic Significance of China's Policy toward Egypt, 1955–1957," *The Chinese Historical Review* 21, no. 1 (May 2014), pp. 56–8.
5   Ibid., p. 59.
6   Yitzhak Shichor, *The Middle East in China's Foreign Policy, 1949–1977* (Cambridge: Cambridge University Press, 1979), p. 98.
7   Joseph Khalili, "Communist China and the United Arab Republic," *Asian Survey* 10, no. 4 (April 1970), p. 313.
8   Nasser cut Egypt's diplomatic relations with China in October 1959 because Beijing had permitted the Syrian communist leader Khaled Bakdash to criticize Nasser during a speech he made at the tenth anniversary celebrations of founding the Chinese republic. Relations were restored in January 1960.
9   Anoushiravan Ehteshami and Niv Horesh, *How China's Rise Is Changing the Middle East* (Abingdon and New York: Routledge, 2019), p. 103.
10 Yitzhak Shichor, "Respected and Suspected: Middle Eastern Perceptions of China's Rise," in *Asian Thought on China's Changing International Relations*, edited by Niv Horesh and Emilian Kavalski (Basingstoke & New York: Palgrave Macmillan, 2014), p. 124.
11 Hashim Behbehani, *China's Foreign Policy in the Arab World, 1955–75: Three Case Studies* (London: Kegan Paul International, 1981), p. 4.
12 For more information on the mounting role of economic considerations in the making of Egyptian foreign policy from the 1970s onwards, see Abdel Monem Said, "From Geopolitics to Geo-Economics: Egyptian National Security Perceptions," in *National Threat Perceptions in the Middle East*, edited by James Leonard, Shmuel Limone, Abdel Monem Said and Yezid Sayigh (New York and Geneva: United Nations, 1995); and Ali Hillal Dessouki, "The Primacy of Economics: The Foreign Policy of Egypt," in *The Foreign Policies of Arab States: The Challenge of Change*, edited by Bahgat Korany and Ali Hillal Dessouki, 2nd Edition (Boulder, CL: Westview Press, 1991).
13 Sherifa Fadel Mohamed, "Egyptian-Chinese Relations between Continuity and Change (2003–2013)," *Al-Mustaqbal Al-Arabi*, no. 420 (February 2014), p. 42.
14 Heba Saleh, "Egypt Sees Chinese Investment, and Tourists as a 'Win-Win' Boost," *Financial Times*, October 30, 2018, https://www.ft.com/content/e490d960-7613-11e8-8cc4-59b7a8ef7d3d
15 Mahmoud Soliman and Jun Zhao, "The Multiple Roles of Egypt in China's 'Belt and Road' Initiative," *Asian Journal of Middle Eastern and Islamic Studies* 13, no. 3 (2019), p. 429.
16 Mohammed Selim, "Egypt and the New Silk Road," *Executive Intelligence Review*, (August 4, 2000), p. 29.

17 Ahmed El-Sayed Al-Naggar, "Developing Egyptian-Chinese Relations," *Ahram Online*, January 24, 2016, http://english.ahram.org.eg/NewsContentP/4/185697/Opinion/Developing-EgyptianChinese-relations.aspx
18 Ashraf Aboul-Yazid, "Egypt and the New Silk Road," *Al-Ahram Weekly*, Issue 1248, May 28, 2015.
19 Quoted in Ehteshami and Horesh, *How China's Rise*, p. 106.
20 Hassan Fayed, "Egypt Should Teach Mandarin at School and Build a Chinese Temple," *Egyptian Streets*, January 18, 2016, https://egyptianstreets.com/2016/01/18/egypt-should-teach-mandarin-at-school-and-build-a-chinese-temple/
21 Ehteshami and Horesh, *How China's Rise*, p. 103.
22 Mohamed Hamshi, "The Political Economy of Arab-Chinese Relations: Challenges and Strategic Opportunities," *Al-Mustaqbal Al-Arabi* (2017), p. 111; and "The Far East and Near East are Meeting Somewhere in the Middle: An In-Depth Look at the Recent Sino-Egyptian Rig Agreement," *Egypt Oil and Gas Newspaper*, December 29, 2014, https://egyptoil-gas.com/features/the-far-east-and-near-east-are-meeting-somewhere-in-the-middle-an-in-depth-look-at-the-recent-sino-egyptian-rig-agreement/11423/
23 Ibrahim Fraihat and Andrew Leber, "China and the Middle East after the Arab Spring: From Status-Quo Observing to Proactive Engagement," *Asian Journal of Middle Eastern and Islamic Studies* 13, no. 1 (2019), p. 4.
24 Anu Sharma, "An Analysis of 'Belt and Road' Initiative and the Middle East," *Asian Journal of Middle Eastern and Islamic Studies* 13, no. 1 (2019), p. 42; and Hamshi, "The Political Economy of Arab-Chinese Relations," p. 123.
25 Emmanuel Matambo, "Sino-Egyptian Industrial and Infrastructure Cooperation: Determinants and Outcomes," *UJ Centre for Africa-China Studies*, May 2019, http://confucius-institute.joburg/wp-content/uploads/2019/06/Belt-Road-Policy-Brief-No-1-desktop.pdf, p. 4.
26 Yousef Saba, "IMF Expects Egypt Economy to Grow 5.9% in Year to End of June," *Reuters*, October 15, 2019, https://www.reuters.com/article/us-egypt-economy-imf/imf-expects-egypt-economy-to-grow-5-9-in-year-to-end-of-june-idUSKBN1WU1TG
27 "Egypt Aims to Reach Growth Rate of 6.4% during 2020/21: Min.," *Egypt Today*, November 11, 2019, https://www.egypttoday.com/Article/3/77668/Egypt-aims-to-reach-growth-rate-of-6-4-during
28 International Monetary Fund, "World Economic Outlook Database, October 2019," https://tinyurl.com/y6xvstrs

29 Enda Curran, "These Could Be the World's Biggest Economies by 2030," *Bloomberg*, January 8, 2019, https://www.bloomberg.com/news/articles/2019-01-08/world-s-biggest-economies-seen-dominated-by-asian-ems-by-2030

30 "Africa Infrastructure Development Index (AIDI), 2019," Africa Infrastructure Knowledge Program, 2019, http://infrastructureafrica.opendataforafrica.org/rscznob/africa-infrastructure-development-index-aidi-2019

31 "Egypt Is Africa's Number One Investment Destination, Says RMB Report," *Enterprise*, September 19, 2019, https://enterprise.press/stories/2019/09/19/egypt-is-africas-number-one-investment-destination-says-rmb-report/

32 Juan Chen, "Strategic Synergy between Egypt 'Vision 2030' and China's 'Belt and Road' Initiative," *Outlines of Global Transformations: Politics, Economics, Law* 11, no. 5 (2018), p. 226.

33 These include the European Union-Egypt Free Trade Agreement, the Greater Arab Free Trade Area Agreement, the Agadir Free Trade Agreement, the Common Market for Eastern and Southern Africa (COMESA), the Southern African Development Community (SADC), the Economic Community of East African States (ECEAS), and the African Continental Free Trade Area (AfCFTA).

34 In its 2017 summit in Xiamen, BRICS introduced the 5+9 mode (which includes the five members as well as nine emerging markets) in an attempt to foster closer economic ties between member states and developing countries. Egypt attended the summit with a huge delegation headed by President El-Sisi.

35 Chen, "Strategic Synergy," p. 223.

36 Soliman and Zhao, "The Multiple Roles," p. 431.

37 Doaa Moneim, "Egyptian Investment Minister Hails China's Belt and Road Initiative," *Ahram Online*, October 22, 2019, http://english.ahram.org.eg/NewsContent/3/12/353403/Business/Economy/Egyptian-investment-minister-hails-China's-Belt-an.aspx

38 "Egypt Vision 2030," Arab Republic of Egypt, Ministry of Communications and Information Technology, http://mcit.gov.eg/Upcont/Documents/Reports%20and%20Documents_492016000_English_Booklet_2030_compressed_4_9_16.pdf, p. 10

39 Wessam Abdel-Alim, "Text of President El Sisi's Speech at the Opening Session of the Belt and Road Forum Summit," *Al-Ahram*, April 26, 2019, http://gate.ahram.org.eg/News/2148829.aspx

40 Gadallah, "An Analysis of the Evolution," pp. 96–7.

41 Olimat, *China and North Africa*, pp. 58–9; and Emma Scott, "Sino-Arab, Sino-Egyptian Relations: 60 Years On," *CCS Commentary* (Centre for Chinese Studies),

April 4, 2016, http://www0.sun.ac.za/ccs/wp-content/uploads/2016/04/CCS_Commentary_Sino-Arab_60_Years_04APR2016.pdf, p. 2; and Farah Halime, "Chinese Firms Brave Uncertainty in Egypt to Gain a Foothold in Middle East," *New York Times*, August 29, 2012, https://www.nytimes.com/2012/08/30/world/middleeast/chinese-firms-brave-uncertainty-in-egypt.html

42 Aya Samir, "Egyptian-Chinese Relations: Historical Similarity and Political Support," *Akhbar El-Yom*, August 30, 2018, https://m.akhbarelyom.com/news/newdetails/2716881/1/العلاقات-المصرية-الصينية-تشابه-تاريخي-ودعم-دبلوماسي; and Farid Farid, "Nightmare as Egypt Aided China to Detain Uighurs," *AFP*, August 18, 2019, https://news.yahoo.com/nightmare-egypt-aided-china-detain-uighurs-024625386.html

43 David Wood, "Egypt Loves China's Deep Pockets," *Foreign Policy*, August 28, 2018, https://foreignpolicy.com/2018/08/28/egypt-loves-chinas-deep-pockets/

44 Matambo, "Sino-Egyptian Industrial and Infrastructure Cooperation," p. 12; and "Trade Exchange Bet. Egypt, China Hits $13.8B in 2018," *Egypt Today*, June 17, 2019, https://www.egypttoday.com/Article/3/71681/Trade-exchange-bet-Egypt-China-hits-13-8B-in-2018

45 Al-Naggar, "Developing Egyptian-Chinese Relations."

46 Assem Abu Hatab, Nada Shoumann and Huo Xuexi, "Exploring Egypt-China Bilateral Trade: Dynamics and Prospects," *Journal of Economic Studies* 39, no. 3 (2012), p. 316.

47 Nada Mustafa, "Cairo-Beijing Have Witnessed Obvious Growth since Sisi's Presidency: Chinese Official," *Sada Elbalad English*, July 9, 2019, https://see.news/egypt-enjoys-attractive-tourist-destinations-chinese-official/

48 Ahmed El-Sayed Al-Naggar, "Developing Egyptian-Chinese Relations."

49 Gadallah, "An Analysis of the Evolution," p. 108; and Matambo, "Sino-Egyptian Industrial and Infrastructure Cooperation," p. 12.

50 Saleh, "Egypt Sees Chinese Investment."

51 Ibid.

52 Tom Mitchell, "Egypt Courts China for Suez Special Zone," *Financial Times*, March 2, 2010, https://www.ft.com/content/5a3445fa-2625-11df-aff3-00144feabdc0; and Janvier Liste, Jacob Kolster and Nono Matondo-Fundani, "Chinese Investments and Employment Creation in Algeria and Egypt," *African Development Bank*, 2012, https://ecdpm.org/wp-content/uploads/2013/10/Chinese-Investments-Employment-Creation-Algeria-Egypt-2012.pdf, p. 12

53 Chen, "Strategic Synergy," p. 229.

54 "Current Development Situation," *TEDA Suez*, April 27, 2017, http://www.setc-zone.com/system/2017/04/27/011260662.shtml

55 "Launch of Expansion Area of China-Egypt TEDA Suez Economic and Trade Cooperation Zone," *TEDA Suez*, April 27, 2017, http://www.setc-zone.com/system/2017/04/27/011260701.shtml

56 "Egypt, China to Cooperate on First Industrial Zone in New Alamein," *Ahram Online*, May 30, 2018, http://english.ahram.org.eg/NewsContent/3/0/301451/Business/0/Egypt-China-to-cooperate-on-first-industrial-zone.aspx

57 "Egypt, China to Establish Electric Train Project Worth $1.2B," *Egypt Today*, July 24, 2017, https://www.egypttoday.com/Article/3/13432/Egypt-China-to-establish-electric-train-project-worth-1-2B

58 "China, Egypt Sign USD 571 mn in Contracts for Electric Train Project," *Enterprise*, October 14, 2019, https://enterprise.press/stories/2019/10/14/china-egypt-sign-usd-571-mn-in-contracts-for-electric-train-project/

59 "New Agreement to Develop Sokhna Port Sees China Cooperation," *Egypt Today*, May 12, 2017, https://www.egypttoday.com/Article/3/5021/New-agreement-to-develop-Sokhna-Port-sees-China-cooperation

60 "CHEC Starts Construction of Second Container Terminal in Egypt's Ain Sokhna," *Ports Europe*, September 5, 2018, https://www.portseurope.com/__trashed-13/

61 "Hutchison Port Holdings Buys Stake in Egyptian Ports Operator—Statement," *Reuters*, March 7, 2016, https://www.reuters.com/article/aict-ma-ckh-holdings/hutchison-port-holdings-buys-stake-in-egyptian-ports-operator-statement-idUSL5N16F0R6

62 Aidan Lewis and Mohamed Abdellah, "Egypt's New Desert Capital Faces Delays as It Battles for Funds," *Reuters*, May 13, 2019, https://www.reuters.com/article/us-egypt-new-capital/egypts-new-desert-capital-faces-delays-as-it-battles-for-funds-idUSKCN1SJ10I

63 "Egypt, China Join Hands to Build Up Egypt's New Capital," *China Daily*, July 10, 2018, https://www.chinadaily.com.cn/a/201807/10/WS5b445cada3103349141e1e00.html; and "Feature: China, Egypt Join Hands to Build CBD Project in Egypt's New Capital City," *Xinhua*, March 19, 2019, http://www.xinhuanet.com/english/2019-03/19/c_137907912.htm

64 "Egypt Signs $3 Billion Loan Deal with Chinese Commercial Bank to Build Business Zone in New Capital," *Ahram Online*, April 28, 2019, http://english.ahram.org.eg/NewsContent/3/12/330776/Business/Economy/Egypt-signs-billion-loan-deal-with-Chinese-commer.aspx

65 Mirette Magdy, "China's $20 Billion New Egypt Capital Project Talks Fall Through," *Bloomberg*, December 16, 2018, https://www.bloomberg.com/news/

66 articles/2018-12-16/china-s-20-billion-new-egypt-capital-project-talks-fall-through
66 "China State Construction Signs a 9.6 Billion US Dollar EPC Contract with Egypt," *CSCEC*, September 2, 2018, https://english.cscec.com/CompanyNews/CorporateNews/201811/2892383.html
67 Mahmoud Saad Diab, "'Belt and Road' Puts Egypt at Forefront of China's New Renewable Energy Projects," *Ahram Online*, March 23, 2019, http://english.ahram.org.eg/NewsContent/1/64/328705/Egypt/Politics-/Belt-and-Road-puts-Egypt-at-forefront-of-Chinas-ne.aspx
68 "Chinese Consortium Wins Contract for Hamrawein Coal-Fired Plant," *Energy Egypt*, June 26, 2018, https://energyegypt.net/chinese-consortium-wins-contract-for-egypts-hamrawein-coal-fired-power-plant/
69 Marwa Yahya, "Chinese Investments in Egypt's Electricity Sector in Continuous Increase: Official," *Xinhuanet*, September 8, 2018, https://mail.yahoo.com/d/folders/1?.src=fp&guce_referrer=ahr0chm6ly9sb2dpbi55ywhvby5jb20v&guce_referrer_sig=aqaaagunarvcaorcnpblq8hb_fe_ffeo0ef2emysdcqa6k2uqjr9pj1nr0apzhtn8sgc8lcucd3l7hgrjbv2vjiz1scug33elvsf1bshntn8n1tktxc_qg16icq8bxqclpabxjfx-i_ro3g0_-1epdofol8o1cp33ix3yuoh1hoc3of-
70 "China's Agribusiness Giant New Hope Expands in Egypt amid Growing Sino-Egyptian Ties," *Xinhua*, March 19, 2018, https://tribune.com.pk/story/1663137/3-chinas-agribusiness-giant-new-hope-expands-egypt-amid-growing-sino-egyptian-ties/
71 "Banque Misr Signs $100 Million Loan with China Development Bank," https://www.banquemisr.com/en/about-us/press/china-development-bank; and "Egyptian, Chinese Banks Sign Loan Deals to Enhance Financial Cooperation," *China Daily*, September 18, 2017, http://www.chinadaily.com.cn/business/2017-09/18/content_32147872.htm
72 Mustafa, "Cairo-Beijing Have Witnessed Obvious Growth."
73 Haddad-Fonda, "The Rhetoric of 'Civilization.'"
74 Saleh, "Egypt Sees Chinese Investment."
75 Chen, "Strategic Synergy," p. 229.
76 Liste, Kolster and Matondo-Fundani, "Chinese Investments and Employment Creation," p. 11.
77 "Egypt Sends Medical Supplies to China to Help Face Coronavirus Spread," *Egypt Today*, January 31, 2020, https://www.egypttoday.com/Article/1/81158/Egypt-sends-medical-supplies-to-China-to-help-face-coronavirus

78 "3rd Chinese Medical Aid to Egypt Weighing 30 Tons Arrives amid COVID-19 Crisis," *Egypt Today*, May 16, 2020, https://www.egypttoday.com/Article/1/86799/3rd-Chinese-medical-aid-to-Egypt-weighing-30-tons-arrives
79 Ibid.
80 Muhammad Mansour, "Egypt Set to Mass Produce China-Developed COVID-19 Vaccine," *Chinafrica*, September 3, 2020, http://www.chinafrica.cn/Homepage/202009/t20200904_800219713.html
81 "COVID-19 Has 'Little Impact' on Egypt-China Bilateral Trade: Chinese Ambassador," *Xinhua*, June 19, 2020, http://www.xinhuanet.com/english/2020-06/19/c_139149954.htm; and Shaimaa Al-Aees, "Egypt-China Economic Cooperation Will Further Grow Post-COVID-19: Chinese Ambassador," *Daily News Egypt*, July 28, 2020, https://dailynewsegypt.com/2020/07/28/egypt-china-economic-cooperation-will-further-grow-post-covid-19-chinese-ambassador/
82 "Trade Exchange Bet. Egypt, China Reaches $5.2B in 7 Months," *Egypt Today*, August 26, 2020, https://www.egypttoday.com/Article/3/91279/Trade-exchange-bet-Egypt-China-reaches-5-2B-in-7
83 John Calabrese, "Towering Ambitions: Egypt and China Building for the Future," *Middle East Institute*, October 6, 2020, https://www.mei.edu/publications/towering-ambitions-egypt-and-china-building-future
84 "Egyptian-Chinese Consortium Wins Ain Sokhna–Alamein High-Speed Rail Contract," *Enterprise*, September 6, 2020, https://enterprise.press/stories/2020/09/06/egyptian-chinese-consortium-wins-ain-sokhna-alamein-high-speed-rail-contract-21245/; and Dan Weatherley, "China-led Consortium Wins High-Speed Rail Project in Egypt," *Construction Global*, September 16, 2020, https://www.constructionglobal.com/construction-projects/china-led-consortium-wins-high-speed-rail-project-egypt
85 Mai Shaheen, "Ain Shams Univ. Opens 'Silk Road' Research, Studies Center," *Sada Elbalad English*, January 13, 2019, https://see.news/ain-shams-univ-opens-silk-road-research-studies-center/
86 Chen, "Strategic Synergy," p. 230.
87 "Egyptian-Chinese University Adds New Aspect to Growing Egypt-China Cooperation," *Xinhua*, September 9, 2019, http://www.xinhuanet.com/english/2019-09/09/c_138378202.htm
88 Mahmoud Fouly, "Suez Canal University Model of Fruitful Educational Cooperation between Egypt, China: University Chief," *Xinhua*, September 21, 2018, http://www.xinhuanet.com/english/2018-09/21/c_137484410.htm
89 Scott, "Sino-Arab, Sino-Egyptian Relations," p. 2.

90 Elena Aoun and Thierry Kellner, "The Crises in the Middle East: A Window of Opportunity for Rising China," *European Journal of East Asian Studies* 14 (2015), p. 199.
91 "Sisi's Attendance of Parade in Beijing Highlights Egypt-China Close Ties," *China Daily*, September 2, 2015, http://www.chinadaily.com.cn/world/2015victoryanniv/2015-09/02/content_21774686.htm
92 "Chinese Fleet Arrives in Egypt for 5-Day Visit," *Egypt Independent*, September 3, 2015, https://ww.egyptindependent.com/chinese-fleet-arrives-egypt-5-day-visit/
93 "Egypt, China Naval Forces Carry Out Joint Military Drills Off Egypt's Mediterranean," *Ahram Online*, August 21, 2019, http://english.ahram.org.eg/NewsContent/1/64/344171/Egypt/Politics-/Egypt,-China-naval-forces-carry-out-joint-military.aspx
94 Mahmoud Gamal, "Egypt: Policies of Military Armament, 2018," *Egyptian Institute for Studies*, April 5, 2019 (https://eipss-eg.org/2018-العسكري-التسليح-سياسات-مصر/); and "Egypt Inducts Armed Chinese Drones," *Arabian Aerospace*, April 29, 2019, https://www.arabianaerospace.aero/egypt-inducts-armed-chinese-drones.html
95 Kyle Mizokami, "For the First Time, Chinese UAVs Are Flying and Fighting in the Middle East," *Popular Mechanics*, December 22, 2015, https://www.popularmechanics.com/military/weapons/news/a18677/chinese-drones-are-flying-and-fighting-in-the-middle-east/
96 Shaimaa Galal, "The Alliance of the Seven: How Egypt Handles the File of Military Production," *Al-Dostour*, March 6, 2018, https://www.dostor.org/2081187; and Maha Salem, "Get to Know the Most Important Milestones of Egyptian-Chinese Military Cooperation," *Al-Ahram*, September 3, 2017, http://gate.ahram.org.eg/News/1575795.aspx
97 "Chinese-Egyptian Relations," *Marefa*.
98 Daniel Ritter, *The Iron Cage of Liberalism: International Politics and Unarmed Revolutions in the Middle East and North Africa* (Oxford: Oxford University Press, 2015), p. 5.
99 Ibid.
100 Ibid., p. 214.
101 For more on strained American-Egyptian relations in the tumultuous years from 2011 to 2013, see Nael Shama, "Egypt and Obama: Turbulent Times, Bouncy Relations," in *The World Views of the Obama Era: From Hope to Disillusionment*, edited by Matthias Maass (London: Palgrave Macmillan, 2018), pp. 72–3.

102 "Trump Administration Cuts, Delays $300M in Aid to Egypt," *CBS News*, August 22, 2017, https://www.cbsnews.com/news/egypt-united-states-delays-military-economic-aid/
103 Shama, "Egypt and Obama," pp. 72–3.
104 Lally Weymouth, "Rare Interview with Egyptian Gen. Abdel Fatah al-Sissi," *The Washington Post*, August 3, 2013, https://www.washingtonpost.com/world/middle_east/rare-interview-with-egyptian-gen-abdel-fatah-al-sissi/2013/08/03/a77eb37c-fbc4-11e2-a369-d1954abcb7e3_story.html
105 The paper stated that "China upholds the Five Principles of Peaceful Coexistence, namely, mutual respect for sovereignty and territorial integrity, mutual non-aggression, mutual non-interference in each other's internal affairs, equality and mutual benefit, and peaceful co-existence" ("China's Arab Policy Paper," *Ministry of Foreign Affairs of the People's Republic of China*, January 13, 2016, https://www.fmprc.gov.cn/mfa_eng/zxxx_662805/t1331683.shtml).
106 Aoun and Kellner, "The Crises in the Middle East," pp. 218–19.
107 The term was originally coined by Joshua Ramo in his 2004 book that carried the title *The Beijing Consensus*.
108 Suisheng Zhao, "The China Model and the Authoritarian State," *East Asia Forum*, August 31, 2011, https://www.eastasiaforum.org/2011/08/31/the-china-model-and-the-authoritarian-state/
109 Wang Jin, "Selective Engagement: China's Middle East Policy after the Arab Spring," *Strategic Assessment* 19, no. 2 (July 2016), p. 110.
110 Ibid.
111 Mohamed, "Egyptian-Chinese Relations," p. 42.
112 "Egyptian Diplomat: China Has Decided to Stand Beside Egypt in Any Discussions at the Security Council," *Al-Quds Al-Arabi*, August 28, 2013, https://www.alquds.co.uk/%D8%AF%D8%A8%D9%84%D9%88%D9%85%D8%A7%D8%B3%D9%8A-%D9%85%D8%B5%D8%B1%D9%8A-%D8%A7%D9%84%D8%B5%D9%8A%D9%86-%D8%AA%D9%82%D8%B1%D8%B1-%D8%A7%D9%84%D9%88%D9%82%D9%88%D9%81-%D8%A8%D8%AC%D8%A7%D9%86%D8%A8/
113 Mohamed Mostafa and Mohamed Nagi, "'They Are Not Welcome': Report on the Uyghur Crisis in Egypt," *Association for Freedom of Thought and Expression and the Egyptian Commission for Rights and Freedoms*, https://afteegypt.org/en/academic_freedoms/2017/10/01/13468-afteegypt.html, p. 5.

114 Nour Youssef, "Egyptian Police Detain Uighurs and Deport Them to China," *New York Times*, July 6, 2017, https://www.nytimes.com/2017/07/06/world/asia/egypt-muslims-uighurs-deportations-xinjiang-china.html

115 "Agreement between Abdel-Ghaffar and China's Deputy Security Minister on Combatting Terrorism," *Al-Tahrir*, June 19, 2017, https://www.eltahrer.com/Story/789836/اتفاق-بين-عبد-الغفار-ونائب-وزير-الأمن-بالصين-على-مكافحة-الإرهاب.

116 Farid, "Nightmare as Egypt Aided China to Detain Uighurs."

117 Ibid.

118 Ahmed Abu El-Gheit, *My Testimony: Egyptian Foreign Policy, 2004–2011* (Cairo: Nahdet Misr, 2013), pp. 407–9.

119 Abu El-Gheit is probably referring to the speech the Pope gave at the University of Regensburg in September 2006, in which he quoted harsh criticism of Islam by the fourteenth century Byzantine emperor Manuel II Palaeologus.

120 Ibid., p. 409.

121 "Data Leak Reveals How China 'Brainwashes' Uighurs in Prison Camps," *BBC*, November 24, 2019, https://www.bbc.com/news/world-asia-china-50511063

122 Zamira Rahim, "Prisoners in China's Xinjiang Concentration Camps Subjected to Gang Rape and Medical Experiments, Former Detainee Says," *The Independent*, October 22, 2019, https://www.independent.co.uk/news/world/asia/china-xinjiang-uighur-muslim-detention-camps-xi-jinping-persecution-a9165896.html

123 Chris Baynes, "Muslim Women 'Forced to Share Beds' with Male Chinese Officials after Husbands Detained in Internment Camps," *The Independent*, November 5, 2019, https://www.independent.co.uk/news/world/asia/muslim-china-uighur-forced-share-beds-male-officials-detention-camps-a9185861.html

124 Catherine Putz, "Which Countries Are for or against China's Xinjiang Policies?" *The Diplomat*, July 15, 2019, https://thediplomat.com/2019/07/which-countries-are-for-or-against-chinas-xinjiang-policies/

125 Haisam Hassanein, "Arab States Give China a Pass on Uyghur Crackdown," *Policy Watch* 3169 (The Washington Institute for Near East Policy), August 26, 2019, https://www.washingtoninstitute.org/policy-analysis/view/arab-states-give-china-a-pass-on-uyghur-crackdown

126 Nick Cumming-Bruce, "More Than 35 Countries Defend China over Mass Detention of Uighur Muslims in UN Letter," *The Independent*, July 13, 2019, https://www.independent.co.uk/news/world/asia/china-mass-detentions-uighur-muslims-un-letter-human-rights-a9003281.html

127 Ahmed El-Sayed Al-Naggar, "Egypt and China: The Potential for Stronger Economic Ties," *Ahram Online*, October 21, 2016, http://english.ahram.org.eg/NewsContentP/4/246289/Opinion/Egypt-and-China-The-potential-for-stronger-economi.aspx; and Gadallah, "An Analysis of the Evolution," p. 102.
128 "FDI in Figures," *OECD*, April 2018, http://www.oecd.org/daf/inv/investment-policy/FDI-in-Figures-April-2018.pdf
129 Barassou Diawara and Kobena Hanson, "What Does the Evidence Say about Contemporary China-Africa Relations," in *Innovating South-South Cooperation: Policies, Challenges, and Prospects*, edited by Hany Besada, Evren Tok and Leah Polonenko (Ottawa: University of Ottawa Press, 2019), p. 225.
130 Al-Naggar, "Developing Egyptian-Chinese Relations."
131 "Foreign Direct Investment (FDI) in Egypt by Country," *Central Bank of Egypt*, https://www.cbe.org.eg/_layouts/15/WopiFrame.aspx?sourcedoc={554C10B8-7EA4-4514-9670-AF1068A22148}&file=External%20Sector%20Data%20271.xlsx&action=default. During President Sisi's visit to China to attend the 2018 Forum on China-Africa Cooperation, Egypt signed scores of contracts with Chinese firms at a total worth of $18.3 billion. If implemented, which is far from certain, China will be the top foreign investor in Egypt. However, as Scott rightly noted, many of the deals Egypt signed with China are MoUs "signifying early-stage negotiations rather than actual investment commitments" (Emma Scott, "China-Egypt Trade and Investment Ties: Seeking a Better Balance," Policy Briefing [Centre for Chinese Studies], June 2015, p. 3).
132 "Minister: China World's Largest Source of Tourists," *The Telegraph*, March 28, 2019, https://www.telegraph.co.uk/china-watch/travel/china-world-tourist-numbers/
133 "Ease of Doing Business in Egypt," *Trading Economics*, https://tradingeconomics.com/egypt/ease-of-doing-business
134 "China's Role in Egypt's Economy," *TIMEP Brief* (The Tahrir Institute for Middle East Policy), November 21, 2019, https://timep.org/reports-briefings/timep-brief-chinas-role-in-egypts-economy/
135 Dang Yuan, "Malaysia's Mahathir Dumps Chinese Projects amid 'New Colonialism' Fear," *DW*, August 21, 2018, https://www.dw.com/en/malaysias-mahathir-dumps-chinese-projects-amid-new-colonialism-fear/a-45160594
136 Christian Fraser, "China's Chequebook Draws African Nations," *BBC*, November 9, 2009, http://news.bbc.co.uk/2/hi/8350228.stm
137 Personal communication, January 18, 2020.
138 Sharma, "An Analysis of 'Belt and Road' Initiative," p. 37.

139 "China's Role in Egypt's Economy."
140 Leslye Davis, A.J. Chavar, Abe Sater and David Frank, "Exclusive Interview: Obama on the World," *New York Times*, August 9, 2014, https://www.nytimes.com/video/opinion/100000003048414/obama-on-the-world.html?playlistId=1194811622299

3

Libya & China: A Tale of Two Eras

Tarek Megerisi

Introduction

They've had the best of relationships; they've had the worst of relationships. China, as a very systematized global power used to building out its relationships formulaically, has often been troubled by Libya as a country which doesn't quite fit into either the African or Arab mold that China has cast. This is the product of Libya's relatively unique characteristics, the mercurial nature of its long-time leader Muammar Gaddafi and his own shifting expectations of the relationship, as well as the pervasive instability and unpredictability that have come to define Libya since its 2011 Arab Spring Revolution.

This chapter will seek to explore the contours of this changing relationship categorized into two distinct eras separated by trauma. By exploring this relationship's unique dynamic in both China and Libya's wider international relations we can better understand how various shared experiences—such as the earlier period of Gaddafi and China as "revolutionary allies" or indeed the February 17 revolution—have stimulated evolutions in either side or their foreign policy. Despite the distinct eras of the relationship demarcated by Libya's internal situation, there are clear, consistent, and meaningful trends that run throughout. This chapter will further seek to identify and unpack them. By doing so, greater insight can be provided into the tenets of the relationship vis-à-vis the ambitions and expectations each party has, as well as into better understanding how the China–Libya relationship and dynamic will evolve in the future and what ramifications that may have.

This is particularly poignant given the periods of change that both countries are currently undergoing, as Libya battles through a nationally defining era of transition and civil war, China continues to steadily build itself out as a global economic superpower through its Belt and Road Initiative (BRI), redefining the region's web of international relations. Indeed, various features that the chapter seeks to examine will likely play a defining role in the future of this relationship, from the increasingly prominent driving force that is economic interest, to China's savvier foreign policy following its traumatic experiences with Libya during the chaos of the revolution, as well as China's own unique characteristic of being a third power distinguishable from Russia and the West in ideology but increasingly able to match the economic and military incentives that have historically drawn the region toward the other two. If peace should come to the shores of Tripoli, then China's nonalignment with any of the parties to Libya's current bout of civil war and its good relationship with each party's backers should leave it well placed to secure a prominent position in Libya's lucrative reconstruction and its valuable hydrocarbon sector—likely at the expense of now-tainted European actors. While the longer the war burns on, the more Western multilateral ideals such as right to protect will be embattled, the more prominence China's defense sector will gain and the greater the risk for weapons proliferation and other destabilizing trends to cross the wider Middle East, Maghreb, Sahel, and perhaps even the Mediterranean.

Relationship Building in the Time of Gaddafi

Initially, Gaddafi had high hopes for a relationship with China. In March 1970[1]—only six months after his assumption of power—he dispatched his prime minister Abdulsalam Jalloud to Beijing with a brief to obtain technological and nuclear assistance, and to buy tactical nuclear weapons.[2] He was seemingly rebuffed on both requests, with Chinese premier Zhou Enlai reportedly suggesting that whilst China could assist Libyans with the research, Libya would have to develop its own production capacity.

Although the relationship cooled afterward, Libya did vote in favor of China's accession to the UN in 1971, unilaterally recognizing the People's Republic of China (PRC) even while it maintained recognition of Taiwan. While China never demanded Libya sever relations, it took until 1978 for formal diplomatic relations between China and Libya to be established, which resulted in Taiwan suspending relations with Libya anyway. Gaddafi's willingness to sacrifice relations with Taiwan, after having maintained a balance for so long, suggested that this was a development of his own foreign policy doctrine of power balancing. Indeed, the interplay between PRC and Taiwanese relations would be a reoccurring feature in relations with Gaddafi. At the time, China had risen in great power status and Gaddafi seemingly recognized that relations with China could be a way of counterbalancing a growing Libyan dependency on the USSR. It has further been argued that Gaddafi saw this as an opportunity to bridge a growing dichotomy in the third world between Soviet partners and those who preferred China's less transactional approach to relationship building. After formalizing the relationship, he dispatched Jalloud to Beijing once more, this time to sell a rapprochement in Sino-Soviet relations.[3]

Whilst Gaddafi always maintained an element of grand politics in his modus operandi, the underlying realpolitik remained. Gaddafi hoped to obtain technologically advanced military assistance from a country he believed was genuinely interested in supporting developing nations without necessarily obtaining a quid pro quo. Indeed, this wider notion of China as a weapons provider that is separate to the traditional Western-Russian divide, and seemingly operating under different political principles, remains just as relevant today as then.

These elements created a solid foundation for a relationship, and Gaddafi was eventually vindicated as China remained one of the few powers to not place economic sanctions on Libya even as Gaddafi developed Libya's reputation as a rogue state in the 1980s and 1990s drawing sanctions from Europe and the United States. This strengthened the perception of the two as "revolutionary allies"[4] as trade grew into the 1990s. In that crucial period, the security partnership also developed with China supplying a variety of "missile related technology and production assistance[5]" between 1997 and 2001. It was later discovered that Gaddafi had even procured a Chinese 25 kiloton nuclear warhead design via Pakistan.[6]

As Libya renounced its weapons of mass destruction (WMD) program in 2003 and sought a rapprochement with the West, the raison d'être of its relationship with China fundamentally shifted. After all, with the likes of the United States, France, and the United Kingdom queuing up to do business with a rehabilitated Gaddafi, he was no longer in such desperate need for a great power sponsor. China too had evolved in its status and needs. Having launched its "Going Global strategy" in 1999 encouraging its corporations to invest worldwide, China was a global economic powerhouse looking to establish itself in new markets and find fresh supplies of raw materials to fuel its furnaces.

China's evolution had provoked a change in the relationship even before Gaddafi's reformation, instigating considerable growth as Chinese companies were drawn to Libya's oil industry and infrastructure needs. Between 2002 and 2003 trade increased 91.3 percent to $216 million and exponentially grew from there, by 211.4 percent the next year to $670 million, and to over $1.3 billion in 2005.[7,8]

Although much is made of China's interest in Libya's oil, given China's insatiable hunger for fuel and Libya's unique brand of "sweet" crude, it was Libya's need to upgrade infrastructure where real resonance was found between the two. China, which did indeed have interest in Libya's oil exporting potential given Libya holds an estimated 3.4 percent of world reserves, initially took an approach similar to other African partnerships, whereby it took contracts to develop infrastructure that may enhance future exports. In 2004 the China National Petroleum Corporation (CNPC) constructed two pipelines linking the Wafa oil field with the port of Mellitah in western Libya on behalf of a

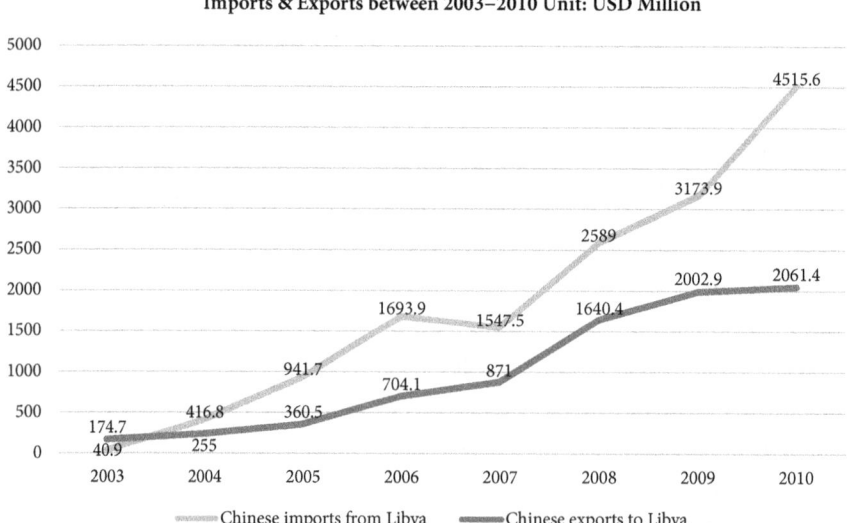
Imports & Exports between 2003–2010 Unit: USD Million

joint venture between Italy's ENI and Libya's National Oil Corporation (NOC). China retained ambitions to develop this further and connect Libya's network of oil pipelines south to enable Niger access to Mediterranean terminals.[9]

However, China never really drew the benefit of Libya's oil potential, partly because larger players such as BP, ENI, Shell, and Total were already present and partly due to Gaddafi's politicization of Libya's oil resources. As Libya hosted a round of oil concessions in 2004, following its "opening up" to the world, China only obtained limited prospecting rights. Any disappointment only soured further over 2006 as a year of terse relations ended with Taiwan's Chinese Petroleum Corporation[10] obtaining an exploitation concession in the lucrative Murzuq basin. It was a year which highlighted that Gaddafi saw oil concessions as a primarily political tool, to be used in relationship building and diversifying allies. In early January 2006, Gaddafi's son and heir-apparent Seif al-Islam had visited Taipei extending diplomatic recognition and striking an agreement to exchange representative offices. This provoked a diplomatic scandal with Chinese foreign minister Li Zhaoxing going to Tripoli on a two-day visit to extract a reassurance from his Libyan counterpart Abdulrahman Shalgam that Tripoli "only recognises one China."[11] Nevertheless, Taiwanese president Chen Shui-Ban would go on to visit Libya in May, furthering the economic relationship that resulted in December's concession and the opening of a trade representation in 2008.[12]

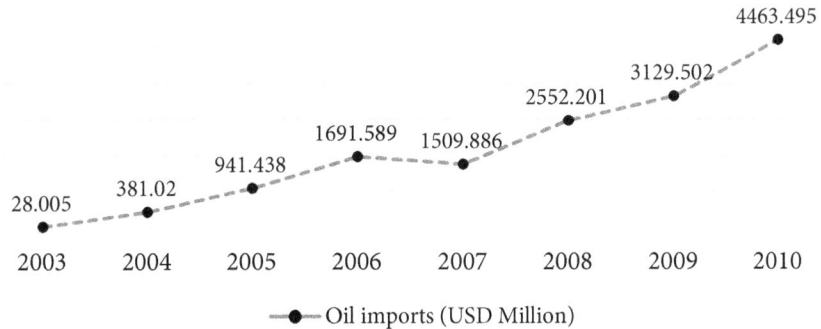

VALUE OF CHINESE OIL IMPORTS FROM LIBYA (2003–2010)

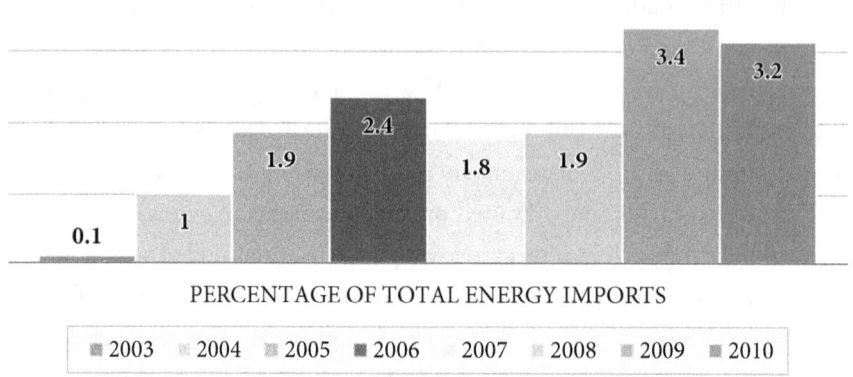

Chinese dependence on energy imports from Libya

PERCENTAGE OF TOTAL ENERGY IMPORTS

2003: 0.1, 2004: 1, 2005: 1.9, 2006: 2.4, 2007: 1.8, 2008: 1.9, 2009: 3.4, 2010: 3.2

Gaddafi's game of realpolitik, wielding oil to gain his desired political concession, and the place he saw for China in his wider geopolitical chessboard is further evidenced by China's first exploration concession coming a month after CNPC sealed a contract to build what would be Libya's largest new gas pipeline for $34 million.[13] Despite China's usefulness in the sanctions years, Gaddafi was as fickle a friend to them as anyone else. After all, he only visited China once in 1982, in one of his infamous outbursts had claimed that China had betrayed socialism, and in the China–Africa summit in Beijing in 2006 while fifty other nations had sent premiers he sent a deputy foreign minister— the lowest ranked amongst all the delegations.[14] Ultimately Gaddafi never felt comfortable with overreliance on foreign nations or exclusivity, often shirking Chinese interests for deeper partnerships with Russia and the United States given their technological edge, as can be seen with the multi billion dollar oil, arms, and infrastructure deal signed during President Vladimir Putin's visit to Libya in 2008.[15]

However, that didn't necessarily mean that there was no "mutual interest" to be found in the Sino-Libyan relationship. Ultimately, Libya was in desperate need of infrastructure upgrades and investment in construction. Here, the expertise of Chinese corporations in a range of infrastructure and large-scale construction specializations, as well as their competitive pricing, made them exciting partners. The fact that Libya, as an authoritarian state with a highly restricted private sector, was relatively immune to certain characteristics of

China's typical economic partnerships which drew ire elsewhere such as limited re-investment, imported labor, and offshored profits was where the mutual interest lay. Not to mention that a developed Libya could help improve other areas of Chinese interest and contracted projects was considered by China as a means to that end, such as oil extraction (despite all of the drama, roughly 11 percent[16] of Libya's oil still went there), priming the market and facilitating future inroads in various sectors as Libya developed. As Libya's infrastructure investment rose, so did the number of Chinese contracted projects, in 1999 Libya had only 0.19 percent of Chinese contracted projects in Africa which grew to 9.6 percent by 2010.[17] Moreover, as China itself developed technological parity or even superiority over others so did the depth of its involvement. In 2008 Chinese telecommunications company Zhong Xing Telecom Equipment (ZTE) signed an agreement to build Africa's first WiMAX network across Libya.

Just as China had finally found its feet in Libya, learning to navigate Gaddafi's mercurial diplomatic style and was deepening ties to the degree it had contracted fifty large-scale projects across multiple sectors totaling $18 billion,[18] the Arab Spring came to Libya. On February 15, 2011, protests against the Gaddafi regime erupted in Libya's second city, Benghazi, and quickly spread across all major population centers. Gaddafi's violent response only strengthened the resolve of the protestors, drove them to develop militarily, and provoked a rapid snowballing of the situation. By February 27 the protest movement had hunkered down, established a political representation, the National Transitional Council (NTC), and with Gaddafi as belligerent as ever the country was doomed to civil war.

The Great Evacuation

As Libya descended into violence and lawlessness, Chinese project sites became vulnerable. Early in the conflict China's Ministry of Commerce (MOFCOM) reported attacks on "at least" twenty-seven construction projects resulting in a 45 percent fall in contracted projects[19] and on February 24 CNPC announced that facilities had been attacked.[20] The losses started to quickly pile up. A week into Libya's revolution MOFCOM had estimated losses at over $1.5 billion,[21] China Railways Construction Corporation was forced to suspend three projects at a loss of $3.6 billion and China State Engineering Corporation suspended a half finished $2.7 billion housing project.[22] The situation went from bad to worse for China as harrowing videos began to be posted on Chinese microblogging website Weibo by some of the roughly 36,000 Chinese nationals working in Libya at the time, showing the destruction caused by attacks on project sites which drew significant media attention back home.

This fed into a dynamic that had accompanied the Chinese government's "Going Global" program, whereby Chinese citizens were increasingly pressuring their government to protect them while they answered the government's call to go abroad. The situation in Libya exemplified this issue and tested the government's system of "overseas citizen protection" with China's government fully aware that their response to this crisis would impact their "legitimacy and credibility"[23] and the future willingness of Chinese nationals to go global. As such, on February 22 the order for an evacuation came from the highest level, with President Hu Jintao and Premier Wen Jiabao issuing an order for all relevant arms of the state to work in concert to guarantee the safe evacuation of Chinese nationals and others under their care (such as from Hong Kong, Macau, Taiwan, and other nationalities working on Chinese projects).

However, a rapid evacuation of so many people so far from home is far easier said than done especially for a state with little experience in such matters or infrastructure for dealing with it—though it had conducted evacuations from East Timor in 2006 and evacuated 1,800 nationals from Egypt during their own revolution, this was a unique scenario given the distance, time constraints, environment of civil war, and the sheer scale of people requiring assistance. For example, even the United States' largest citizen evacuation of modern times, 15,000 people out of Beirut in 2006, was conducted by the US military over a two-week period. China would have to rely on civilian and diplomatic infrastructure instead and remarkably would accomplish it in a similar timeframe.[24]

The entire Chinese state was mobilized to manage this complex, high-pressure, foreign operation under the media's eye, activating a ministerial-level joint conference system established in 2004. The state council created an emergency headquarters led by Vice Premier Zhang Dejang to organize the evacuation. Multiple ministries coalesced and rallied resources to organize land, air, and sea evacuations out of Libya. Some evacuees were sent to Tobruk in eastern Libya and over the border to Salum in Egypt where the Chinese embassy in Egypt had organized 100 buses. The Civil Aviation Administration of China chartered a plane from Tripoli to China on February 23, from March 1 onward they were chartering multiple Chinese airlines to dispatch twenty flights a day from various neighboring countries. The People's Liberation Army (PLA) also flew in two cargo planes to evacuate workers in more remote parts of the country to Khartoum, Sudan. However, most escaped via the naval route with assistance from the Greek (which chartered seven vessels from Benghazi to Crete) and Maltese governments, Chinese shipping companies with nearby vessels, and a PLA Navy frigate.[25]

This operation was a huge test for China's growing consular capacity, involving the coordination of embassies across the region, and overall the Chinese government had managed to fulfill the old adage of turning a crisis into an opportunity. The evacuation, of twice the citizens as in the United States' operation in an equivalent timeframe, became a point of pride for the Chinese government. This extended to China's foreign policy as some claimed the operation highlighted the success of China's "people-first diplomacy,"[26] pointing to the helpfulness of foreign governments in the endeavor. It also enabled the Chinese government to defend its go global strategy which has continued to develop since, evolving into the One Belt One Road (OBOR) initiative of current president Xi Jinping. Moreover, this act has emboldened China's own government to continue going global. The trauma in Libya has been widely considered to have been a major driver of China's decision to establish a naval base in Djibouti in 2017 which will enable them to project power and protect interests (such as oil traffic through the Mandeb straits). As a result, events in Libya and the Chinese government's successful response to it can be considered to have triggered further developments in China's position as a global power. However, China managed the geopolitical aspects of Libya's crisis much less smoothly.

Foreign Policy Lessons from Libya's Revolution

China has long established its foreign policy positions on the basis of various principles. If these principles can be considered exemplified by the multilateral assistance and consular networks that facilitated the evacuation, then their weaknesses were made apparent by events at the United Nations Security Council (UNSC) that were developing alongside. Indeed, the complexities of the still maturing web of interests and games of realpolitik that swirled around Libya's revolution exposed the inherent paradoxes of these principles. China's failure to reconcile these paradoxes in a confused abstention of the crucial UNSC resolution 1973 that enabled the NATO intervention meant it ultimately lost face, and its once-lucrative presence in the heart of North Africa.

The guiding light of China's foreign policy is a principle of "noninterference" or "friends with all nations," that is, a layered principle in and of itself. It is established on respect for the sovereignty of nations and an unwillingness to project its own political beliefs or preferences on partner countries, something it has long attacked the West for doing as a form of neocolonialism. It was this principle that led to China's reticence to support Libya's revolution; indeed, it was the last member of the UNSC to recognize Libya's revolutionary authorities, the NTC. However, in the multilayered world of the contemporary era nations are never truly isolated entities being members of regional organizations and having tight alliances of their own which deeply influence their national character and decision-making.

China is aware of this reality and has placed great weight on regional organizations in its diplomacy and the rolling out of various strategies such as the OBOR initiative, politically perceiving regional organizations as quasi extensions of their member-states. In the case of UNSC resolution 1973 Foreign Minister Yang Jiechi conceded that China's decision to abstain "attached great importance to the requests of the Arab League and the African Union"[27] who both backed the military intervention and who were vital for China's economic ambitions. The influence of these two regional organizations on China's decision-making highlights the loophole that can form between the sovereignty of a nation and the regional organizations it is part of as well as the unsuitability of fixing policy via rigid principles in fluid moments where imperatives overlap. Back home, the abstention was seen as a betrayal of "noninterference" with various nationalists accusing the government of the time of "comprising its principles" and "acquiescing to western demands."[28]

That resolution 1973 was founded upon the principle of Right to Protect (R2P), fed into other Chinese principles of being a responsible power, exceptional circumstances demanding exceptional actions, and not being isolated. China defines itself as a great power nation and believes it has a duty to act responsibly so as to satisfy this definition. This sense of duty is largely manifested within the Security Council and has factored in China's growing role in UN Peacekeeping operations and consistent calls for any multilateral international activity to be built upon UN resolutions. That principle has also factored into its role in the development, at UN level, of the principle of R2P. Indeed, China's acquiescence to expanding the mandate of the UN mission to Bosnia despite local consent being "unclear, eroding or non-existant"[29] showed a precedent for its abstention for resolution 1973 which was the first time R2P was used without the target country's consent. Moreover, China had voted for the earlier resolution 1970 which was a unanimous UNSC resolution recognizing the seriousness of the situation in Libya.

As such, China felt itself constrained by circumstance. As a responsible power that had played a role in cultivating R2P, it couldn't veto action having formally recognized the seriousness of the situation. Moreover, China actively avoided being isolated at the Security Council, having not cast a lone veto since 1999. Following its abstention China comforted itself with justifications that Libya's unique circumstances called for unique action with ambassador Li Badong calling it a "special circumstance"[30] and tried to reconcile the abstention with the principle of "nonintervention" through further comments of concern and the need to respect the "sovereignty, independence, unification and territorial integrity of Libya"[31] but the damage had already been done.

From a Chinese perspective, despite methodically adhering to their own foreign policy principles they had undermined themselves on multiple levels. Internationally, they had lost face with their vote raising questions over the independence of Chinese foreign policy and their ability to withstand Western pressure. Neither the West nor Libyans were tangibly appreciative of the vote either. As explained by prominent Chinese strategist Yan Xuetong, China was still labeled an "irresponsible power" for refusing to participate in the military campaign, and their vote would never have done anything to shift the political baseline that "the West will always see China as an undemocratic country with a poor human rights record and the Arab states will always side with the west."[32]

Worse still, their abstention had paved the road for a NATO intervention that fed Chinese fears that NATO could eventually negate the UNSC's role in managing international interventions. Moreover, it became worried that R2P was evolving beyond an obscure principle, and now R2P interventions could be established as a precedent once more negating the UNSC as a forum where China may be able to prevent activities contrary to its interests.

Although it moved to combat the more existential fears at the next available opportunity, by vetoing a UN resolution on Syria alongside Russia, it still felt itself to have lost out. Following the overthrow of Gaddafi, Libya's revolutionaries were pursuing their own policy principle of "to the victors go the spoils" and despite China's abstention there were many factors leading Libyans to classify China as being on Gaddafi's side. While Beijing had initiated contact with the NTC through its embassies in Egypt and Qatar and met its Chairman Mahmoud Jibril in June, they had also met with Gaddafi's representatives in Beijing on July 16 and offered him $200 million worth of weapons that could be covertly delivered via Algeria and South Africa.[33] This played into existing prejudices, entrenched by comments during the revolution by Gaddafi who tried to garner Chinese sympathy by likening the protests to Tiananmen Square and declared "we are ready to bring Chinese and Indian companies to replace Western ones."[34]

That the four BRIC countries all abstained from resolution 1973 only served to liken an abstention to a veto in the eyes of Libyans, especially considering the joint statement they released in March[35] attacking the NATO intervention as egregious and exacerbating civilian casualties, confirming that their abstention lay on the unsupportive side of the spectrum. Indeed, manager of the revolutionary-operated Arabian Gulf Oil Company (AGOCO) AbdelJalil Mayouf summarized the mood well when he claimed that China, Russia, and Brazil (all abstaining nations) could face political obstacles in restoring ties. This mood caused Chinese consternation that they would now lose out regarding a presence in Libya's lucrative reconstruction and even on existing contracts which the NTC could seek to nullify on corruption grounds.[36]

For China, its decision to abstain was the worst of both worlds as it facilitated the intervention and all that went with it whilst creating a scenario that cut it out from an increasingly lucrative partnership in North Africa. Moreover, China's Libya experience at the Security Council highlighted its weakness as a foreign policy player, whereby its rigid adherence to foreign policy principles meant it could be outmaneuvered by those able to keep an eye on long-term interests and play a more nimble realpolitik short game. Although China has shown some evolution in this capacity since, notably alongside Russia in Syria, it remains something of a truism of their foreign policy posturing that is unlikely to change anytime soon and remains open to exploitation at a future moment of crisis.

New Libya, New Relationship?

Chinese commentary around its UNSC veto on Syria, intimating that it was an attempt to stop another Libya and negatively painting the still-fresh Libyan revolution as an example of abuse of power that highlights the risks of regime change,[37] did little to endear China to the still-suspicious revolutionary authorities in Libya. A protest against China's veto, seen as an attack on the Arab Spring, where Libyans hurled eggs and rocks at China's embassy in Tripoli and even attempted to replace China's flag with Syria's, depicted popular sentiments of the time.[38] Indeed, the interwar period in Libya between 2012 and 2014 was a time of high revolutionary fervor and economic opportunism from those nations that did assist the military uprising, typified by Italian oil giant ENI dispatching engineers to restore infrastructure as soon as the revolutionaries had advanced on Tripoli.[39] China, aware that a door had been shut in their face by Libyans drunk on their victory and Western powers keen to exclude unwanted competition, were ruminating over their losses as well as the opportunity costs of their decisions, and seemingly growing bitter over it.

Widespread acrimony in China, fueled by a sense of betrayal by the West over how the situation in Libya had developed, was laid bare in the reactions to the grisly murder of US Ambassador to Libya Christopher Stephens on September 11, 2012, by jihadists in Benghazi. On Weibo, an initial post reveling in the act, depicting the mild-mannered ambassador as the epitome of American hegemony and gloating over the consequences of American overreach, was shared more than 3,000 times and attracted 800 comments in only twenty-four hours. Even more cultured figures such as the editor-in-chief of the Chinese People's Political Consultative Conference Journal stoked up this daily hate[40] and by September 13 it ranked in Weibo's top 10 list. This revealing affair depicts how a narrative that China had been played by the West over Libya was widely internalized, a narrative that naturally bled into the denigration of the Libyan revolution as an American fabrication and in some cases even an anti-Chinese conspiracy.

This politicized animosity toward Libya and an attempt to combat the perceived Western hegemony it was now under was also evident in China's UNSC diplomacy. Shortly after the formalization of the end of the revolution and a new transitional government, on January 26, 2012, Ambassador Wang Min used his Security Council platform to convey African narratives around the revolution and call for more formal involvement of Africa and assistance to them in dealing with Libya's negative externalities.[41] This is notable given key African states, such as South Africa, and the AU had remained incensed over how they were shut out of the revolutionary process and sympathetic to Gaddafi who had heavily patronized the African Union. This developed further over the year into formal criticisms from China that the NATO intervention violated the mandate provided by resolution 1973 as well as Chinese attempts to trigger further investigations into the intervention in what appears to be clear attempts to subvert the possibility of NATO interventions becoming an international norm, to strengthen a narrative that the West violated the trust of countries like China in 2011, and of course to potentially even ward Western nations off of Libya in an attempt to create a more level playing field.

However, notwithstanding the political pageantry between China and the West over the situation, and of course the Libyans stuck in the middle, economic ties remained largely governed by the very separate logic of business. Despite threats from the NTC that China would no longer have preferential access and their existing contracts would be investigated and potentially nullified due to corruption through Gaddafi, his sons, or inner circle, these threats don't seem to have materialized. In the years following the revolution, the fluctuations in Chinese imports seem to tack alongside Libya's oil output and dip during times when Libya's NOC was forced into declaring force majeure due to politicized oil embargoes. Moreover, Chinese exports to Libya bounced to $2.4 billion in 2012—up from $720 million in 2011 which was likely deflated due to the revolution—and then steadily decreased from there over the subsequent years. The gradual drop-off suggests that this was more

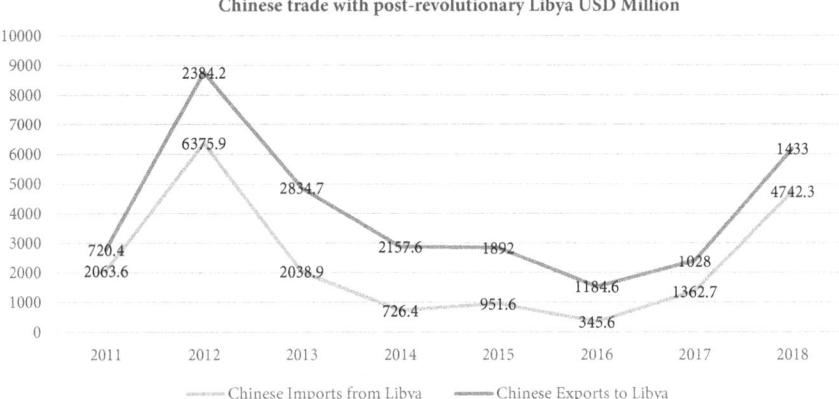

down to the shrinking of the Libyan economy as Libya's general instability and failing state in the years following the revolution gradually froze the regular economy and facilitated the rise of a powerful shadow economy. That trade figures are more likely linked to Libya's internal dramas than any fundamental problem in the relationship is further buttressed by the $697 million dollars[42] of contracts awarded to Chinese companies in 2013.[43]

Once Bitten, Twice Shy

As time has passed the basis of the political hostility has largely been forgotten about. Libya of course has had its own problems to deal with. In 2014, following two years of steady decline across the political, economic, and security sectors the transitional process was completely derailed in a year which saw the formation of competing governments, a new civil war, and the beginnings of a coup by an ex-army general which is still being felt today. Indeed, the ferocity of Libya's collapse and the already fractious environment in which it took place meant that it took some time for a new status quo to crystalize. By 2018 there was some modicum of stability in the political scene with a Government of National Accord (GNA) in the capital Tripoli, created by a UN-backed political negotiation process in 2015 and internationally considered the legitimate government of Libya as a result. Rivaling the GNA in the east of Libya was essentially a military-style autocracy, run by 2014's putschist Khalifa Haftar, which maintained a government and a bulk of the last elected parliament to provide it a façade of civilian governance and as such a claim to legitimacy despite these institutions not being in control of any of the levers of state.

As the GNA was increasingly challenged by Haftar and put through multiple "peace processes" designed to form some political consensus between the two, the administration looked to the outside world for friends and for business. In March 2018, China's state-owned PetroChina Company signed a deal to buy crude oil and help Libya's NOC upgrade its oil production capacity.[44] Given its general environment of instability and violence, and Libya's very real need to repair and upgrade civilian and hydrocarbon infrastructure, Libya was on the look out for countries that may be willing to stomach more risk than Western corporations for the payoff of working through a government that enjoys next to no financial oversight. As such, China was a prime target. On July 13, the foreign minister of the GNA Mohammed Siyala signed a memorandum of understanding in Beijing for Libya to join into China's flagship international project, the BRI.[45] Shortly after, Libya's NOC sent a senior delegation to Beijing to discuss "investment and enhanced cooperation opportunities[46]" in Libya's hydrocarbon sector.

At the sidelines of the Beijing Summit of the Forum on China Africa Cooperation that year, attended by GNA's prime minister Fayez el-Sarraj in a far cry from the days when Gaddafi sent junior officials to such occasions, Sarraj actively courted Chinese companies speaking of the "good reputation" they had acquired and Libya's multiple investment opportunities.[47] This was not limited to the business sector. In January 2019, the GNA's interior minister Fathi Bashagha requested assistance from the Chinese ambassador in his quest to rebuild Libya's security institutions.[48] Although China was far from the only country Bashagha reached out too, to have made a request on such a sensitive topic is a clear symbol that any revolutionary-era animosity was long gone. As the other events show Libya had gone fully in the other direction, almost desperate for China to return for economic and political reasons.

Having once been bitten, China was still shy to return, however. Not only did Libya seem capable of collapsing into civil war at any moment, but the complexities of its domestic politics were mirrored in the foreign dynamics that continued to envelop Libya's transition. With the events of 2011 still being remembered traumatically back in Beijing, despite the successful evacuation,

China looked at Libya more as another global crisis than a potential opportunity to rebuild a once-lucrative relationship. Moreover, with Libya's competing sides each being backed by different close regional partners of China and a final outcome still uncertain, China was keen to remain as visibly neutral as possible to avoid a repeat of the reputational damage it incurred over 2011. In many ways China's caution was prudent as just days before a planned for national conference intended to re-orient Libya's wayward transition, Haftar attacked Libya's capital triggering an all-out war that lasted fifteen months and transformed the country once more.

China's Long Game in Libya

Given this perspective on Libya, China's policy position—based on its usual principles—has deepened as Libya's situation worsened following Haftar's assault. Never one to miss an opportunity China also used Haftar's callous belligerence to continue to harangue the West over its failures in Libya. An editorial in China's global times[49] shortly after Haftar's attack highlights China's remaining angst over 2011's developments and the continuation of a policy—shared by Russia—that leverages the failure of Western follow through in Libya to denigrate the principle of R2P or Western intervention more generally. UNSC statements by Chinese representatives[50] since the start of Haftar's war in April 2019 highlight an enduring reliance on policy making based on core foreign policy principles. This includes pushing for a multilateral resolution mechanism that goes through the UN's support mission, and more recently calling on its partners involved in Libya to work toward an "earnest implementation"[51] of the Berlin conference which sought to create a framework for progress amongst the menagerie of states interfering in Libya. China's wider position is centered on various elements of the "noninterference" principle that has led China to repeatedly call for greater African involvement in resolving Libya's crisis and respect for Libyan sovereignty which should manifest in a Libyan-led and owned political process rather than one imposed from outside.

However, despite China's active neutrality and calls for Libyan sovereignty and respect for the UN, China has played an indirect role in perhaps Libya's most destructive bout of violence since its colonial era. Haftar's principal military backers, both the United Arab Emirates (UAE) and Egypt are prolific customers of Chinese weapons which have found their way across Libya's borders (in direct contravention of the UNSC Arms Embargo in place since 2011) and into Haftar's arsenal.[52] During Haftar's onslaught, Libya has quietly become the world's most intense theater of drone warfare, in which Chinese manufactured drones have played a central role. On November 18, 2019, then UN Special Representative to the Secretary General for Libya Ghassan Salamé accused Haftar's forces of having carried out 800 drone strikes.[53] All of these strikes have almost certainly been carried out on Haftar's behalf by foreign[54] pilots using Chinese Wing Loong II drones firing Chinese Blue Arrow 7 missiles, which is the only drone technology available to the UAE and Egypt.[55] Although the GNA has repeatedly called on China to "take a stand"[56] over this use of their weaponry, China has done little in response other than call for an investigation[57] that has seemingly produced no results. This is partially down to China's unwillingness to put strains on relations with these two very important countries to the BRI but also likely down to the benefits this exposure is accruing to China's military industrial complex. Chinese weapons have begun to build a reputation in Libya for being just as effective as Russian or Western counterparts, but considerably cheaper and therefore more practical for proxy wars and less costly if destroyed or captured. This is also relevant to China's drones, in direct competition in Libya with Turkey's Bayraktar models which have flown sorties on behalf of the GNA. In essence, the war in Libya is giving Chinese weaponry "field tested" status that will increase its value and customer base and is showcasing its drones to be an effective way to access technology that the United States is loathe to sell.

China's aloofness during Libya's worsening war displays that it may have learned the lessons of 2011 and is playing the long game rather than the moment. It can be read as an evolution of its foreign policy principle of noninterference to one of nonalignment,[58] which in this context reflects a refusal to take sides even as seemingly everyone else does. The value of such an approach, while exhibited in the unexpected boons to areas such as China's military industrial complex which occurred without a worsening of ties between China and the GNA, is centered around maximizing what may come after the war. China's limited participation to officially siding with a UN multilateral approach means that should Haftar lose, China will suffer no reputational damage in Libya as it did in 2011 and President Serraj's pledge to participate in the BRI will likely proceed unhindered. Should Haftar prevail, the lack of a strong Chinese voice in any Libya-related diplomacy will mean that the existing cooperation, given CNPC's activity in Libya and Haftar's de facto control of the country's oil terminals, will lay the groundwork for further Chinese involvement. This shows a savvier approach by China and a reconciling of its once-multifaceted political, ideological, and economic foreign policy interests into an economic pole star that is pursued through prioritizing certainty and stability. In this case, Chinese prominence in Libya's post-conflict reconstruction and ensuring Libyan participation in the BRI is most likely China's preferred endgame.

This evolution from noninterference to nonalignment can also be seen in the region's other internecine conflicts of Iraq, Syria, and Yemen, where political involvement is spurned and channels are maintained with all potential winners under a policy focused entirely on ensuring a leading Chinese role in the postwar reconstruction. However, this principle of nonalignment can be considered as framed by a dependence on the conflict zone in question remaining predictable and not being dominated by another outside power. These borders to China's nonalignment principle can be seen in the Chinese commentariat's[59] response to Ankara's powerful intervention beginning in late 2019 as Turkey's surprise will considerably dent China's hopes of swooping in to claim the economic gains once rival powers had exhausted themselves fighting one another. Turkey effectively ended Haftar's assault setting themselves up as the dominant foreign power alongside Libya's legitimate government and immediately began the process of capitalizing on their boldness and tapping into Libya's vast opportunities in the construction and hydrocarbon market which China so keenly eyed. However, Libya's divide has yet to be bridged and the response to this may well be more subtle Chinese support to Russia in the hopes that they may frustrate Turkish hopes of hegemony.

As opposed to China's experiences in 2011, it seems that China is in a win-win situation in today's Libyan conflict. Current dynamics in Libya, whereby the GNA remains exporting oil to China and trying to attract Chinese businesses, suggest that China will not suffer any reputational damage or throttled access to the country regardless which way the war goes. This is in stark contrast to the host of regional and European states that have clearly taken sides. At the same time, the longer the war drags on the more benefits will accrue to its still nascent defense industry, and the worse Libya's situation becomes the more ammunition provided to Chinese and Russian attempts to counteract any chance 2011 may still have of being used as a precedent for future R2P interventions.

This is partially due to Libya fitting much cleaner within China's various foreign policy puzzles. Libya is already signed up to the BRI and China is well positioned to benefit from its oil and reconstruction when the time is right, and China is comfortable enough to wait, not needing influence in Libya as a gateway to elsewhere in the region or Africa like Turkey and Russia do.[60] It seems that Libya finally fits in one of China's many foreign policy molds, and the emerging relationship is much like any other MENA or conflict state in how China plans its economic and diplomatic outreach. This extends to expected events that nevertheless showcase how normalized Libyan-Chinese relations are since 2011 such as Libya being party to China's initial bout of Covid-19-related aid as it tried to distance itself from being the source of 2020's definitive crisis. Covid-19 initially didn't seriously affect Libya, only taking hold toward the end of summer once the Chinese association was long gone and thus it seems unlikely that China will receive any blowback despite the devastation wrought by the virus in Libya. More typically China's increased comfort with Libya can also be seen in how Libya is standardized enough for China to simply pursue its generic tacking to Russia's policy lead at the Security Council level where it assisted Moscow in blocking the release of a report by the UN Panel of Experts on Libya which documented arms embargo violations by Russia.[61] This shows a continuing closeness between the two powers with China knowing that traveling in Moscow's wake won't affect its own long-term, well-balanced, economically centered plans that are often separate enough from Russia's hard politics and in the Libyan case it could even help ensure that Turkey doesn't upset that plan either.

Libya's placement into the mold of another Middle Eastern perennial conflict country can also be seen in the encroachment of counterterror rhetoric into China's commentary on Libya. Given PRC's operations in East Turkestan and long-standing fears that an armed resistance to this could be fed through the movement of jihadists from Afghanistan and elsewhere, China's security lens toward the wider region has long been one of counterterrorism. Whilst it fears this potential threat, it is more than happy to let the Western world's counterterrorist apparatus take the lead in fighting it whilst it keeps attention focused on its most feared facets of jihadism to ensure they remain central parts of the conversation over conflict zones in the region. A recent interview with Foreign Minister Wang Yi, where his analysis on Libya revolved around the standard dig at interventionism, the expected call for a multilateral solution, but then also the need to keep counterterrorism prioritized, specifically how to "prevent cross-border flows of Foreign Terrorist Fighters,"[62] highlights another way in which for the PRC, Libya has finally been standardized.

Conclusion: Guns, Oil, and Mutual Interest

Although China's relationship with Libya has been trying on many levels for the global power that can't quite fit this desert country into any of its standardized frameworks, there are lessons to be gleaned and suggestions for where the relationship may go in the future.

The first, and perhaps most obvious, is how China will seek to leverage the example of Libya on the global stage and the potential consequences of that. One of China's greatest fears in 2011 was that R2P mandates could become a standardized model for interventions in their own right, weakening the UN Security Council's authority as a rule setter as a result. Given China's deep-seated anxiety that human rights issues will be used to persecute China in the future, and potentially even wielded punitively against it as the United States "pivots" east, Libya's precedent is something they will combat ferociously. It is a policy position they hold in common with Russia. This doesn't mean that China will work against any attempts at a resolution in Libya, but they will always try to draw a distinction between the intervention of 2011 and whatever form a future resolution takes. Moreover, apart from being a core foreign policy principle of theirs, their preferred solution for Libya—one led by regional actors and carried through the UN—will likely be held up as proof of its superiority over Western-led policies if it comes to pass. This could become problematic in the future as the Libyan crisis is so beset by the interferences of influential foreign states which actively subvert UN resolution attempts that it becomes increasingly likely that a successful transition will only come to pass in Libya if it's sponsored by a great power. In such a scenario, if a European or American initiative should seek to replace the current UN process, then Chinese fears could lead them toward obstructionism alongside Russia.

However, these same fears can also be weaponized alongside the predictability of China's position vis-à-vis Libya, and its preferred resolution that can be used to try to constrain the current hostilities and the benefits it provides to China's weapons industry. China is eternally anxious over isolation within the UN and prides itself on being a responsible member of the Security Council, as well as not interfering in other nation's sovereign matters. At the same time, many unaligned states invested in the Libya crisis are finding it difficult to sacrifice their Gulf and Egyptian relationships to push for an enforcement of the arms embargo. Using the presence of Chinese weapons in Libya, especially the reliance on Chinese drones, to cause China reputational damage for being party, even if indirectly, to the destabilizing war in Libya could be a good way of getting China to pressure its regional partners and even to constrain the means at the disposal of the belligerents.

After all the risk profile of continued proliferation and the growth of China's weapons industry to the stabilization of the region should not be neglected. A similar dynamic to Libya's, regarding regional powers identifying Chinese armaments as a cheap yet effective solution for arming their proxies, is also occurring in Yemen and could easily become a new standard as the MENA region becomes engulfed in its own internal power struggle. Moreover, at a time when regional powers are becoming more belligerent and are more actively pursuing their own foreign policy interests, which often run antithetically to the interests of the target countries and the West, policy makers should retain awareness of China's growing industry that is increasingly providing a competitive alternative to their own producers and increasing the autonomy of these actors to pursue potentially destabilizing policies.

Ultimately, China has far more interest in a stable region and stable Libya than in the current dynamic, which is a practical foundation to build working relationships on Libya and possibly even garnering greater Chinese involvement in the resolution process. China's current lens for viewing the region is through the BRI. Many of the leading belligerents prosecuting Libya's proxy war, such as Egypt, Turkey, and the UAE, are key partners for this region. As such China could be another avenue through which to push diplomacy, given it's a country with a unique relationship with all these states and an effective vehicle for economic arguments. The fact that Libya hasn't yet factored into the BRI in any meaningful way should not downplay its potential geostrategic significance. Libya sits at the heart of the Mediterranean, serving as a key node in shipping routes between Europe, Africa, and through the Suez. Its central location, large borders, and proximity to Europe makes it the bridge between Europe and Africa—a historically lucrative characteristic. This serves Chinese purposes of using North Africa to test products for the European market[63] and more generally provides innumerable potential economic benefits to Libya, China, Europe, and the regional economy. So, not only does it fulfill the BRI criteria of being a potentially key trading node if for some stability and infrastructure investment, but of course its considerable reserves of sweet crude makes it even more appealing. As such, Libya's potential within the BRI framework and the seemingly wide-ranging economic benefits therein could be an avenue for leveraging greater Chinese involvement in forcing a resolution to the benefits of all concerned.

Indeed, it is far better to get ahead of this issue and (to use China's own principle) work multilaterally to create a mutually beneficial resolution rather than allow a potentially destructive competition to take place in the future which could have harmful consequences for Libya. Many European countries, such as France and Italy, have had their credibility burned in Libya through partisan actions during the national split that's been ongoing since 2014. This extends to regional countries such as Egypt, Turkey, and the UAE too. This raises a risk for the West that Libya's oil resources and the vital Greenstream pipeline which feeds gas under the Mediterranean to Italy could be offered to China instead. Although this is clearly a sovereign Libyan decision, a high-stakes competition between Western powers and China for Libya's oil, also including Turkey, Russia, and Gulf powers if the reconstruction is to be included, could be incredibly destabilizing for Libya's fragile political climate. Trying to work in concert to secure Libya is the best route toward guaranteeing mutual benefit and the wider stability on which everybody's economic interest lies.

Overall, it seems that China has learned the lessons of 2011 far better than anyone else. Their determination to remain outwardly neutral has caused a transformation in Libyan perceptions of them from being a malignant counterrevolutionary force, to the predictable well-intentioned and potentially helpful great power that Gaddafi once saw them as. As a result, there is a very real potential for China to leverage Libya to boost its military industry complex, capture vital energy resources, and dominate the eventual reconstruction to garner huge profits, raising their general status and regional influence to the exclusion of others. Instead of doubling down on the mistakes of the past nine years, and ignoring China or engaging with them antagonistically, regional and Western powers should instead be exploring avenues of cooperation to advance mutual benefit. Moreover, given the increasing complexity of the Libyan crisis, and the difficulties in halting such an advanced proxy war let alone unrolling the years of destruction, mismanagement, and accumulated grievance to generate real stability in Libya, those who prize stability over partisanship in Libya need as many allies and as many tools as they can get.

Notes

1 Malfrid Braut-Hegghammer, *Unclear Physics: Why Iraq and Libya Failed to Build Nuclear Weapons* (New York: Cornell University Press, 2016), p.141.
2 Joseph V. R. Micallef, "A Nuclear Bomb for Libya?," *Bulletin of the Atomic Scientists* (August 1981), p. 14.
3 American University, *Libya, A Country Study* (Washington, DC: Federal Research Division, Library of congress, 1979), p. 233.
4 Stephanie Erian, "China at the Libyan Endgame," *Policy magazine* 28, no. 1 (Autumn 2012), p. 49.
5 Centre for International Trade and Security (CITS), Export Control's in the People's Republic of China, University of Georgia (February 2005), p. 9
6 CITS, *Export Controls in the PRC*, p. 6
7 See Embassy of the People's Republic of China in Libya, "The Economic Cooperation between China and Libya," 2012, http://ly.china-embassy.org/eng/jmgx/t297043.htm
8 All data from China Med project, https://www.chinamed.it/chinamed-data/north-africa/libya
9 Francois Lafargue, "China in North Africa," *MED* (2008), p. 66.
10 In ibid.
11 "Libya Says It Only Recognises One china" *JANA*[Official Libyan News Agency] (January 19, 2006).

12 All Data from China Med Project, https://www.chinamed.it/chinamed-data/north-africa/libya
13 Joshua Eisenmann, *China and the Developing World: Beijing's Strategy for the Twenty First Century* (New York: M.E Sharpe, 2007), p. 117.
14 The Diplomat, "*China's Prickly Gaddafi Ties*," 2011, https://thediplomat.com/2011/03/chinas-prickly-gaddafi-ties/
15 Reuters, "*Russia, Libya Seal Debt Accord, Eye Arms Deal*," 2008, https://www.reuters.com/article/us-russia-libya-idUSSHC61895920080417
16 Steve Sotloff, "China's Libya Problem," *The Diplomat*, March 14, 2012, https://thediplomat.com/2012/03/chinas-libya-problem/
17 Juan Zhang and William X. Wei, "Managing Political Risks of Chinese Contracted Projects in Libya," *Project Management Journal* 43, no. 4 (2012), p. 44
18 Erian, "China at the Libyan Endgame," p. 49.
19 Leslie Hook, "China's Future in Africa, after Libya," *Financial Times*, March 04, 2011, http://blogs.ft.com/beyond-brics/2011/03/04/chinas-future-in-africa-after-libya/
20 Leslie Hook and Geoff Dyer, "Chinese Oil Interests Attacked in Libya," *Financial Times*, February 24, 2011, https://www.ft.com/content/eef58d52-3fe2-11e0-811f-00144feabdc0
21 Zerba, "China's Libyan Evacuation Operation," p. 1094.
22 Erian, "China at the Libyan Endgame," p. 50.
23 Zerba, "China's Libyan Evacuation Operation," p. 1099.
24 In ibid., pp. 1100–1.
25 In ibid., p. 1100.
26 Ding Ying, "Out of Libya," March 6, 2011, http://www.bjreview.com/print/txt/2011-03/06/content_338897.htm
27 Christopher Holland, "Chinese Attitudes to International Law: China, the Security Council, Sovereignty, and Intervention," *NYU Journal of International Law and Politics Online Forum*, (July 2012), p. 28.
28 Yun Sun, "Syria: What China Has Learned from Its Libya Experience," *East-West Center Asia Pacific Bulletin*, no. 152, February 27, 2012, https://www.eastwestcenter.org/system/tdf/private/apb152_1.pdf?file=1&type=node&id=33315
29 Holland, "Chinese Attitudes to International Law," p. 26.
30 Ibid., p. 29.
31 Ibid., p. 36.
32 Yun Sun, "What China Learned from Its Libya Experience," p. 2.

33. Graeme Smith, "China Offered Gadhafi Huge Stockpiles of Arms: Libyan Memos," *The Globe and Mail*, September 2, 2011, https://www.theglobeandmail.com/news/world/china-offered-gadhafi-huge-stockpiles-of-arms-libyan-memos/article1363316/

34. Pepe Escobar, "China's Interests in Gaddafi," *Aljazeera*, April 14, 2011, https://www.aljazeera.com/indepth/opinion/2011/04/201141195046788263.html

35. Andrew Jacobs, "China Urges Quick End to Airstrikes in Libya," March 22, 2011, https://www.nytimes.com/2011/03/23/world/asia/23beiijing.html

36. James Dorsey, "Fall of Gaddafi: Policy Challenge for China and Russia," *RSIS Commentaries*, September 5, 2011, https://dr.ntu.edu.sg/bitstream/10356/94773/1/RSIS1262011.pdf

37. Chris Buckley, "China Defends Syria Veto, Doubts Wests Intentions," *Reuters*, February 6, 2012, https://www.reuters.com/article/us-china-syria-un/china-defends-syria-veto-doubts-wests-intentions-idUSTRE8150NY20120206

38. Reuters, "Syria Protestors Hurl Rocks at China Embassy in Libya," February 6, 2012, http://english.ahram.org.eg/NewsContent/2/8/33848/World/Region/Syria-protesters-hurl-rocks-at-China-embassy-in-Li.aspx

39. Erian, "China at the Libyan Endgame," p. 51.

40. Yi Lu, "U.S. Ambassadors Death Draws Cheers and an Ugly Rumour on China's Web," *The Atlantic*, September 18, 2012, https://www.theatlantic.com/international/archive/2012/09/us-ambassadors-death-draws-cheers-and-an-ugly-rumor-on-chinas-web/262514/

41. Permanent Mission of the PRC to the UN, "Statement by Ambassador Wang Min, Deputy Permanent Representative of China to the United Nations, at the Security Council Briefing on the Impact of the Sahel Region Caused by the Libyan Conflict," January 26, 2012, http://www.china-un.org/eng/chinaandun/securitycouncil/regionalhotspots/africa/lib/t930690.htm

42. All figures in this paragraph are from China Med, "ChinaMed index for Libya," https://www.chinamed.it/chinamed-data/north-africa/libya

43. Ibid.

44. Salma elWardany and Laura Hurst, "PetroChina Is Said to Agree to 2018 Deal to Lift Libya Oil," *Bloomberg*, March 1, 2018, https://www.bloomberg.com/news/articles/2018-03-01/libya-crude-output-is-said-to-be-stable-despite-key-field-s-halt

45. Safa alHarathy, "Libya Joins China's Belt and Road initiative," *The Libya observer*, July 13, 2018, https://www.libyaobserver.ly/economy/libya-joins-china%E2%80%99s-belt-and-road-initiative

46 Abdulkader Assad, "Libya's NOC mulls cooperation with Chinese oil firms," *The Libya Observer*, July 25, 2018, https://www.libyaobserver.ly/economy/libyas-noc-mulls-cooperation-chinas-oil-firms

47 Xinhua, "Interview: Libya Welcomes Return of Chinese Companies, PM Says ahead of FOCAC Beijing Summit," August 31, 2018, http://www.xinhuanet.com/english/2018-08/31/c_137434072.htm

48 Alwasat, "GNA Interior Minister Bashagha Affirms Libya's Desire for Security Cooperation with China," January 9, 2019, http://en.alwasat.ly/news/libya/232190

49 Global Times op-ed, "West Should Feel Guilty for Resumed Fighting in Libya," April 8, 2019, https://www.globaltimes.cn/content/1145108.shtml

50 Permanent Mission of the PRC to the UN, "Libya," (http://www.china-un.org/eng/chinaandun/securitycouncil/regionalhotspots/africa/lib/)

51 Xinhua, "China Asks for Earnest Implementation of Outcome of Berlin Conference on Libya," February 13, 2020, http://www.xinhuanet.com/english/2020-02/13/c_138778669.htm

52 Reuters, "Libyan Fighters Seize U.S and Chinese Missiles from Haftar's Forces," June 29, 2019, https://www.reuters.com/article/us-libya-security/libyan-fighters-seize-u-s-and-chinese-missiles-from-haftars-forces-idUSKCN1TU0W8

53 UNSMIL, "SRSG Ghassan Salamé Briefing to the Security Council," November 18, 2019, https://unsmil.unmissions.org/srsg-ghassan-salame-briefing-security-council-18-november-2019

54 Tom Kington, "UAE Allegedly Using Chinese Drones for Deadly Airstrikes in Libya," *DefenseNews*, May 2, 2019, https://www.defensenews.com/unmanned/2019/05/02/uae-allegedly-using-chinese-drones-for-deadly-airstrikes-in-libya/

55 Arabian Aerospace Online News Service, "Egypt Inducts Chinese Armed Drones," April 29, 2019, https://www.arabianaerospace.aero/egypt-inducts-armed-chinese-drones.html

56 Safa alHarathy, "Libyan Foreign Ministry Calls on Beijing to Act against the Use of Chinese-Made Drones in Killing Libyans," *The Libya Observer*, November 20, 2019 https://www.libyaobserver.ly/inbrief/libyan-foreign-ministry-calls-beijing-act-against-use-chinese-made-drones-killing-libyans

57 Abdulkader Assad, "China Vows to Probe Use of Its Drones by Haftar's Forces in Libya," *The Libya Observer*, October 16, 2019, https://www.libyaobserver.ly/news/china-vows-probe-use-its-drones-haftars-forces-libya

58 Business Reporting Desk, "Here's the Real Reason China Isn't Taking Sides in Libya," *Belt & Road News*, January 29, 2020, https://www.beltandroad.news/2020/01/29/heres-the-real-reason-china-isnt-taking-sides-in-libya/
59 George Cafiero, "The Geopolitics of China's Libya Foreign Policy," August 4, 2020, https://www.chinamed.it/publications/the-geopolitics-of-chinas-libya-foreign-policy
60 Sandy Alkoutami and Frederic Wehrey, "China's Balancing Act in Libya," *Lawfare*, May 10, 2020, https://www.lawfareblog.com/chinas-balancing-act-libya
61 AP News Wire, "Russia, China Block Release of UN Report Criticizing Russia," *The Independent*, September 26, 2020, https://www.independent.co.uk/news/russia-china-block-release-un-report-criticizing-russia-un-diplomats-security-council-parties-libya-b612738.html
62 Ministry of Foreign Affairs of the PRC, "Written Interview with Asharq al-Awsat by State Councillor and Foreign Minister Wang Yi", November 19, 2020, https://www.fmprc.gov.cn/mfa_eng/zxxx_662805/t1833773.shtml
63 Lafargue, "China in North Africa," p. 66

4

The Burgeoning China–Tunisia Relationship: Short-Term Reward, Long-Term Risk

Sarah Yerkes

Introduction

While China has undertaken a serious investment and interest in the African continent over the past several years, Tunisia has remained largely overlooked. In part due to Tunisia's desire to cozy up to the West following the 2010–11 revolution and ongoing democratic transition, and in part due to geography and historical ties, Europe remains Tunisia's largest trading partner and strategic ally. The United States has also dramatically increased its economic, political, and security relationship with Tunisia over the past decade, making Tunisia a Major Non-NATO Ally in 2015. But following a slight decline in relations in the wake of the Arab Spring, China has begun to pay far more attention to Tunisia, both diplomatically and economically. Tunisia formally joined China's flagship Belt and Road Initiative (BRI) in 2017, and both countries are showing increasingly greater interest in one another.

Tunisia and China have a long-standing historic relationship—one of the oldest in the Arab world. Both President Habib Bourguiba and President Zine el Abidine Ben Ali took a strong interest in China, with Ben Ali, specifically, ramping up ties between the two nations. Following the economic crisis that unfolded in Tunisia following the revolution, President Beji Caid Essebsi and Prime Minister Chahed actively courted Chinese investors, tourists, and officials to become more involved in the country. Today, the relationship is at a potential turning point. The new Tunisian president, elected in October 2019, has yet to make clear his foreign policy priorities, and there is a growing angst in the West (as well as greater alliance between the United States and Europe) against the rise of China. Tunisia therefore must decide how closely it seeks to be tied to China—and how close is too close for Tunisia's Western allies.

China and Tunisia before the Arab Spring

Tunisia and China began their relationship in 1957 when Tunisia sent a cultural delegation to Beijing and the two countries established Tunisia–China associations in each country. These cultural ties were quickly followed up with economic ties through trade agreements. A Chinese-Tunisian trade agreement signed during Chinese vice minister of foreign trade Lei Renmin's visit to Tunisia in 1958 made Tunisia one of the first Arab countries to forge trade ties with China. This was the first of many such agreements.[1]

On a regional level, China had established the All-China Afro-Asian Solidarity Committee in Beijing in 1958 and used the Afro-Asian People's Solidarity Organization, established in 1957 and headquartered in Cairo, to transmit "rhetorical and material support to African parties."[2] Additionally, the Chinese Islamic Association operated in the 1950s and 1960s as a conduit between the Chinese Communist Party (CCP) and African Muslims, distributing propaganda throughout Africa—including North Africa. During this time, China was actively engaged in supporting anticolonial independence movements across Africa. Tunisia thus benefited from a wide array of Chinese support for its efforts to uproot French colonialism, including political support, diplomatic recognition, economic assistance, and some light arms.[3]

In October 1961, China began to open a formal diplomatic channel with Tunisia, beginning with a visit to Tunisia by China's ambassador to Morocco, who held a series of meetings with high-level Tunisian officials. Tunisia reciprocated with a visit by the minister of information and tourism to China in 1961. This came as US–China relations were at an all-time low. Thus, Tunisia needed to figure out how to balance its relationship with the United States with a desire to establish relations with China. At the time, Tunisia was the largest recipient of US economic assistance in Africa (around $60 million a year), and President Habib Bourguiba recognized the need to assuage his American counterparts of any reservations they might have toward Tunisia's turn to the East.[4] Another hiccup arose over China's aggressive stance toward India, a fellow member of the Non-Aligned Movement. Bourguiba stated, "China's stand in the border dispute with India and its refusal to sign the nuclear test ban treaty can't be approved by Tunisia."[5] Nevertheless, China was eager for Tunisian support in its bid to join the United Nations and the two countries were able to put their policy differences aside.

Thus, official diplomatic relations between Tunisia and China began January 10, 1964, with the visit of Chinese premier Zhou Enlai and vice premier Chen Yi, as part of a broader Africa tour, setting up the opening of the Chinese embassy in Tunis on April 20 of that year. The relationship was tested during the late 1960s when Tunisia took a stance toward Taiwan that China found unfavorable. While Tunisia did not explicitly call for recognition of Taiwan, it also failed to adopt an official "One China" policy. This was "sufficient to convince Beijing that the relationship was not worth the price."[6] While China has "never imposed economic conditions" on aid recipients, they have "always insisted that partner countries observe the One China policy," according to China expert Deborah Brautigam.[7]

The relationship suffered further damage in the summer of 1966 when the two countries found themselves in a diplomatic standoff over what Tunisia perceived as Chinese Communist proselytization. Four Chinese table tennis players were sent to Tunisia to teach Tunisian youth how to play table tennis. However, the Tunisian government alleged that the table tennis players were actually there to indoctrinate Tunisians into Communism, as evidenced by demonstrations by Tunisians in June 1967 in Tunis stating, "Long Live Mao" and "China Bravo."[8] Following the demonstrations, on July 14, 1967, the Tunisian police interrogated a table tennis instructor in Bizerte and retuned him to the Chinese embassy. This led to an official note of Chinese protest, which the Tunisian officials ignored, instead limiting the activities of the Chinese embassy staff. The Chinese followed up with a series of diplomatic notes, all of which the Tunisian government ignored, eventually angering the Chinese enough to close their embassy in September 1967. Relations between the two countries did not resume until 1971, followed by a visit from the Tunisian minister of foreign affairs to China in August 1972 and the eventual opening of the Tunisian embassy in Beijing on December 10, 1973.

After the resumption of relations in the early 1970s, economic cooperation between the two countries ramped up. This included economic as well as security assistance, with China transferring $5 million worth of gunboats to Tunisia in the 1970s.[9] In 1977, after providing Tunisia with $57 million in economic assistance, China became the largest communist donor in Tunisia, accounting for one-fourth of total communist economic aid.[10] China's goal in the Middle East had long been to both gain recognition for its One China policy and serve as a counter-weight to Western and Soviet influence throughout the Middle East and North Africa.[11]

In many ways, this was an easy task, as China had the "added value of not carrying any of the political and colonial baggage plaguing Western agency in the region."[12] In states with oil, this was complemented by increasing Chinese access to energy resources. But in the Tunisian case, Chinese influence took many other soft-power forms. China began sending medical teams to Tunisia in 1973, and the two countries began student exchange programs in 1976. This was valuable because Tunisia's healthcare sector had suffered dramatically following independence, after many healthcare personnel left Tunisia for France.[13]

China continues to send medical teams to Tunisia today, with a new medical team arriving every two years and the twenty-fourth medical team arriving in 2019.[14] Since 1973, Chinese medical teams have "provided more than 5 million outpatient services to Tunisian people and performed more than 320,000 operations."[15] The two countries' press organizations (Agence Tunis-Afrique Press and Xinhua) also established cooperation during this time.[16] Furthermore, China was able to strengthen its relationship with Tunisia over its support for the Palestinian cause. China was one of the first non-Arab states to recognize the Palestine Liberation Organization (PLO), which was headquartered in Tunis between 1982 and 1991.[17]

China also began funding some major infrastructure projects at this time like the Medjerdah-Cap Bon Canal, funded by a loan agreement signed on July 14, 1974, and finalized in April 1989. Within the same period, the Chinese funded the construction of the Cultural and Sports Center of Menzah 6 in Tunis via a loan agreement signed on October 23, 1984. This was consistent with China's broader push in the region to take over infrastructure funding in Africa after the West and the World Bank had stepped away from infrastructure projects during the 1970s and 1980s.[18] Recognizing the increase in

Chinese-Tunisian economic relations, the two countries created the Sino-Tunisian Joint Committee of Economic, Trade and Technological Cooperation in 1983, and held the Joint Committee's first meeting in Tunisia in 1984.[19] Meetings continue to be held every few years, alternating between Tunis and Beijing. In part as a result of the increased economic cooperation, there has been a "significant presence of Chinese labor" in a variety of sectors in Tunisia including the manufacturing sectors, light industry, and agricultural sectors.[20]

Tunisia further strengthened political, economic, and cultural ties to China under President Zine el Abidine Ben Ali, who came to power in 1987. Ben Ali's authoritarian regime was simpatico with China and supported China against rising Western anger over China's poor human rights record, particularly China's brutal response to the Tiananmen Square protests in 1989. Ben Ali himself visited China in April 1991. In 1996, the two countries agreed to periodic political consultations and several Tunisian ministers visited China in the 1990s and 2000s.[21] Under Ben Ali, Tunisia welcomed a number of high-level Chinese visitors, including a visit in 1992 by President Yang Shangkun, a visit by Foreign Minister Tang Jiaxuan in 2000, and a visit by President Jiang Zemin in April 2002. During the 2002 visit, the two countries signed several agreements including agreements on economic and technological cooperation; a maritime agreement; an agreement on civil air transport; an agreement on cultural cooperation; and an agreement on the dispatch of Chinese medical teams to work in Tunisia.[22] In 2007, China and Tunisia signed an exchange agreement that allowed China to begin sending youth volunteers to Tunisia in 2008. Between 2008 and 2011 three cohorts of volunteers traveled to Tunisia, including kung fu masters, table tennis coaches, and Chinese teachers with the goal of promoting Chinese culture.[23] Notably, China signed an agreement with Tunisia in 2009 to open a Confucius Classroom in Sfax—the first Confucius Institute in the Arab World.[24]

China also increased its security cooperation with Tunisia, sending a defense attaché to Tunisia for the first time in 2007 and holding four high-level Chinese military delegation visits between 2005 and 2008.[25] China exported around $3,400 worth of small arms to Tunisia between 2001 and 2005.[26] China also invested in some large infrastructure projects during this time, including building two dams in the Tataouine Governorate beginning in 2006, worth about $4.3 million.

Diplomatically, Ben Ali was careful to avoid the mistakes of his predecessor and was clear about his support for a One China policy. In 2010, during a visit to Tunis, Chinese foreign minister Yang Jiechi praised Ben Ali for Tunisia's political support for Taiwan, Tibet, and the Xinjiang Uighur Autonomous Region.[27] While many Arab countries had issues with China's persecution of Muslims, Tunisia managed to avoid the issue. However, because of the close relationship between Ben Ali and the Chinese government, China struggled with how to respond when the Tunisian revolution began in December 2010, calling for Ben Ali's ouster. As one scholar noted, "China's response to the political unrest was somewhat lagging behind."[28] Initially, China took a "wait and see approach," calling for the restoration of stability during and following the overthrow of Ben Ali.[29] While several Western countries sent envoys to examine the situation on the ground in Tunis, China did not engage directly until March 2011, two months after Ben Ali's removal from power. As Degang Sun and Yahia Zoubir stated, the Arab Spring was "so unprecedented and unpredictable that the Chinese government was totally unprepared and disoriented."[30]

Complicating China's response to the Tunisian revolution, the Chinese government feared a copycat revolution at home, seeing the Arab Spring as potentially destabilizing with threats to China's stability, national security, and prosperity.[31] This was a legitimate fear, as minority groups in China, such as the Uighurs as well as Tibetans, saw the popular protests throughout the Arab world as "inspiring," particularly since many of the social and economic factors that led to the Tunisian revolution were present in China.[32] Thus, the Chinese authorities were careful to control news coverage of the revolutions—"trying to steer the debate toward the unsuitability of the Western democratic model for developing countries."[33] Additionally, "The security services unleashed an unprecedented crackdown on foreign journalists in China—tracking, detaining, harassing, and beating them, hacking into their computers, and threatening their expulsion from the country."[34] This put the country at odds with Tunisia's revolutionary leaders who took the reins of the nascent democracy. This was exacerbated by the fact that Chinese-Tunisian relations had largely existed at the bilateral government-to-government level with little connection to Tunisian civil society or the public. The early years of Tunisia's democratic transition thus represented a new challenge for the China–Tunisia relationship.

On March 8, 2011, Vice Foreign Minister Zhai Jun came to Tunis with the goal of reaffirming close ties between the two countries and to help with the repatriation of 36,000 Chinese nationals from Libya, due to the ongoing violence there. During his visit, Zhai announced $6 million in assistance for a new development project in Tunisia.[35] In 2011, China also provided Tunisia with $2 million in cash and about $4.4 million worth of relief supplies to help Tunisia deal with the growing refugee crisis on its border with Libya as a result of the unrest surrounding the Arab Spring. This included around 1,500 tents, 1,000 sets of solar-powered lights, 23,000 blankets, 25 tons of food, and 22 tons of medicine.[36] But these gifts were not enough to paper over the real and major differences between the Chinese authoritarian model and the democratic transition unfolding in Tunisia, putting the relationship on ice for a few years.

Relations between Tunisia and China Today

The relationship between China and Tunisia has grown steadily since the Tunisian revolution. After a bumpy start in the early years post-2011, relations normalized beginning in 2013. While China is less involved in Tunisia than in neighboring North African states, there is an interest on both sides—the Chinese and Tunisian—for additional Chinese investment, particularly in infrastructure, a sector with tremendous need. During the government of President Beji Caid Essebsi, from 2014 to 2019, there was a steady stream of bilateral diplomatic engagement and efforts by Prime Minister Chahed and his government to woo Chinese investors and draw Chinese tourists to Tunisia. Under the government of President Kais Saied, elected in October 2019, that outreach is likely to continue, although Prime Minister Mechichi had just formed his government at the time of this writing and it was not clear what Saied's or Mechichi's approach to China would look like. Tunisia is eager to show China that it can serve as a gateway to Africa and sees the growing interest in Chinese development globally through the BRI as a chance for Tunisia to get its hands on much-needed capital.[37]

Tunisia's prized geostrategic location, just 100 miles from Sicily and at the crossroads of Europe, Africa, and the Middle East, puts it on China's radar and makes it an attractive place for Chinese investment. Tunisia also offers China a large quantity of skilled laborers, a large middle class with "relatively high purchasing power" and the ability to facilitate political and economic ties throughout the Maghreb—particularly to neighboring Libya and Algeria.[38] Furthermore, Tunisia's neutral foreign policy posture and commitment to the One China policy have prevented any major ruptures in the relationship since the Arab Spring. Tunisia's unique location as a gateway between the Middle East and Africa has also allowed it to play a large role in the various Chinese multilateral bodies such as the Forum on China-Africa Cooperation and the China-Arab States Cooperation Forum (CASCF).

Tunisia has also benefited from China's approach toward great power competition. As Sulmaan Khan notes, China sees great power competition differently from the West. It seeks out friendships across the globe, meaning that while great powers matter, "smaller powers matter too."[39] Similarly, Jon Alterman states that China "does not have a natural network of allies, instead it seeks out friendships wherever it can" making relationships with smaller countries as important as larger ones.[40] Thus, while other states may not prioritize relations with Tunisia, China has recognized the importance of Tunisia's geostrategic location and the access Tunisia can provide for China to the African market.

Today, the bulk of the China–Tunisia relationship is in the economic sphere. China has limited security cooperation with Tunisia but remains interested in its stability. While in much of Africa, China is involved in peacekeeping missions or other security mechanisms, this is absent in Tunisia due to the country's lack of ongoing external conflict. However, there is some interest in expanding the security relationship, particularly in the counterterrorism sphere. Last year, the two countries reportedly signed a $4.8 million grant from China to Tunisia. The deal includes military procurements for Tunisia's National Army. In China's broad strategy for relations with the Arab world, it promises to "strengthen exchange of visits of military officials, expand military personnel exchange, deepen cooperation on weapons, equipment and various specialized technologies, and carry out joint military exercises."[41] Furthermore, China seeks to strengthen the counterterrorism capacity of Arab states and "establish a long-term security cooperation mechanism" to address the growing terror threat.

Diplomatic Relations

There has been a steady stream of Tunisian and Chinese diplomatic engagements since the Arab Spring. In 2012, each foreign minister visited the other's country, signaling the beginning of the repair in the post-revolution relationship. The Tunisian foreign minister visited China in April, and the Chinese foreign minister reciprocated with a visit to Tunisia in June. The following year, the pace of Chinese visits to Tunisia picked up, including visits by vice chairman of the Provincial People's Political Consultative Conference of Ningxia Hui Autonomous Region Hong Yang, member of the Foreign Policy Advisory Committee of the Chinese Foreign Ministry Ji Peiding, vice minister of the National Health and Family Planning Commission Ma Xiaowei, and Vice Agricultural Minister Niu Dun. Cultural cooperation also increased. In October 2013, the Chinese embassy in Tunisia and the Tunisian Ministry of Culture jointly hosted the first China Movie Week.[42]

Regular high-level visits continued throughout the 2010s, including a May 2016 visit by Chinese foreign minister Wang Yi to Tunisia, a July 2017 visit by Tunisian foreign minister Khemais Jhinaoui to Beijing, a September 2018 meeting between Chinese president Xi Jinping and Tunisian prime minister Youssef Chahed, and a July 2019 visit by the head of the International Department of the Central Committee of the CCP Song Tao to Tunisia.

Tourism is another important tool of Chinese soft power.[43] By 2014, China had overtaken the United States as the largest source of outbound tourism globally (based on the number of trips and money spent abroad), meaning that Chinese tourism has the potential to offer tremendous economic benefits to recipient countries.[44] One Chinese tool for control over tourism is the Approved Destination Status program, which Tunisia joined in 2004, which determines whether countries can accept Chinese tour groups and whether they can promote their country as a tourist destination inside of China.[45] As a result, Tunisia saw a dramatic uptick in Chinese tourism in the years after 2004. However, the numbers remained small. In 2016 only around 8,000 Chinese tourists visited Tunisia. The following year, Tunisia allowed visa-free entry for Chinese tourists for the first time, which resulted in a growth to around 20,000 tourists a year. If that growth continues, Karim Jatlaoui, representative of the

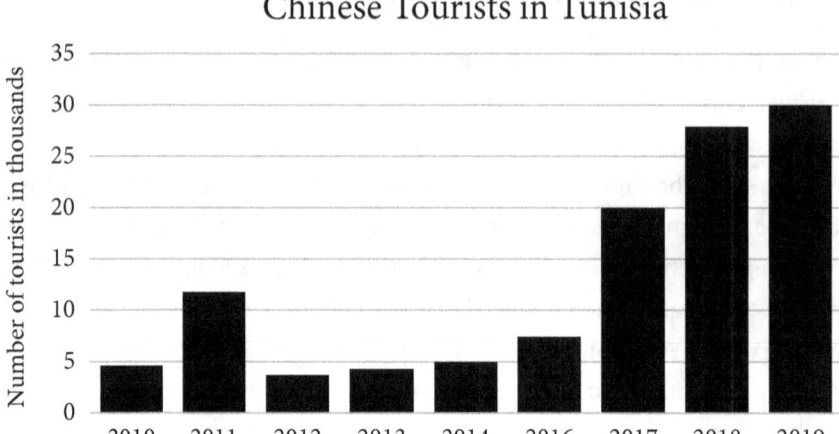

Chinese Tourists in Tunisia

Tunisian National Tourism Office Beijing Bureau, expects Chinese tourists to increase to 50,000 by 2020.[46]

While that number might be unrealistic, the Tunisian government is working to attract Chinese tourists in a variety of ways. According to former minister of tourism and handicrafts Salma Elloumi Rekik, "We are trying to draw more Chinese tourists, by upgrading payment methods, setting up Chinese logos, launching direct flights, as well as running Chinese restaurants, to make Chinese visitors' trips in Tunisia more convenient and enjoyable."[47] As of August 10, 2019, 18,935 Chinese tourists had visited Tunisia, an increase of more than 10 percent over the previous year.[48] However, Chinese tourists still make up only a small fraction of the nearly nine million tourists who visited the country in 2019, the bulk of whom came from Europe and neighboring North African states. And as a point of comparison, 100 times as many Chinese tourists visited France in 2017 as Tunisia, meaning Tunisia still has a long way to go to be a real tourist destination for China.

Education and Exchanges

Education and cultural exchanges have been a cornerstone of the Chinese-Tunisian relationship. Tunisia began offering Chinese-language courses in the 1980s, the first Arab country to do so.[49] Tunisians have also increasingly come to view China as a desirable destination to study abroad. Since 2009, more than 1,000 Tunisians have participated in courses and workshops in Chinese training centers and universities with the goal of gaining expertise in diplomacy, economic management, health, and agriculture.[50] Furthermore, in July 2018 China agreed to help fund a $32 million Diplomatic Academy of Training and Studies. The Academy, a 22-year-old institution affiliated with the Tunisian Ministry of Foreign Affairs, has been operating out of rented offices in Tunis. Under the new deal, the Chinese agreed to fund a new building to train Tunisian officials, as well as potentially diplomats from across Africa and the Middle East, in foreign languages, international studies, international trade, and laws. The groundbreaking took place on May 3, 2019.

Educational cooperation has also increased, with the University of Carthage, for example, now partnering with four different Chinese universities and hosting three cohorts to date of thirty Chinese students learning Arabic. One of the main tools China uses to expand its outreach is through Confucius Institutes and Confucius Classrooms. Institutes are aimed at the university level, while classrooms are aimed at the secondary level. Both serve as hubs for Chinese language and culture, similar to the French Alliance Française model or the German Goethe Institute model and provide Chinese-language classes as well as a variety of cultural classes such as "Chinese medicine, history, culture, society, martial arts, theater, flower arranging, paper cutting, and occasionally contemporary topics."[51] The first Confucius Institute was established in Seoul in 2004, and China's goal is to establish 1,000 Institutes and Classrooms globally by 2020.[52]

A Confucius Classroom was set up in Sfax in 2009 and Tunisia's first Confucius Institute opened in November 2018, a joint venture between Dalian University of Foreign Languages and the University of Carthage.[53] The Institute is open to all Tunisian students and researchers, as well as the general public.[54] At the Institute's inauguration, its director Xu Rixuan said, "Our specific objective is to teach Chinese language, to train teachers in Chinese and to promote cultural and academic exchanges between Tunisia and China."[55] Both Chinese and Tunisian officials have been pleased with the success of the Institute at the University of Carthage and have discussed plans to open additional Institutes in Tunisia.[56]

Economic Relations

China has steadily increased its economic relationships across the Arab world, beginning with the establishment of the CASCF in 2004. Today, the emphasis is on the twenty-first-century Maritime Silk Road and China's "1+2+3 Cooperation Pattern," which includes (1) energy at the core; (2) infrastructure and trade and investment facilitation as the two wings; and (3) nuclear energy, space satellites, and new sources of energy as the three final pillars.[57] As part of its Arab strategy, China also seeks to increase people-to-people engagement and cultural cooperation in the fields of science, education, health, and media.[58]

While China did not undertake substantial investment in Tunisia until recently, China has come to recognize the strategic importance of Tunisia as a hub between Europe, Africa, and the Middle East. Tunisia has also tried to sell itself to China as the gateway to the wider Muslim world. At the 2013 Ningxia Expo, the Tunisian Minister of Trade and Tourism, speaking about the possibility of partnering with China's halal food market, argued, "We need more Chinese investors to come to Tunisia, which can serve as a platform for access to a wider market of over 1.5 billion Muslims."[59] China is also interested in North Africa as a way to get closer to the European market. The preferential trade agreements that Tunisia (and others) have with the European Union allow goods manufactured in Tunisia to be exported to Europe with lower tariffs. China is interested in band-wagoning onto this agreement after a change in the rules of origin for North African goods in Europe means that Tunisia can source products from China and still get the preferential treatment as if goods were fully sourced in Tunisia.[60]

But despite the opportunities for both sides, there are some major challenges facing the Tunisian-Chinese economic relationship. One issue is around labor. Tunisia continues to confront high rates of unemployment, particularly among university graduates. While Tunisia is eager for Chinese cash flow, most Chinese investment comes with Chinese, not local, labor, meaning that Tunisia would not likely see a concomitant influx of jobs with greater Chinese investment. A second area of contention is around the Chinese economic model. As Michael Singh notes, "Just as China is seeking to make its own difficult transition to a more market-oriented economy, many Middle Eastern governments need to shrink their public sectors, reduce their spending, bolster their social safety nets, and encourage private sector-led growth. China is not the ideal partner for such a transition, given its own similar challenges."[61]

Another challenge is around Tunisia's legal system. Tunisia's public procurement law has turned off some Chinese investors, who would prefer a no-bid process for projects, which is illegal in Tunisia. China is able to operate more easily in countries with less transparent procurement processes, which has been frustrating for some Chinese investment efforts. Furthermore, while Chinese trade with Tunisia has grown dramatically over the past two decades, the trade balance has steadily shifted in China's favor. In the early 1990s, Chinese exports to and imports from Tunisia were largely balanced. In 1992, for example, China exported $28.5 million worth of goods to Tunisia and imported $23.5 million. However, the trade imbalance began to widen substantially around 2002, when China exported $144.11 million worth of goods and only imported $38.3 million. In 2018, the most recent year for which data is available, the gap is extremely large, with China exporting $1.4 billion worth of goods and importing only $195 million. In comparison, the Chinese trade balance with the United States is much more even, with 2017 US exports reaching only $544 million and imports of $477 million.[62] Evidently, despite this increase in Chinese exports, Europe remains Tunisia's primary trading partner, with China as number three following France and Italy.

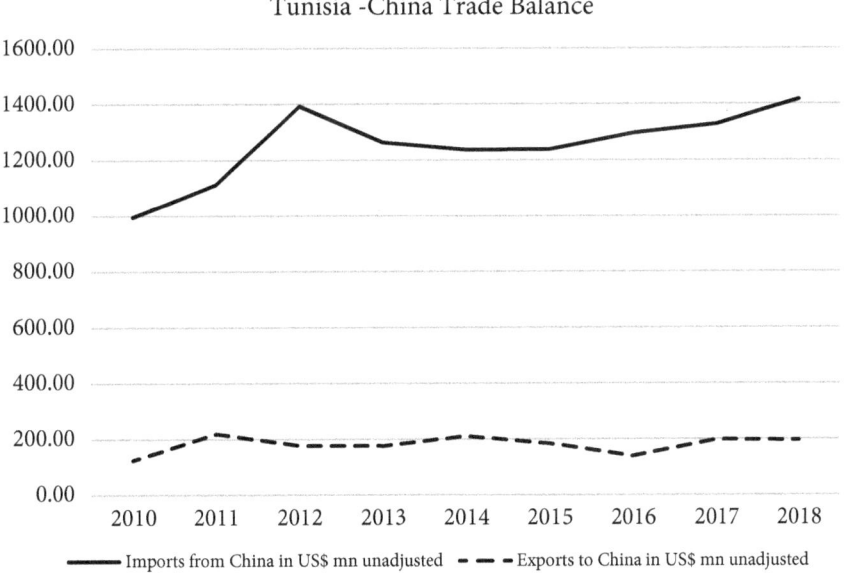

Tunisia-China Trade Balance

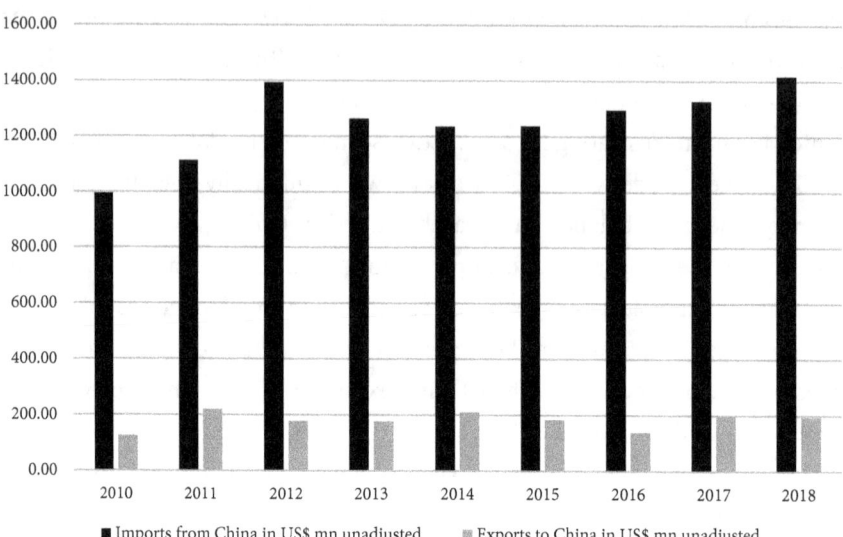

Tunisia's main export to China is diammonium phosphate. Other exports include olive oil, electrical cables, marble, clothing, electronic batteries, automotive components, wine, mineral, and leather waste. Tunisia imports a wide variety of goods including tea, coffee, silk and cotton fabrics, synthetic textiles, leather, sports equipment, and electrical and electronic equipment. One success story is the Sino-Arab Chemical Fertilizers Company (SACF), founded in 1985 as a joint venture between China, Tunisia, and Kuwait. SACF is now one of China's primary fertilizer companies. The original investment cost $58 million and it quickly expanded, producing, processing, and selling fertilizer in China and exporting products to Thailand, South Korea, Japan, Pakistan, and Indonesia.[63] Another example of a successful venture is the Haier plant, operating under the name HHW in Tunisia. Haier, a Chinese appliance conglomerate founded in 1984, opened its Tunisia factory in 2001, where it assembles and markets Haier brand products. This is a joint venture between China and Tunisia, and is unique in that it hires foreigners, rather than just Chinese employees, into senior management and marketing staff.[64]

Today, both countries are working to deepen cooperation in tourism, agricultural products (primarily olive oil), as well as aerospace.[65] In May 2011 Tunisia participated in the World Travel Fair in Shanghai for the first time, in an attempt to introduce the Chinese tourism industry to Tunisia as an attractive tourism destination. In November 2019, Tunisia increased its participation in China's annual International Import Expo, sending a twenty-seven-participant delegation headed by then minister of commerce Omar Behi compared to a five-member delegation in the past. This was also the first year that Tunisia put a focus on tourism at the expo, sending a representative from the Tunisian National Tourism Office. But to fully take advantage of tourism, the countries need to work on the civilian aviation sector. Attempts to this end have been previously made but have not produced any results. For example, Tunisia and China signed an MOU on air transport in 2014 to allow the national air carrier, Tunisair, to fly twenty-one direct flights per week to China. However, there are no flights from Tunisair to any Chinese city at this writing.

Another small area of economic cooperation is the energy sector. In 2004 the China National Petroleum Corporation (CNPC) acquired some oil exploration rights in the NK exploration block in Tunisia as well as 50 percent equity in the SLK Oilfield. Together, these two blocks constitute 3,332 square kilometers.[66] However, according to energy expert Erica Downs, these oilfields were not used to shore up Chinese oil imports, as China did not export any of the oil pumped by the CNPC in Tunisia in 2007.[67]

Belt and Road Initiative

China's largest global investment vehicle is the BRI. Tunisia formally joined China's twenty-first-century Maritime Silk Road Initiative, a part of the broader BRI, on July 11, 2018, in a signing ceremony in China on the sidelines of the eighth Ministerial Meeting of the CASCF. The BRI consists of two tracks—a land-based "belt" and a maritime-based "road," both designed to increase trade and build the Chinese footprint in Central Asia, Europe, and the Middle East. According to the Chinese government, the BRI "is designed to uphold the global free trade regime and the open world economy in the spirit of open regional cooperation."[68] As China expert Doug Paal notes, the BRI was originally designed to "deploy China's excess industrial capacity abroad."[69] Utilizing primarily infrastructure investment, such as ports, bridges, railways, highways, and upgraded power grids, the Maritime Silk Road has the potential to provide recipient countries with a significant influx of funds, while simultaneously providing China with new markets for its goods and a way to indirectly confront US and European supremacy in the region. But little as far as statistics are available to the public, including a budget and list of projects, meaning there is little public knowledge regarding the extent of the BRI to date.

Tunisia has long been eager to take part in the BRI as a way to increase the Chinese investment portfolio in Tunisia and to develop the country's crumbling and insufficient infrastructure. Currently, there are only 10 Chinese enterprises in Tunisia, compared to 4,000 European enterprises, which leaves a significant amount of room for Chinese expansion. During the signing of Tunisia's ascension to the Maritime Silk Road Initiative, Foreign Minister Jhinaoui expressed his desire to see Tunisia as an "important fulcrum" for the BRI in North Africa—a gateway for Chinese investment into the rest of the region.[70] So far, there are plans under the BRI to improve the port of Zarzis in the south into an economic and trade hub; to build a bridge connecting the island of Djerba, already an attractive tourist destination, to the southern region of Medenine; and to build a railway linking Gabes to Zarzis.[71] There is also an agreement for China to build a 200,000 square meter commercial center worth $65 million in Tunis.[72]

However, there is some real fear about China's long-term goals in investing billions of dollars into the BRI. In the Tunisian case, given the country's strategic location and proximity to Europe, there is a fear on the part of the United States and Europe that China may slowly insert a military component or intelligence presence into the ports it constructs and oversees, something the United States and Europe would not tolerate. Additionally, because of the transactional nature of China's foreign policy and economic relationships, these massive infrastructure investment projects provide China with substantial leverage over recipient countries and give China something to cash in on later. In the case of Tunisia, a young democracy seeking to consolidate its democratic gains, this has the potential to put the Tunisian government at odds with its Chinese benefactors. For example, with Tunisia taking a seat on the UN Security Council in 2020, China could use its promise of cash and development funds to push Tunisia towards adopting positions friendly to China in the multilateral arena—positions that could be in opposition to Tunisia's traditional Western allies.

Infrastructure Investment

Tunisia's infrastructure is in desperate need of updating. There remains a dramatic difference between the quality of infrastructure—from roads to hospitals to wireless networks—between the country's coastal regions and interior/southern regions. While the country's 27-year-long decentralization plan, begun in 2018, seeks to address some of these issues by instituting a "positive discrimination" process to funnel government funds disproportionately to the interior, there remains a tremendous need to improve all manner of infrastructure in order to enable Tunisia to reach its economic potential.[73] Furthermore, as one US official noted, the United States no longer does the sort of infrastructure investment at which China has become expert, thus it is not surprising that Tunisia would be seeking additional sources of infrastructure support, which China has provided through grants and loans as well as construction projects.[74]

Over the past few decades, China has become the global leader in infrastructure investment. In 2012, China signed several agreements, including giving Tunisia $1.3 million toward upgrading local hospitals and healthcare centers affected by flooding; $30 million to build a hospital at the Sfax School of Medicine; funding shrimp farms in the Mediterranean Sea and providing Chinese expertise in shrimp farming; and building solar panels to provide lighting to marinas.[75] In 2013, China agreed to grant Tunisia 37 million dinars (about $23 million) for development assistance.[76] In 2014, China signed an agreement to build a solar lighting project at the Rades Port.[77] There is some speculation that China is also seeking inroads into the Bizerte port, on Tunisia's northernmost point, which would give China much easier access to Europe and serve as a hub of fiber optic submarine network cables.[78]

In addition to investments, China has provided Tunisia with some grants and loans. Between 2011 and 2014, China provided Tunisia with five separate grants for unspecified development purposes, totaling around $49 million.[79] Between 2000 and 2017, Tunisia borrowed $145 million from China. The last loan was in 2009 for $80 million. Most of the loans ($123 million) came from the Exim Bank. The loans were primarily in the transport and communications sectors.[80] The value of Chinese foreign direct investment stocks in Tunisia peaked in 2015 at $20.85 million, up from $1.56 million in 2003.[81]

The annual revenue of Chinese construction projects in Tunisia has steadily climbed from $10 million in 1999 to $219 million in 2017.[82] Yet the number of Chinese workers in Tunisia has remained relatively stable, from 292 in 2009 to 289 in 2017. There was a peak of 650 workers in 2013, but overall the numbers suggest that despite a significant increase in the size of infrastructure projects, China has not imported increasingly larger numbers of workers.

One key area of infrastructure investment is through Huawei, the Chinese telecom giant, who seeks to provide global 5G connectivity and has already made a tremendous investment in Tunisia. Huawei first came to Tunisia in 1999 where it began as an internet infrastructure provider and has since evolved to also build and market its own smartphones. Today it is the leading operator of 3G modems in Tunisia. In 2006, Huawei opened a training center in Tunisia to support its Tunisian and African partners. And in 2009, Huawei Marine Networks built the Hannibal cable, a 170-kilometer Tunisie Telecom cable linking Tunisia to Italy.[83]

Huawei also organizes and hosts training programs for Tunisians in the field and in September 2019 held a Northern African Innovation Day Forum in Tunis that was attended by more than 300 Arab and African officials and communications specialists. Huawei is also involved in training young Tunisian engineers through its Seeds for the Future initiative, started in 2008. Tunisia has participated in the program since 2017 and is the first Francophone African country to do so. Through the program, China selects ten Tunisian ICT engineering students each year to study in China. The program is wildly popular, with more than 1,900 Tunisian students participating in the competition for the chance to study in China between 2017 and 2019.[84]

The Impact of the COVID-19 Pandemic on Sino-Tunisian Relations

The COVID-19 pandemic has had little impact on the Sino-Tunisian relationship. Tunisia has been neutral in its reaction to the onset of the COVID-19 pandemic, failing to publicly blame China for the virus. While there has been some disinformation and conspiracy theories circulating around Tunisia related to the virus, these have largely focused on potential vaccines or other controversial ways to combat the virus, rather than the conspiracy theories regarding the weaponization of the virus by China as have been popularized by President Trump and others in the United States.

Chinese-Tunisian economic cooperation has continued, in spite of the virus. In Fall 2020, Tunisia (through the Tunisian embassy in Beijing) participated in the third China International Imports Fair in Shanghai. And discussions between Tunisian and Chinese officials over economic development and infrastructure projects continued throughout the pandemic. Additionally, China has provided Tunisia with significant support during the pandemic, mostly in the form of medical equipment. On March 28, 2020 two Chinese foundations (the Jack Ma Foundation and the Alibaba Foundation) provided Tunisia with 100,000 masks, 20,000 screening tests, and 741 protective suits.[85] And between April 3 and September 21, 2020 the Chinese government sent Tunisia three separate shipments of medical and personal protective equipment including more than 30,000 masks, more than 100,000 pairs of medical gloves, 13,000 rapid screening tests and cleaning and disinfection products. The Chinese assistance received widespread coverage in the Tunisian press.

Furthermore, the decline of Gulf investment, brought on by the fall in oil prices, might open some doors for China. Gulf states, in particular Qatar and Saudi Arabia, have made significant investments in Tunisia.[86] Qatar helped organize the "Tunisia 2020" donor conference, making the second-largest pledge of $1.25 billion, and China and the Gulf have often supported similar types of investment projects, such as large, showy infrastructure projects. With the Gulf unable to make good on some of its pledges, China might seize the opportunity to step up its footprint in Tunisia.

How Does China's Rise Impact Tunisia's Western Allies?

While Tunisia has the potential to gain a lot from its burgeoning relationship with China, there is also the potential risk of alienating Tunisia's Western allies—the United States and Europe. Under the Trump administration, the United States has grown increasingly concerned with the rise of China. Pentagon officials regularly discuss their role in Africa as part of great power competition and are seeking ways to counter the growing Chinese power and influence across the continent.[87] Secretary of State Mike Pompeo has described China as "the central threat of our times," noting that the United States sees China as a direct threat to democracy and the US way of life, and stating that it "will take a concerted effort, not just by the United States, but by all of us who love freedom and cherish democracy and the rule of law to ensure that [the US] remains the predominant model for the world for the next century."[88] The State Department has thus begun placing "China watchers" across the US missions in the MENA region, and is devising a "China strategy" for the Near Eastern Affairs bureau. This reflects a real worry on behalf of the United States that China's long-standing effort to unseat the United States as the sole superpower may be working. At the same time, this is also a pragmatic recognition that China is filling in the gaps—particularly in infrastructure investment—that the United States and other Western powers have left unfilled. Thus, US officials may be concerned about China's rise in Tunisia, but they are not surprised. As one US official said, "of course Tunisia is turning to China" given their ability to throw large sums of money at the country; and "of course China is interested in Tunisia" given its important geostrategic location.[89]

Politically, there is no question that the post-revolutionary Tunisian government is more compatible with the United States and Europe than with China. But, despite large influxes of assistance in the years right after the revolution, the West has been unable (or unwilling) to satisfy all of Tunisia's demands for economic aid. Furthermore, Tunisia has long prided itself on its neutral foreign policy, allowing it to simultaneously seek stronger Western relations as well as closer ties to Western adversaries like China and Russia. As Douglas Paal notes, China's relationships are "transactional" and not based on a shared set of values, which is how China was able to maintain a relationship with both the Ben Ali regime and the democratic leaders in Tunisia in the same way that China has maintained relationships with a variety of MENA states, including those who are at odds with one another.[90]

China has been able to maintain relationships with a variety of Arab states due to its "Five Principles of Peaceful Coexistence," which precludes China from interfering in domestic affairs or promoting a political agenda. The Five Principles include "mutual respect for sovereignty and territorial integrity, mutual nonaggression, mutual noninterference in each other's internal affairs, equality and mutual benefit, and peaceful coexistence." Importantly, China has also been clear in its support for an independent Palestinian state on the 1967 borders, with East Jerusalem as its capital.[91] This, combined with Tunisia's support for a One China policy, has allowed the two states to avoid any major diplomatic ruptures. However, China also "supports Arab states in exploring their own development paths suited to the national conditions," meaning that China is neither promoting democracy nor fighting it. This is problematic in the case of a transitioning country like Tunisia. As one US official noted, China enables Tunisia to indulge its worst habits, rather than promoting good governance and reform.[92]

The United States

But one need only look at the dust up in United States–United Kingdom relations over Britain's desire to allow Huawei to build some of its 5G network to see that China has the potential to divide even close friends and allies. The United States lobbied the United Kingdom hard to prevent Huawei from taking a foothold there, over intelligence fears that the Chinese government could force Huawei to include backdoors into their equipment, "allowing access to encrypted data for spying or sabotage purposes."[93] But as one columnist noted, "London appears to have already calculated that China is a land paved with gold it cannot afford to stay away from."[94] So one can hardly expect that Tunisia, a country with much greater economic need than the United Kingdom, would be willing to forgo Chinese assistance simply to appease the United States, a far lesser donor.

In contrast to its relationship with China, one of the strongest pillars of the Tunisia–US relationship is that of shared values. Thus, there is concern in the West that should China increase its engagement with Tunisia, it could have a negative impact on Tunisia's democratic progress. This fear is not unique to Tunisia. One of the critiques of Chinese aid globally is that it has the potential to indoctrinate or negatively influence local populations toward authoritarianism or communism. But the way China carries out its assistance has, at times, had the opposite impact. As China expert David Shambaugh notes, "Much of China's aid comes in the form of hard infrastructure: roads, rails, buildings, stadiums, etc. Even though these do have a positive impact on the recipient country in the end, they are normally built entirely with imported Chinese labor and by Chinese construction companies with contracts from the Chinese government."[95] Thus, recipient states such as Tunisia, where unemployment is high, often end up resentful of Chinese development projects, which fail to benefit the local labor market. Furthermore, while Beijing may be trying to buy influence in Tunisia through the promise of massive amounts of funding, some scholars note that throughout the Middle East, China has "symbolic power that does not always reflect its real capacities and ambitions."[96]

This is borne out in public opinion data, where Tunisians are split in their perception of China and its role in promoting much-needed economic development. Tunisians overwhelmingly believe that China has an influence on their economy, with 74 percent of those surveyed by the 2014/2015 Afro Barometer stating that China has either "a lot" or "some" influence on the economy.[97] But they are split on their view of China and its role in their country. A total of 42 percent of Tunisians surveyed said China's economic and political role in Tunisia is either very positive or somewhat positive, while 39 percent said the role was very negative or somewhat negative.[98] When asked what contributes to the positive image of China in Tunisia, the largest percentage (30 percent) said the quality and cost of Chinese products; however, when asked what contributes to a negative image of China, more than half (53 percent) also said the quality of Chinese products. China also gets positive scores on its business and infrastructure investment, which 18 and 16 percent, respectively, list as the main thing contributing to a positive image of China.[99] Thus, it is not surprising that nearly half (47 percent) of Tunisians surveyed said that China's economic assistance meets Tunisia's needs.[100]

In the 2018 Arab Barometer, about 63 percent of Tunisians said they would like economic relations with China to get stronger over the next few years.[101] This is generally on par with Tunisian desires for economic relations with other global powers. For example, 45 percent of Tunisians said they want to see economic relations with the United States get stronger, 51 percent said the same about the United Kingdom, 50 percent about Russia, and 57 percent about Turkey. Regional powers performed worse, with 44 percent of Tunisians saying they want to see stronger relations with Qatar, 39 percent with Saudi Arabia, and 31 percent with Iran.[102] Half of Tunisians surveyed (50 percent) said they want foreign aid from China to increase.[103] Only the European Union performs better, with 52 percent of Tunisians saying that they want to see foreign aid from the European Union increase, compared to 44 percent for the United Kingdom, 46 percent for Russia, 45 percent for the United States, and 39 percent for Saudi Arabia.[104]

In good news for the West, some research has found that Chinese aid is "diminishing Chinese soft power in Africa, while US aid is bolstering American soft power, both in absolute terms and relative to China."[105] One study found that Chinese aid has a net negative effect on the belief that elections are good, as well as on the belief that citizens should be able to join any civil society organization they choose, but a net positive effect on the belief that democracy is the best system.[106] The same study finds that US aid "induces greater alignment with the liberal democratic values typically associated with the US, and typically not associated with China."[107] Counterintuitively, they find that completion of a Chinese aid project tends to decrease ideological affinity for China but boost affinity for the United States and other Western powers while completed US projects boost affinity for the United States and other Western powers.[108] One explanation is that China is accused of "prioritizing speed and cost at the expense of quality and fair play" and that relying on Chinese, rather than local, labor alienates the local population. Finally, China's lack of values-based conditionality (other than adherence to the One China policy) might hurt China. Because Western powers are pushing for liberal democracy, while China remains silent, there is no real alternative to the Western model at play. David Shambaugh argues that "China is not shaping events and actively contributing to solving problems. Rather, it is quite risk-averse and narrowly self-interested."[109] Thus, he states, China "punches way below its weight" in international diplomacy. Beijing is not doing enough to shoulder its appropriate share of international responsibility and to be a world leader.[110]

While China does not have the same footprint in Tunisia that it does in other MENA countries, it is growing as a competitor to Western influence in the region. The Tunisian government seems to recognize the need to balance out its desire to grow its relationship with the United States with a need for the levels of financial support that China is willing to provide. As one Tunisian diplomat stated, "China is our friend. America is our ally."[111]

Europe

When it comes to Europe, the situation is more complicated. Europe remains the top trade partner of Tunisia and Tunisia is a member of the European Neighborhood Policy. Thus, China's growing investment in Tunisia could, in the long term, begin to encroach on Europe's trade relations. China has already begun to invest significantly on the other side of the Mediterranean, buying up assets in Portugal, Greece, and Italy following the 2008 financial crisis. In Greece, for example, China Overseas Shipping Company has a substantial stake (67 percent control) in the Port of Piraeus, the largest seaport in Greece.[112] These investments have a much deeper impact than purely economic assistance. As Philippe Le Corre notes, "Since these investments, many of the targeted countries are becoming soft supporters of China on the international stage."[113] He argues that Greece and Portugal "have become cautious in criticizing China on the world stage on issues of human rights or diplomacy to avoid damaging prosperous economic relations."[114] Furthermore, more and more European countries—particularly those along the Mediterranean—are signing on to the BRI, despite the objection of other European states. Italy was the first member of the G-7 to sign on to the BRI, going against the "US and EU strategic posture" toward China.[115]

Thus, there is far less outcry in Europe over China writ large than there is in the United States. Most of Europe does not see China as the Great Power rival in the same way that the United States tends to characterize China, although there are some signals that that may be changing with the publication of an EU document in March 2019 using uncharacteristically bold language and calling China "an economic competitor … and a systemic rival promoting alternative models of governance."[116] But, Europe is concerned about China's potential to threaten its business interests, particularly in the southern Mediterranean.

The European Union did not really think about China strategically until a few years ago, but today there is tremendous concern in Europe over China's impact on European businesses and its lack of "fair" play.[117] Nevertheless, Europe remains very divided over China. The European Commission, who has proposed more screening of foreign investments and has pushed China to liberalize, is the most hawkish European actor. But the major European powers, like Germany, France, and the UK, have taken a less confrontational posture toward China than the European Commission. And when it comes to China's role in North Africa, most European actors welcome Chinese investment if it will lead to increased economic development—something with a direct influence on Europe due to the growing numbers of North African migrants heading toward Europe's southern shores.

Conclusion

While China has been late to the game in recognizing Tunisia's strategic location, the China–Tunisia relationship has been taking off in leaps and bounds over the past few years. Nevertheless, there remain several areas with significant room for growth—particularly tourism and infrastructure development. Tunisia is making some efforts to attract larger numbers of Chinese tourists, but to compete with other North African and Mediterranean destinations it must do a lot more. Tunisia's tourism ministry should be careful not to alienate the European and North African tourists who make up the bulk of the nine million annual visitors but should take a proactive effort to reach out to the millions of potential Chinese tourists, once the COVID-19 pandemic is under control. First, the countries should begin Tunisair direct flights to China, as approved in the MOU. Second, Tunisia should embark on a more intensive marketing campaign to directly compete with other Mediterranean destinations, like Morocco, Greece, and Italy, showcasing the country's beaches, historic sites, and affordable prices.

Tunisia should also be more proactive in the infrastructure space and should use China's infrastructure investment to assist with job creation. Tunisia should take advantage of the Chinese interest in infrastructure, particularly hospitals, cultural centers, and railways, but should also work with China to incorporate more opportunities for job creation at the local level. China has expressed a lot of interest in building out Tunisia's ports. This investment serves China more than Tunisia; thus, the Tunisian authorities should use port access as a bargaining chip to push China toward allowing more Tunisian workers and better integrating local management of Chinese construction projects in the country. In encouraging Chinese investment, Tunisia should recognize the risks of further Chinese investment in sensitive areas. While Tunisia is eager for further investment in ports, as well as ICT, it is not clear what China's long-term intentions are regarding security and intelligence. While it makes sense, economically, for Tunisia to take advantage of China's investment opportunities, the young democracy should be very weary of China's long-term interests and protect itself against Chinese attempts to gain access to sensitive data and industrial information, particularly through Huawei. While it is possible for Tunisia to fully embrace Huawei's network, Tunisian authorities should ensure its dealings with Huawei offer the same protections that other democracies (like the UK) are demanding, or risk ruptures in intel sharing with the West.

But, Tunisia should also seriously consider the long-term implications of a dependency on foreign infrastructure—whether digital or physical. All of China's "gifts" come with a price, which may not be evident for years to come. One price could be the United States and Europe should also keep a careful eye on the growing Chinese presence in Tunisia and seek to counter-balance China's influence with further assistance commitments. The West should recognize China's strategic advantage as well as their own. While the Western countries could cede the infrastructure space to China, they might also consider growing their trade with Tunisia through a US-Tunisia Free Trade Agreement, something the Tunisians have been asking for from the United States for several years. The Western democracies should also continue to fund and support the country's democratic transition as it enters a fragile period following the economic challenges exacerbated by the pandemic.

Notes

1 Chinese Foreign Ministry, "Tunisia," China.org.cn, October 10, 2006, http://sars.china.com.cn/english/features/focac/183413.htm
2 David H. Shinn and Joshua Eisenman, *China and Africa: A Century of Engagement* (Philadelphia: University of Pennsylvania Press, 2012).
3 Muhamad S. Olimat, *China and North Africa since World War II: A Bilateral Approach* (Washington DC: Lexington Books, 2014).
4 Ibid.
5 Ibid.
6 Shinn and Eisenman, *China and Africa*.

7   Deborah Brautigam, *The Dragon's Gift: The Real Story of China in Africa* (Oxford: Oxford University Press, 2009).
8   "Peking's Envoys Ousted by Tunis." *New York Times*, September 24, 1967.
9   Shinn and Eisenman, *China and Africa*.
10 Ibid.
11 Emilian Kavalski, *China and the Global Politics of Regionalization* (London: Routledge, 2016).
12 Ibid.
13 Olimat, *China and North Africa since World War II*.
14 Axel Dreher et al., "Aid, China, and Growth: Evidence from a New Global Development Finance Dataset," Working Paper (AidData, October 2017), https://www.ssrn.com/abstract=3051044
15 "Chinese Embassy in Tunisia Welcomes New Batch of Chinese Medical Team," *Xinhua*, November 4, 2019, http://www.xinhuanet.com/english/2019-11/04/c_138525855.htm
16 David H. Shinn, "China's Approach to East, North and the Horn of Africa," Testimony before the U.S.-China Economic and Security Review Commission, China's Global Influence: Objectives and Strategies, Dirksen Senate Office Building, July 21, 2005, https://www.uscc.gov/sites/default/files/7.21-22.05shinn_david_wrts.pdf
17 Kavalski, *China and the Global Politics of Regionalization*.
18 Brautigam, *The Dragon's Gift*.
19 Chinese Foreign Ministry, "Tunisia."
20 Muhammad Zulfikar Rakhmat, "China and Tunisia: A Quiet Partnership," *The Diplomat*, June 28, 2014, https://thediplomat.com/2014/06/china-and-tunisia-a-quiet-partnership/
21 Shinn, "China's Approach to East, North and the Horn of Africa."
22 Chinese Foreign Ministry, "Tunisia."
23 Dreher et al., "Aid, China, and Growth."
24 Ibid.
25 Shinn and Eisenman, *China and Africa*.
26 Arthur N. Waldron (Ed.), *China in Africa*, 1st Edition (Washington, DC: The Jamestown Foundation, 2009).
27 Shinn and Eisenman, *China and Africa*.
28 Zhongmin Liu, "On Political Unrest in the Middle East and China's Diplomacy," *Journal of Middle Eastern and Islamic Studies (in Asia)* 6, no. 1 (March 1, 2012), pp. 1–18, https://doi.org/10.1080/19370679.2012.12023195

29 Ibrahim Fraihat and Andrew Leber, "China and the Middle East after the Arab Spring: From Status-Quo Observing to Proactive Engagement," *Asian Journal of Middle Eastern and Islamic Studies* 13, no. 1 (January 2, 2019), pp. 1–17, https://doi.org/10.1080/25765949.2019.1586177

30 Degang Sun and Yahia Zoubir, "China's Response to the Revolts in the Arab World: A Case of Pragmatic Diplomacy," *Mediterranean Politics* 19 (January 2, 2014), https://doi.org/10.1080/13629395.2013.809257

31 Muhamad S. Olimat, *China and the Middle East: From Silk Road to Arab Spring*, 1st Edition (Milton Park, Abingdon, Oxon: Routledge, 2012).

32 Ibid.

33 John Calabrese, "The Risks and Rewards of China's Deepening Ties with the Middle East," *China Brief* 5, no. 2 (May 24, 2005), https://jamestown.org/program/the-risks-and-rewards-of-chinas-deepening-ties-with-the-middle-east/

34 David Shambaugh, *China Goes Global: The Partial Power*, 1st Edition (Oxford & New York: Oxford University Press, 2013).

35 David H. Shinn and Joshua Eisenman, "China's Relations with North Africa and the Sahel," in *China and Africa*, *A Century of Engagement* (Philadelphia: University of Pennsylvania Press, 2012), pp. 228–48, https://www.jstor.org/stable/j.ctt3fhwkz.12

36 Dreher et al., "Aid, China, and Growth."

37 Author's interview with Tunisian diplomat. January 2020.

38 Nizar Ben Salah, "The Construction of the Community with a Shared Future for Mankind: Chinese Investment in Africa, The Maghreb and Tunisia," *Economy & Finance, MEF Reflections* (Maghreb Economic Forum [MEF], 2019), https://www.slideshare.net/MAGEF/chinese-investment-in-africa-the-maghreb-and-tunisia

39 Jon Alterman et al., "China in the Middle East: Part One," *Babel: Translating the Middle East*, https://www.csis.org/podcasts/babel-translating-middle-east

40 Ibid.

41 Government of the People's Republic of China, "China's Arab Policy Paper," Embassy of the People's Republic of China in the Kingdom of Saudi Arabia, January 2016, http://sa.china-embassy.org/eng/xwdt/t1331633.htm

42 "China and Tunisia," Ministry of Foreign Affairs of the People's Republic of China, https://www.fmprc.gov.cn/mfa_eng/wjb_663304/zzjg_663340/xybfs_663590/gjlb_663594/2893_663786/

43 Mordechai Chaziza, "China in the Middle East: Tourism as a Stealth Weapon," *Middle East Quarterly* 26, no. 4 (Fall 2019), https://www.meforum.org/59293/mordechai-chaziza-china-in-the-middle-east

44 Ibid.
45 Shawn Arita, Sumner La Croix, and James Mak, "How China's Approved Destination Status Policy Spurs and Hinders Chinese Travel Abroad," Working Paper (University of Hawai'i at Manoa: The Economic Research Organization at the University of Hawai'i, October 19, 2012).
46 "Chinese Tourists to Tunisia Witness Boom in 2018," *Xinhua*, October 28, 2018, http://www.xinhuanet.com/english/2018-10/28/c_137562912.htm
47 Ibid.
48 "Chinese Tourists in Tunisia up by 10.1 Pct by Aug. 10," *Xinhua*, August 21, 2019, http://www.xinhuanet.com/english/2019-08/21/c_138324265.htm
49 "Cultural Exchange Builds a Bridge for Tunisia and China," *China Daily*, September 27, 2019, http://www.chinadaily.com.cn/a/201909/27/WS5d8da36ea310cf3e3556ddf3.html
50 "China-Sponsored Training Courses Help Enhance China-Tunisia Cooperation: Embassy," *Xinhua*, January 11, 2020, http://www.xinhuanet.com/english/2020-01/11/c_138695151.htm
51 Shambaugh, *China Goes Global*.
52 Ibid.
53 Adel Abdel Ghafar and Anna Jacobs, "Beijing Calling: Assessing China's Growing Footprint in North Africa," Policy Briefing (Brookings Doha Center, September 2019), https://www.brookings.edu/research/beijing-calling-assessing-chinas-growing-footprint-in-north-africa/
54 "1st Confucius Institute in Tunisia Inaugurated," *Xinhua*, April 11, 2019, http://www.xinhuanet.com/english/2019-04/11/c_137966337.htm
55 "Confucius Institute Opens Classroom in Tunisia," *Xinhua*, November 13, 2018, http://www.xinhuanet.com/english/2018-11/13/c_129992290.htm
56 Mo Hong'e, "Cultural Exchange Builds a Bridge for Tunisia and China," *China Daily*, September 27, 2019, http://www.ecns.cn/news/2019-09-27/detail-ifzpknpx2078795.shtml
57 Government of the People's Republic of China, "China's Arab Policy Paper."
58 Ibid.
59 Olimat, *China and North Africa since World War II*.
60 Chris Alden and Faten Aggad-Clerx, "Chinese Investments and Employment Creation in Algeria and Egypt," Economic Brief (African Development Bank [AfDB], 2012), https://www.afdb.org/fileadmin/uploads/afdb/Documents/Publications/Brochure%20China%20Anglais.pdf

61 Michael Singh, "Chinese Policy in the Middle East in the Wake of the Arab Uprisings," in *Toward Well-Oiled Relations? China's Presence in the Middle East Following the Arab Spring* (London: Palgrave Macmillan, 2016).
62 Dreher et al., "Aid, China, and Growth."
63 "Index," Sino-Arab Chemical Fertilizers Co., Ltd., http://www.sacf.com/en/index.aspx
64 Shambaugh, *China Goes Global*.
65 "Xi Meets Tunisian Prime Minister." Ministry of Foreign Affairs of the People's Republic of China, https://www.fmprc.gov.cn/mfa_eng/wjb_663304/zzjg_663340/xybfs_663590/gjlb_663594/2893_663786/2895_663790/t1593095.shtml
66 Waldron, *China in Africa*.
67 Shambaugh, *China Goes Global*.
68 National Development and Reform Commission, Ministry of Foreign Affairs, and Ministry of Commerce of the People's Republic of China, "Vision and Proposed Actions Outlined on Jointly Building Silk Road Economic Belt and 21st-Century Maritime Silk Road," *China Daily*, March 30, 2015, http://language.chinadaily.com.cn/2015-03/30/content_19950951.htm
69 Alterman et al., "China in the Middle East: Part Two."
70 "Wang Yi Holds Talks with Foreign Minister Khemaies Jhinaoui of Tunisia," Ministry of Foreign Affairs of the People's Republic of China, https://www.fmprc.gov.cn/mfa_eng/wjb_663304/zzjg_663340/xybfs_663590/gjlb_663594/2893_663786/2895_663790/t1576877.shtml
71 Sarah Souli, "Tunisia Hopes Boost in Chinese Investment Can Ease Economic Woes," *Al-Monitor*, March 19, 2018, https://www.al-monitor.com/pulse/originals/2018/03/boost-china-investment-tunisia-europe-trade.html
72 Djallel Khechib, "One Belt, Different Aims: Beyond China's Increasing Leverage in The Grand Maghreb," *IHH Humanitarian and Social Research Center*, October 4, 2018, http://insamer.com/en/one-belt-different-aims-beyond-chinas-increasing-leverage-in-the-grand-maghreb_1665.html
73 Sarah Yerkes and Marwan Muasher, "Decentralization in Tunisia: Empowering Towns, Engaging People," *Carnegie Endowment for International Peace*, May 17, 2018, https://carnegieendowment.org/2018/05/17/decentralization-in-tunisia-empowering-towns-engaging-people-pub-76376
74 Author's interview with State Department official, January 2019.
75 Dreher et al., "Aid, China, and Growth."
76 Ibid.

77   Ibid.
78   Souli, "Tunisia Hopes Boost in Chinese Investment Can Ease Economic Woes."
79   Dreher et al., "Aid, China, and Growth."
80   "China's Public Diplomacy Dashboard," *AidData*, 2019, http://china-dashboard.aiddata.org
81   Ibid.
82   Dreher et al., "Aid, China, and Growth."
83   Ghafar and Jacobs, "Beijing Calling."
84   "Huawei Awards Prizes to Tunisian ICT Students, Instructors," *Xinhua*, December 21, 2019, http://www.xinhuanet.com/english/2019-12/21/c_138647189_4.htm
85   "Coronavirus: Le gouvernement chinois fournira à la Tunisie un autre lot de dons," *La Presse. Tn*, May 14, 2020, https://lapresse.tn/61967/coronavirus-le-gouvernement-chinois-fournira-a-la-tunisie-un-autre-lot-de-dons/
86   Sarah Yerkes, "Tunisia: Gulf's Loss Could be China's Gain," in *As Gulf Donors Shift Priorities, Arab States Search for Aid,* edited by Michele Dunne (Carnegie Endowment for International Peace, June 2020), https://carnegieendowment.org/2020/06/09/tunisia-gulf-s-loss-could-be-china-s-gain-pub-82012
87   Author's discussions with Pentagon officials, 2019.
88   Tom McTague, "Britain and the United States Have a China Problem—The Atlantic," *The Atlantic*, January 30, 2020, https://www.theatlantic.com/international/archive/2020/01/britain-us-huawei-china-mike-pompeo-dominic-raab/605806/
89   Author's interview with US official, January 2020.
90   Alterman et al., "China in the Middle East: Part Two."
91   Government of the People's Republic of China, "China's Arab Policy Paper."
92   Author's interview with State Department official, January 2019.
93   Erik Brattberg and Philippe Le Corre, "Huawei and Europe's 5G Conundrum," *National Interest*, December 27, 2018.
94   McTague, "Britain and the United States Have a China Problem."
95   Shambaugh, *China Goes Global*.
96   Camille Lons et al., "China's Great Game in the Middle East," Policy Brief (European Council on Foreign Relations, October 2019).
97   "Data," *Afrobarometer*, https://www.afrobarometer.org/data
98   Ibid.
99   Ibid.
100 Ibid.

101 "Data Analysis Tool," *Arab Barometer*, https://www.arabbarometer.org/survey-data/data-analysis-tool/
102 Ibid.
103 Ibid.
104 Ibid.
105 Robert A Blair, Robert Marty, and Phillip Roessler, "Foreign Aid and Soft Power," Working Paper (AidData, August 2019).
106 Ibid.
107 Ibid.
108 Ibid.
109 Shambaugh, *China Goes Global*.
110 Ibid.
111 Author's interview with Tunisian diplomat, 2019.
112 Philippe Le Corre, "This Is China's Plan to Dominate Southern Europe," *National Interest*, October 30, 2018.
113 Ibid.
114 Ibid.
115 Philippe Le Corre, "On China's Expanding Influence in Europe and Eurasia," Testimony before the House of Representatives Foreign Affairs Committee, May 9, 2019.
116 "EU-China—A strategic outlook." March 12, 2019: https://ec.europa.eu/commission/sites/beta-political/files/communication-eu-china-a-strategic-outlook.pdf
117 Author's interview with Europe expert. January 2020.

5

China's Relations with Algeria: From Revolutionary Friendship to Comprehensive Strategic Partnership

Yahia H. Zoubir

Introduction

In the Middle East and North Africa (MENA) region, and assuredly in the Maghreb, Algeria is unquestionably the country that has maintained the strongest ties with the People's Republic of China (PRC). Indeed, Algeria's relations with China are not limited to economic transactions, as is the case with China's relations with many countries across the MENA region. The two states enjoy relatively robust political, diplomatic, economic, trade, and, to a lesser degree, cultural relations. Algeria is a pivotal Maghreb, Arab, African, Mediterranean, and Muslim country, a reality that makes the country's geopolitical position quite attractive for outside powers, China included. Indeed, its proximity to the European Union reinforces the geostrategic importance of Algeria, situated between Europe, the Sahel with its multiple security and economic challenges, and the Maghreb, prey to the rivalry between Algeria and Morocco.[1]

This chapter focuses on the varied interests that Algeria and China share and seeks to provide a realistic assessment of the real significance of those relations. It will review the multifaceted political, economic, trade, military, and cultural relations, which have been developed since prior to Algeria's independence in 1962, with special focus on the last two decades. It will conclude with a discussion of the potential for further developments, the limitations of those ties.

Sino-Algerian Relations from Pre-independence to the Post-independence Era

Algerian and Chinese officials point out quite correctly that the two countries developed friendly rapport when Algeria was still a French colony and was fighting a brutal war against French colonialism (1954–62). Chinese government officials, whose delegation was led by Zhu Enlai, and the Algerian mission led by members of the National Liberation Front (FLN) met in Indonesia at the Afro-Asian Bandung Conference in April 1955,[2] five months after the launch of Algeria's war of independence. That meeting marked the beginning of close ties between China's Communist Party and the nationalist FLN at a time when China's foreign policy was markedly revolutionary and infused with a strong degree of ideology. For Algerians, the meeting in Bandung allowed the FLN to plan numerous visits to Beijing to secure China's diplomatic and military support. Algeria obtained both; on December 20, 1958, China became the first non-Arab country to recognize the Provisional Government of the Algerian Republic (GPRA), established in September that same year. For the Chinese, the Bandung Conference was consequential in terms of China's foreign policy toward the developing world and Algeria, in particular. Indeed, the meeting provided the context within which China's foreign minister, Zhou Enlai, publicized the Five Principles of Peaceful Coexistence of China's foreign policy, which China, India, and Myanmar had proposed back in 1954: mutual respect for sovereignty and territorial integrity, mutual nonaggression, mutual noninterference in internal affairs, equality and mutual benefit, and peaceful coexistence.[3]

During the Algerian war of liberation, delegations from the FLN traveled to Beijing, where they met with high-level Chinese leaders, including Mao himself.[4] Moreover, unlike the USSR, which wished to maintain good diplomatic relations with France, while supporting the FLN, China supported the Algerian revolution without worrying about the reactions of Paris.[5] Between 1958 and 1962, the Chinese provided assistance to Algerian combatants before the USSR decided to do so. China inspired and taught some of the guerrilla tactics that Algerian fighters in the National Liberation Army (ALN) used against French colonial troops.[6] The FLN leaders were persuaded that assistance to Algeria could come only from the socialist states, the Soviet

Union and China in particular.[7] And that assistance did come and without conditions as.

China trained many Algerian fighters in its military institutes.[8] Not only did China provide arms and military training, it also offered financial aid estimated at $10 million,[9] despite the PRC's limited resources. Unquestionably, Algerians have never forgotten China's support during their war of independence, even though Sino-Algerian relations at the time were not free of self-interested calculations.[10] Regardless, this laid the foundations of long-standing relationship.

Between 1963 and 1975, China signed twenty agreements, including a friendship accord, covering many fields, such as economic and technical cooperation, health, cultural cooperation, communication, scientific and military cooperation, and maritime cooperation, among other fields.[11] Throughout the 1960s and 1970s, China's ties with Algeria, as with other African countries, were nevertheless at the heart of the rivalry between the PRC and the USSR.[12] Politically, the most significant event took place in 1971, when Algeria, despite its close relations with Moscow, mobilized the African countries, which had become independent in the 1960s, to support the PRC in its bid to become a permanent member of the UN Security Council and remove Taiwan from the seat it had occupied hitherto. Both Algeria and Albania sponsored Resolution 27588,[13] a vote which allowed China to acquire its permanent seat on the Security Council. During this period, Algeria was instrumental in the consolidation of ties between China and Africa. Because of the commonality of their foreign policy interests, Algeria and the PRC worked closely together at the United Nations on questions related to liberation movements, such as the African National Congress (ANC) or the Palestinian Liberation Organization (PLO).[14]

With Deng Xiaoping's accession to power in 1978, Mao's ideologically charged diplomatic policy gave way to a new, more pragmatic, and economically oriented diplomacy. China's foreign policy, including its policy toward the MENA, rested now on its own development/modernization strategy, thus undergoing a threefold transformation: a shift from ideological orientation to ideological neutrality, from unitary form to multiple channels in bilateral trade, and from single aid to a "win-win" strategy in the area of cooperation.[15] Progressively, China has displayed since then its ambition to offer—not to impose—a new development model ("authoritarian market system"[16]) to generate mutually beneficial (win-win) relations, an aspect of China's policy that has been rather attractive to developing countries, especially those wishing to reduce their dependency on or bargain with the West, while keeping their authoritarian political systems unaltered.

It would be erroneous to assume that China's emphasis on the primacy of the economy means absence of geopolitical calculations and convergences, notwithstanding its noninvolvement in conflict resolution in the region.[17] Algeria, for instance, was one of China's diplomatic supporters in the aftermath of the April 1989 crackdown on students in Tiananmen Square, which saw the imposition of Western sanctions against China. Like it did in 1970–1 to help China gain its seat at the UNSC, Algeria mobilized this time African countries within the Organization of African Unity (OAU) to reject the application of sanctions which were hindering economic relations between China and the African continent. This orientation eventually bore fruit with the creation of the Forum on China-Africa Cooperation (FOCAC) in 2000 from which China–Africa relations took on a strategic dimension for both sides.

In 1978, China launched its "reform and opening up" policy ("Socialism with Chinese characteristics"); this pragmatic foreign policy shift, gradually developed away from the radical, confrontational foreign policy of the 1950s–70s. The PRC focused instead on economic development and unrelenting modernization. Although this did not mean an abandonment of Marxist principles, it was trade and economic development, not ideology, that became the major driver of China's exchanges with developing countries. China's new policy focused on economic and cultural cooperation, while upholding the foreign policy principles such as noninterference in states' domestic affairs which Chinese officials reiterate constantly, insisting that they are immutable.

China's drive for modernization entailed seeking new providers of energy and raw materials, especially hydrocarbons, of which China needed in massive quantities, mostly in sub-Saharan Africa and, later, the Gulf region. Probably because 90 percent of Algeria's oil exports go to Europe and because it exports most of its natural gas to the European Union, it did not represent an important source of hydrocarbons for China,[18] even if Chinese oil companies are present in Algeria's oil sector (building refineries, oil recuperations, and oil exploration). Energy and other raw materials have become strategic for the country's economy; this meant that China would pay little regard to those suppliers' ideological and political inclinations.

Since then, China has relied on "oil diplomacy"[19] based on strengthening political partnerships and trade relations with other countries, as well as on increasing foreign direct investments (FDI). This is precisely the vision that determined its relations with many developing countries. This begs the question as to why Sino-Algerian relations, especially in the economic realm, developed concomitantly to the changes in the PRC in the early 1980s, i.e., during China's "opening up"; the obvious answer is that this growth owes much not only to the long-lasting relationship between the two, but also because of Algeria's own political, economic, and military needs (diversification of partners at all levels). Thus, although the impressive growth, especially in economic relations, would happen in the late 1990s and 2000s, both countries decided in the 1980s to meet their respective and mutual interests through the consolidation of their multifaceted relations. For China, Algeria's geopolitical position offered an opportunity for the PRC to extend its influence onto Europe and sub-Saharan Africa. One way for China to extend that influence in the region was through encouraging its corporations to export their commodities, especially low-cost products affordable to the lower-middle class populations. Algeria's location as a Mediterranean, African, and Middle Eastern country offers such an advantage for Chinese investors and traders, particularly regarding transport expenditures (air, sea, and land transport routes linking Algeria to Africa and Europe).[20]

The takeoff in Sino-Algerian relations occurred in the early 1980s. Indeed, from the early 1980s onward,[21] bilateral economic and trade cooperation had begun to increase. The major sectors involved cooperation in construction of housing projects, agriculture, and water reservoirs. Until then, though, economic and trade relations were negligible compared to what they are today. Algeria's considerable trade relations with Europe, particularly France, constrained greater cooperation with China, especially since China was focused on its own domestic political and economic transformation. Sino-Algerian trade volume amounted merely to US$ 170 million in 1982; it rose insignificantly to US$ 199 million in 2000 and to US$ 292 million in 2001.[22] Considering the potential of economic exchanges and given their relatively close relations, it is evident that Sino-Algerian trade volume in the 1980s was insignificant.

In 1982, China and Algeria established a Joint Committee for Economic, Commercial, and Technical Cooperation which later included agriculture, energy, scientific research,[23] and nuclear power. According to the Algerian ambassador to China, from 1982 to 2007, six rounds had been held.[24] Later, cooperation expanded, and encompassed almost all fields: energy, agriculture, construction, scientific research, culture, military, and nuclear sector, as well as animal production, irrigation, and combating desertification.[25]

Politically, because of their old ties and friendship, during the armed Islamist insurgency in Algeria in the 1990s, Algeria and China signed an agreement to hold regular political consultations, while Western countries maintained a tacit diplomatic embargo on the Algerian government.[26] Thus, the authorities in Algiers were able to count on China's unwavering support during the internal crisis which almost brought down the state. Given that Western countries had imposed a quasi-embargo on military supplies to Algeria, China's political support proved a real relief.

Close to the end of President Abdelaziz Bouteflika's first presidential term in 2004, President Hu Jintao visited Algeria. His political discussions with Bouteflika focused on the prospects for a new economic and political international order.[27] This reflected the growing intensity of political relations between the two states. Bouteflika stated during his visit to Beijing in November 2006 that "our relations intensified during the last years, they have been consecrated by a declaration about a strategic partnership initiated during my visit in 2004."[28] During the FOCAC held in Beijing, the PRC and Algeria signed the Declaration on Strategic Partnership and Cooperation. In 2014, this partnership was elevated to a Comprehensive Strategic Partnership (CSP),[29] the highest type of partnership that China offers reflecting a given significance of the partner in its international relations.[30] This CSP coincided with the fifty-fifth anniversary of the establishment of Sino-Algerian diplomatic relations and the tenth anniversary of the conclusion of Strategic Cooperation relations between the two nations; the main objective was "to raise [bilateral cooperation] to the highest level for mutual benefit, thus enabling the two friendly countries and peoples to achieve further progress, prosperity and development."[31]

Following the signing of the CSP, consolidation of relations at all levels continued. In April 2015, for instance, during the Algerian-Chinese Trade and Investment Forum, held in Beijing, the two sides signed fifteen draft agreements, two agreements, and a memorandum of understanding (MoU) on industry, mining, agriculture, and tourism.[32] This took place during Algeria's prime minister Abdelmalek Sellal's four-day official visit to Beijing at the invitation of his counterpart Li Keqiang. During the visit, Sellal met with Xi Jinping; the two sides reiterated the importance of Sino-Algerian relations.[33]

Political relations witnessed even more frequent high-level official visits henceforth, while the growth of economic ties had already resulted in the establishment of air links, the coming of tens of thousands of Chinese construction workers, as well as the flow of Algerian business people to China, especially to Yiwu (Zhejiang Province), in search of cheap Chinese consumer goods.[34] In 2018, on the sixtieth anniversary of the establishment of diplomatic relations, Xi Jinping reiterated China's commitment to foster further development of the CSP between China and Algeria.[35] In their exchanges during the same occasion, the two sides pledged to intensify cooperation within the framework of the Belt and Road Initiative (BRI).[36]

On the one hand, this sustained cooperation and partnership at all levels has allowed China to counterbalance French and US interests not only in Algeria, but also in Africa[37]; on the other hand, it has contributed to Algeria preserving its independent foreign policy and foreign policy principles (similar to China's), as illustrated by the diversification of its relations with the outside world and rejection of foreign powers' interference in states' domestic affairs. For the PRC, as for the European Union and the United States, Algeria remains an important regional power not only due to its size, geographical location, and geopolitical position, but also because it boasts mineral resources, such as zinc, iron-ore, uranium, gold, and phosphates, as well as hydrocarbon resources, such as oil and gas. Major states see Algeria, a middle power,[38] as a key player in regional stability in both North Africa and the Sahel.[39] For Beijing, Algeria's assets and potential are attractive for reasons other than economics. Its influence and role in the Mediterranean, sub-Saharan Africa, and in the African Union are real assets for the PRC, for, both economically and politically, Algeria fits into China's policy in the Mediterranean and in sub-Saharan Africa, as well as in the BRI (land and maritime). Having Algeria as a reliable strategic partner on the continent is a significant advantage, especially since Beijing holds Africa as an indispensable strategic asset for China's modernization.

Since February 22, 2019, Algeria has undergone a major crisis; on April 2, the military removed forcibly Bouteflika, who, despite his severe illness, sought a fifth term in office. China remained cautious toward the events[40]; it reiterated its principle of noninterference in other countries' internal affairs, stating that China "hopes to see Algeria make smooth progress on its political agenda" and that the PRC was "convinced that the Algerian people have the wisdom and capacity to explore a path that meets their country's requirements."[41] The Chinese were much more assertive in defending Algeria. Indeed, when the European Parliament passed on November 28, 2019, a resolution on the situation concerning liberties in Algeria,[42] Chinese ambassador Lie Lianhe declared that "we will oppose the interference of any foreign power in the internal affairs of Algeria. China will always remain at Algeria's side," insisting that Beijing will also oppose "any intervention by foreign forces in Algeria's internal affairs."[43] Clearly, without rejecting the protest movement, which had not abated for a year (until it decided to suspend in March 2020 the marches due to the Covid-19 pandemic), in Beijing's eyes, Algeria's stability is paramount and foreign interference in its domestic affairs is unacceptable. Any chaos in the country, as has happened in Libya since 2011, would prove detrimental to China's vested interests.

Despite its close relations, China has not sided with Algeria regarding the question of Western Sahara, an important diplomatic and national security interest for Algerians who support a referendum on the former Spanish territory, which Morocco has occupied illegally since 1975. Instead, it has sought to play a balancing act between Algeria and Morocco.[44] China has adopted a seemingly neutral position and has favored unconvincingly a negotiated solution between Morocco and the POLISARIO Front (the Frente Popular de Liberación de Saguia el Hamra et Río de Oro) based on UN Security Council resolutions to reach "a just, lasting, and acceptable settlement," as inscribed in UN documents. It is Beijing's ambiguous position at times that Algerian officials find quite puzzling. They are disappointed with China's detached attitude, especially since Beijing gives the impression at times that it favors Morocco's offer of autonomy to the Sahrawis rather than adhere to the right to self-determination. China's position on the conflict, though its officials do not say so explicitly, derives from its erroneous perception that the conflict falls perhaps within the scope of one of its five principles, i.e., respect of sovereignty and territorial integrity of states, even if only the United States[45] and a handful of insignificant African countries and the Gulf monarchies recognize Moroccan sovereignty over Western Sahara.[46]

This Chinese position baffles Algerian officials who question how China could confuse Western Sahara with the principle of noninterference or territorial sovereignty. Algerian ambassador to China told the author during an interview in November 2016 that "we have supported China on many issues, including the PRC's gaining a seat at the UN Security Council. We told our Chinese partners that Western Sahara is a different question from Tibet or Xinjiang, to no avail."[47]

Undoubtedly, China's position derives from Morocco's implicit threat that should China recognize the Sahrawi Arab Democratic Republic (SADR) or support Algeria's position openly, Morocco would recognize Taiwan or raise the issue of Tibet.[48] China's neutrality derives partly from avoiding a potential change of Morocco's position on Taiwan or Tibet or induce Morocco to raise concerns about China's treatment of the Uyghurs in Xinjiang. Nevertheless, China's position on Western Sahara is not constrained by political reasons only. Since 2016, China's economic interests in Morocco (e.g., the *Tanger Med* meta-project) have grown considerably and have the potential of increasing further. Trade and investments have also increased.[49]

Furthermore, China is cognizant of Morocco's strategic location and its favored economic association with the European Union, particularly France and Spain, its major trade partners, and its closeness to most French-speaking sub-Saharan countries.[50] Undoubtedly, these and several other factors provide a big advantage to Morocco from Beijing's perspective.[51] True to its realist policy, China puts aside ideological considerations—that would induce it to support the Sahrawis—to enter more easily the European and West African zones, while preserving its close relations with Algeria, which, as a former Chinese ambassador to Morocco told the author, are much more important and more comprehensive than those with Morocco.[52] Besides, under Bouteflika's rule, Algeria did not press the question of Western Sahara in its relations with China, an attitude that has changed in 2020. Sino-Algerian political relations have continued to expand. For instance, in March

2019, the agreement between the two countries to exempt each other from visa requirements for holders of diplomatic and service passports entered into force.⁵³

Regarding the Muslim Uyghurs question in Xinjiang, Algeria has taken a favorable position toward China. Indeed, along with other Arab and Muslim countries, Algeria was a signatory to the letter sent to the United Nations, supporting counterterrorism and deradicalization measures in Xinjiang, as well as the opening of "vocational education and training centers," which Westerners label as concentration or at best internment camps. Unmistakably, Algeria's decision derives from its friendship with Beijing, but also because, economically, "Algiers, whose economy is deteriorating, could consider Beijing as a real alternative to recourse to the IMF."⁵⁴ Another explanation is Algeria's own experience with domestic violent Islamist extremism in the 1990s and its devastating consequences. Algeria, like some other Arab countries, has sided in 2020 with China on Taiwan and Hong Kong, a position that the Chinese government has appreciated. Foreign Minister Wang Yi declared at the China–Arab States Cooperation Forum (CASCF) meeting that "China appreciates the Arab brothers' support to its just position on Hong Kong, Xinjiang, Taiwan and other matters that are China's internal affairs."⁵⁵

Before focusing on Sino-Algeria economic relations, one should point out that although those relations evolved since the 1980s, and even if there was mutual interest in developing them bilaterally, they must also be seen within the context of the One Belt, One Road (OBOR) initiative (2013), or BRI since 2015, which 138 countries had joined as of March 2020.⁵⁶

China's Belt and Road Initiative: The New Framework of Chinese Cooperation

Since the launch of the BRI, the importance of the MENA region has taken on an added dimension. Creating connectivity between different continents, seas, waterways, rails, and telecommunications required not just financial resources but energy and minerals, as well. In the past two decades, China has increased its presence not only in Algeria but in the Greater Maghreb countries—Algeria, Libya, Mauritania, Morocco, and Tunisia—and the Gulf region, in terms of trade, investment, and economic cooperation. It has become active in these countries, focusing on bilateral relations while also working within two frameworks: the FOCAC and the CASCF, created in 2000 and 2004, respectively. As stated above, Beijing's political, diplomatic, economic, and commercial relations in the Maghreb region are strongest with Algeria,[57] although economic relations with Morocco and Tunisia have also grown, especially with Morocco, which has gained the status of "strategic partner" in 2016. China is strengthening its ties with the MENA and acquiring important segments in those markets. Thus, the North Africa region is part of China's overarching political strategy, known as the "Great Rejuvenation of the Chinese Nation," the "China Dream," what Xi Jinping rephrased at the nineteenth CPC National Congress in 2017 as the "Great Modern Socialist Country" by the mid-twenty-first century.[58] Undoubtedly, the aim is to do this through economic development at home and economic exchanges as the primary driver of relations around the world and with North Africa.[59]

Since the launch of the BRI, to which most African countries have signed up, China has reaffirmed its "strategic" interests in the MENA, where seventeen countries have joined the BRI. At the Ministerial Meeting of the CASCF in 2014, President Xi Jinping declared that "the establishment of the China–Arab States Cooperation Forum was a strategic step the two sides took for the long-term development of the China–Arab relations."[60] As to China's 2016 *Arab Policy Paper*, it states that China will continue its traditional friendship with the Arab states and promote cooperation at all levels. The paper reiterated the strategic nature of those relations whose objective is to preserve peace and stability.[61] The *Arab Policy Paper* incorporates many elements, which are also upheld by Algeria. In addition to reemphasizing the Five Principles, which Algeria adheres to, the paper insists that "China supports the Middle East peace process and the establishment of an independent state of Palestine with full sovereignty, based on the pre-1967 borders, with East Jerusalem as its capital," a position that coincides with Algeria's. As important is the statement that "China respects choices made by the Arab people, and supports Arab states in exploring their own development paths," another similarity with Algeria's principles. Thus, when analyzing China's political and economic relations in the MENA, one should keep in mind the policy orientations that the Chinese government has laid out for the region, the institutional frameworks that have been set up (FOCAC, CASCF), as well as China's "Great Rejuvenation of the Chinese Nation" strategy. To this, one should also include the novel approach, known as the "1+2+3" cooperation pattern, which President Xi Jinping advanced in 2014 that involves closer cooperation in the energy sector, infrastructure-building, trade and investment, and collaboration in development plans to "improve people's welfare," as well as setting up institutions to encourage bilateral trade and investment into various sectors (energy, petrochemical, agriculture, manufacturing, and services).[62]

Indubitably, in the context of the BRI and China's other initiatives, Algeria's geopolitical position would prove even more valuable from a Chinese perspective. In September 2018, Algeria signed a MoU to join China's BRI. In the framework of the MoU, the two states committed to cooperate in the areas of policy coordination, infrastructure interdependence, and a multitude of other areas; Algeria ratified the MoU in July 2019,[63] through a presidential decree that interim President Abdelkader Bensalah signed. By way of that agreement, the two countries "are working to consolidate political relations, strengthen economic ties and intensify people-to-people and cultural exchange, contributing to the achievement of common development goals" and "to establish fruitful cooperation and sustainable development through the integrated potentials, opportunities and advantages offered by the economies of the two countries." In addition, they declared that they are also working to "strengthen cooperation with the states participating in the initiative and consolidate their economic development achieving progress," as well as to "strengthen mutual exchange and support, in accordance with the concept of the BRI based on cooperation, development and mutual gain, through the full use of existing bilateral cooperation mechanisms and multilateral mechanisms that bind the parties."[64] In sum, the BRI aims to consolidate the already strong Sino-Algerian economic and other relations.

In a phone discussion between Algeria and China's prime ministers, Abdelaziz Djerad invited Li Keqiang for an official visit when the Covid-2019 was over; the purpose of the planned visit is "to activate the elaboration, by both parties, of a new five-year plan of global strategic partnership for the years 2020–2024."[65] Undoubtedly, the two parties will renew the CSP to expand on their multifaceted relations.

Sino-Algerian Economic Relations

Economic relations between Algeria and China have increased exponentially since the early 2000s, around the time when FOCAC was established. Algeria had just regained security and stability after the civil strife, the so-called "black" or "bloody decade." Benefiting from exceptional oil revenues, the authorities were able to revitalize the economy and international relations after the relative isolation of the 1990s.[66] These two aspects went hand in hand, as the economy was in shambles and Algeria was isolated internationally. To remedy the economic situation, in the early 2000s, the government launched public investment plans in the field of infrastructure. Housing needs in particular were immense, and Bouteflika, who had been elected through a contentious election—six candidates withdrew on the eve on what appeared to be a rigged election—was aware that, beyond the policy of national reconciliation, his wresting legitimacy from the population depended in part on resolving the housing crisis.

The actual transformation of economic relations started in 2002, marking exponential growth henceforth. The Chinese authorities had come to the realization that Algeria, the second largest country in Africa (the largest since 2011, after South Sudan became an independent state), has an important geopolitical position in the Mediterranean,[67] the Middle East, and Africa, a major asset. Not only are those regions essential for China, but Algeria represented an attractive, lucrative market for China's companies in that area. The transformation was considerable, for Chinese companies had secured billions of dollars in contracts in Algeria, mostly in housing construction, roads, highway, rail, and hydrocarbons; the trade volume has revolved between $8 billion and more than $9 billion in recent years. According to Algerian customs, in 2019, China remained the country's main supplier; in 2019, China contributed 18.25 percent of Algeria's imports, $7.654,26 billion, followed by France, Italy, Spain, and Germany with respective shares of 10.20 percent, 8.13 percent, 6.99 percent, and 6.76 percent. The total trade volume with China amounted to $9.294,21 billion.[68] France remains Algeria's main customer with a share of 14.11 percent, followed by Italy, Spain, the United States, and Turkey with respective shares of 12.90 percent, 11.15 percent, 6.42 percent, and 6.27

percent. China imported in the same period $1.639,95 billion, representing 4.58 percent of the shares.[69] In 2019, Algeria's top five suppliers were China, France, Italy, Spain, and Germany.

In the early 2000s, the Algerian government chose to rely on China rather than on its traditional European partners; in part, though pro-Western, Bouteflika wished to fulfill the electoral pledge he had made to reduce the huge deficit in construction and thus offer housing for the population at an affordable price. For him, resolving the housing issue rested on political considerations, namely, to gain a degree of legitimacy following his controversial, rigged election in April 1999.[70] Certainly, Europe could not compete with China in building so many dwellings with similar cost and speed. Prior to China's involvement, Algeria had suffered extremely from an acute housing shortage, which had real social implications, and triggered cyclical social unrest. Unquestionably, China could deliver housing speedily and at inexpensive, government subsidized cost. The authorities could afford such domestic investment as a result of the rocketing financial revenues cumulated from the rapid and huge increase of oil prices in the world energy market. They called on China to build not merely housing but many other major civilian infrastructures that could address the country's inadequate or deteriorating transportation, communication, water supply and rail systems.

The construction projects took on strategic importance for Bouteflika's regime, whose legitimacy and popular support rested on the president's promises to improve the welfare of the citizens, create new jobs, and stimulate economic growth. Thus, China secured a contract worth over $7 billion for the construction 2/3rd of the 1,200-kilometer-long highway from the border with Morocco to the frontier with Tunisia. Other examples of cooperation included the 3,000-kilometer North-South Trans-Saharan Highway linking Algeria to Nigeria, the most difficult portion of which was built by the China State Construction Engineering Corporation.[71]

The Trans-Saharan highway project crosses through Algeria, Chad, Mali, Niger, Nigeria, and Tunisia. It has a total stretch of 4,500 kilometers on the route linking Algiers to Lagos.[72] The Chinese have also worked on the extension of the country's railroad network and telecommunications systems. They obtained a $3.5 billion contract for the development of a railway assigned to the Chinese Civil Engineering Construction Corporation (CCECC).[73] In the telecommunications sector, companies, such as Huawei and Zhongxing Telecom Equipment, made direct investments in Algeria, while ZTE signed an agreement with Algérie Télécom to modernize the telecommunication sector in the country.[74] Huawei has built training divisions and provided scholarships for training at Huawei centers in China.[75] The China State Construction Engineering Corporation (CSCEC) has built tens of thousands of dwellings in different towns, as well as different types of edifices. They have been involved in virtually all the major projects: the new Algiers airport and the new terminal inaugurated in April 2019, the great mosque of Algiers ($1.5 billion)[76] completed in April 2019,[77] the Olympic stadium in Oran, the Ministry of Foreign Affairs, the site of the Constitutional Court on the heights of Algiers, large five-star hotels (Sheraton, Hilton, etc.), as well as large shopping centers, like the Dounia Park, the extension of the railway network, the construction of 750 kilometers of an aqueduct linking In Salah to Tamanrasset (in the deep south), etc. In addition, China has offered as a gift an opera house in Ouled Fayet, a suburb of Algiers. For these major projects, Algeria has awarded since 2013 fifty construction contracts to Chinese companies worth a total of $25 billion. The CSCEC, which in 2016 had 245 projects in the country,[78] and the CCECC dominate the construction market in the country.

All these constructions have obviously required a large workforce, most of which has come from China. In response to the charge that they favor the Chinese workforce to the locals, officials often reply: "But the Chinese are very efficient, reliable and active."[79] For the Algerian government, the Chinese enterprises of the 3/8 system, i.e., three teams that take turns nonstop, day and night, is quite attractive. This helps in the timely delivery of the projects. Furthermore, the Chinese workforce is not submitted to the same favorable local labor laws. The main problem the workforce has created relates to cultural clashes and to the stereotypes that Algerians hold vis-à-vis the Chinese. In fact, there have been some skirmishes between Chinese residents and/or workers, on the one hand, and the locals, on the other. The most notable scuffle occurred in 2009 in Baz Ezzouar in the eastern suburb of Algiers, a small dispute that escalated to a brawl that caused some injuries.[80] Another fight occurred in 2016 in a construction site but this time it was among Chinese workers some of whom were intoxicated.[81] This might have added to the negative perception that the Chinese do not respect the local culture although similar behavior occurs among Algerians.

There are no reliable data on the number of Chinese workers in Algeria, especially since it is a mobile workforce that returns to China after the completion of the work for which it came to accomplish in the country.[82] While there were reports of 55,000 Chinese workers in 2016,[83] for some, this number is underestimated.[84] Although the number of Chinese workers in Algeria is not known accurately, the Chinese community in Algeria is or was at some point in time the second largest in Africa, if not the largest.[85] In 2017, it was estimated at 40,000, half of whom in Algiers alone.[86] In 2019, the Chinese ambassador to Algeria gave the number as 30,000 workers[87]; this, of course, does not include the thousands of permanent Chinese residents settled throughout the country. In sum, Chinese citizens in Algeria are not only workers; there are also thousands who are permanent residents.[88]

Among the big projects, one stands out as a major development for China's Maritime Silk Road. On January 17, 2016, the two countries signed an agreement for a mega port at El-Hamdania, 80 kilometers west of Algiers, the construction of which is to be carried out by a company under Algerian law made up of the Public Port Services Group and two Chinese companies, CSCEC and the China Harbor Engineering Company (CHEC). A long-term Chinese credit, guaranteed by the Algerian government, will finance the port infrastructure. If materialized, El-Hamdania will be among the 30 largest ports in the world. The construction was expected to be completed by 2024,[89] and gradually brought into service by 2020, with the entry of Shanghai Ports, which will ensure its operation.[90] The port will consist of 23 docks and a handling volume of 6.5 million containers and 25,7 million tons/year of freight. Algerian authorities anticipate that the yearly cargo traffic of the future harbor will reach 35 million tons by 2050.[91] The objective of the project is also to create industrial undertakings and to make the port a development hub. Once the port becomes operational, it will connect Algeria with Southeast Asia, the United States, and the rest of Africa and would augment Algeria's current maritime traffic capacity. China's state-owned shipping line, COSCO Shipping, indicated that it could make El-Hamdania its hub in the western Mediterranean Sea.[92] The new hub might compete with northern Mediterranean ports, such as the ones in Spain (e.g., Valencia and Barcelona).[93]

Whatever the case, in view of Algeria's long coast and geopolitical location, it is fairly certain that the Chinese will build a port in Algeria, especially since this falls within its port construction policy to support the Maritime Silk Road.[94] For Algeria, such port and the industrial hub constitute a badly needed undertaking to put Algeria's economy back on track. In summer 2020, the mega-project, which was delayed due to the political turmoil in the country, has been revived. It will be financed by a loan from the National Investment Fund (NIF) and a long-term loan from the Exim Bank of China.[95] The cost of the seven-year construction is estimated between US$5–6 billion. This port will compete with those in Morocco and Spain; from a Chinese perspective, this is an additional port that will serve the MSR and strengthen connectivity.

There exist other important sectors in Sino-Algerian economic relations. Construction has begun in April 2021 According to the China Automobile Manufacturers Association (CAAM), Algeria was the leading destination for China's vehicle exports in 2012 and 2013.[96] In 2013, China's FAW had signed an agreement with Arcofina for the assembly of its vehicles in Algeria, a plant with a capacity of 10,000 passenger vehicles annually.[97] Chinese companies have become quite involved in the automotive and automobile industry, an important market in Algeria long dominated by French companies. Algeria's automotive sector ranks among the largest on the African continent (alongside South Africa, Egypt, and Morocco); the country imports more cars from China than any other.

In 2018, the heavy truck of Shaanxi Automobile Group opened a production line in Algeria, the country's first Chinese vehicle assembly plant in production[98]; the plan was to assemble and manufacture about 3,000 trucks yearly under the brand of Shacman. The company would serve not only the local market, but will also export to Tunisia and Mali, among others. Its first truck Shacman "made in Algeria" came out from the factory in Sétif (eastern Algeria) on May 10, 2018.[99] Earlier, the KIV Group and Chinese car manufacturer Foton had signed a deal in 2017 on the setup of a joint company, Foton Motors Algeria, for the establishment of truck assembly and manufacturing plant in the eastern city of Annaba.[100]

Energy Relations

Although Algeria is not a major oil supplier to the PRC, Chinese oil companies, such as CNPC, CNOOC, and SINOPEC, are present in the country. In 2017, Algeria was ranked sixteenth in the world in energy production[101]; it also boasts "20 trillion cubic meters of technically recoverable shale gas, representing 707 Tcf of technically recoverable shale gas, the third-largest quantity of untapped shale gas resources in the world."[102] In 2018, Algeria's proven natural gas reserves amounted to 4,504.0 billion cubic meters.[103] This might provide China with an investment opportunity. Indubitably, China is interested in this market, especially after the loss of its investments in Libya following the chaos that ravaged it since 2011. In view of Algeria's announced decision in May 2020 to move away from dependence on oil and focus on other natural resources (phosphates, gold, zinc, etc.), it is certain that Chinese firms will be involved in those sectors.

Chinese oil companies have been involved in the energy sector, particularly in well recovery and exploration which is their domain of expertise. China is engaged not only in wells development (Zarzaitine, Illizi, etc.) and other activities in the energy sectors, but also in the construction of refineries (Adrar, operational since 2007; Skikda, etc.). Certainly, cooperation between China and Algeria in the field of nuclear research, which began in the 1980s,[104] and civil nuclear energy for electricity production will also grow. Many officials in Algeria are pushing for solar energy, suggesting that China could be one of the candidates for such a project.[105]

Despite the presence of the Chinese oil companies, the relationship with Algeria in the energy sector remains limited; however, this might change in the future because of the US export of shale oil to Europe. Like other MENA suppliers, there is fear that this might result in the reduction of Algerian gas supplies to Europe, a traditional market for Algerian hydrocarbons, and would compel Algeria to seek other markets for its energy outputs in countries like China and India. China's growing and stronger presence in Algeria's oil sector was also the effect of the withdrawal of some Western companies (BP and Norway's Statoil in particular) following the terrorist attack in January 2013 against the gas plant in Tiguentourine, near In Amenas,[106] close to the border with Libya. In February 2020, reports indicated that BP sought to sell its 45.89 percent share in the gas plan in In Amenas.[107]

Algeria, which has the fourth largest phosphate reserves in the world, has been in the process of concluding a very important agreement with China; until now, Algeria has produced and exported raw phosphates at a great loss because, unlike other producers, it does not transform it into phosphoric acid or fertilizer. Phosphoric acid sells for two to three times more than a barrel of oil. Due to domestic political and social turmoil in the country since February 2019, the promising $6 billion project with China had been put on hold.[108] However, after resuming discussions, on January 7, 2020, the national oil company SONATRACH and the Chinese CITIC signed an amendment to the MoU, "Tébessa integrated phosphate project," which the two sides had concluded in November 2018. The phosphate complex will purportedly attract an investment of $6 billion and is scheduled to start operating in 2022. The project will create 3,000 direct jobs while its construction sites across the four wilayas [departments] will provide 14,000 indirect jobs.[109] Following Algerian president Abdelmadjid Tebboune's press conference[110] broadcast on May 1, 2020, in which he insisted on the necessity to focus on untapped resources, instead of remaining dependent on oil, phosphates will take certainly added importance, making the deal with China a reality.

Despite the booming economic relations, it is rather surprising that Chinese FDI in Algeria remains quite low. In 2017, total FDI Stock in Algeria amounted to $1,833.66 billion. In 2019, Algeria received a mere $440 million. During the period from 2005 to 2019, Chinese Investments and Contracts in Algeria totaled $23.61 billion, while for Morocco, they were ten times less amounting to $2.3 billion.[111] As a journalist pointed out correctly, "In Algeria, China doesn't invest much, but it counts a lot."[112] And even though Chinese FDI in Algeria is relatively low, it is higher than that in the other Maghreb states.

Sino-Algerian Military Cooperation

Following the "Sand War" with Morocco in 1963 until the last couple of decades, Algeria had purchased 90 percent of its armaments from the Soviet

Union/Russia.¹¹³ China was not a major supplier of weaponry to Algeria, except for light arms, such as the Chinese-made Soviet AK-47s. But, political, economic, and cultural transformations in Algeria in the 1990s and 2000s led the government to expand the sources of armaments and military training. Therefore, the country began purchasing weapons from the United States, Germany, France, Turkey, South Africa, and China, among others. The first major purchase, an insignificant one, occurred in the mid-1990s, when Algeria imported Chinese weapons worth $100 million.¹¹⁴ Algeria's drive to diversify its military procurements began with the huge oil revenues (until 2014). The country decided to professionalize the military but also modernize the Armed Forces, which were in need for new equipment to replace the obsolete arsenals. Thus, the National Popular Army (ANP) began equipping its branches (army, air force, and navy) with modern Chinese weapons, making Algeria one of the nine African emergent customers for Chinese military exports.¹¹⁵ From 2013 to 2017, Algeria increased its imports of Chinese arms significantly,¹¹⁶ resulting in Algeria becoming one of China's primary arms clients in Africa.¹¹⁷ China sold various types of weapons to Algeria, such as the LZ45 155 mm self-propelled howitzers, delivered in 2014, which the ANP uses in tactical maneuvers, the 50 C-802/CSS-N-8 anti-ship missiles, and 50 FM90 surface-to-air missile systems. In July 2016, the Algerian Navy bought the third and final C28A corvette ordered from China in March 2012.¹¹⁸ Those purchases from the PRC also included three frigates,¹¹⁹ as well as Hainan patrol boats, armed with mines and rockets for antisubmarine missions, products of Chinese shipyards.¹²⁰ Algeria has also acquired a number of Chinese UAVs, such as the CH-3 and the CH-4 combat drone.¹²¹

The two countries' military cooperation was elevated to another level with the launch of the Algerian satellite into space in December 2017 from the Xichang Satellite Launch Center (XSLC), aboard a Long March-3B launch vehicle.¹²² This was Algeria's fifth satellite, but the first in the field of telecommunications. Named the Alcomsat-1, this satellite was made by the China Aerospace Science and Technology Corporation (CASC). Although its operation allows Algeria to broadcast from 200 to 300 radio digital radios and a similar number of television channels, Alcomsat-1 also has an intelligence mission since it will optimize the signal quality of geolocation satellites (GPS, GLONASS, Galileo).¹²³ While this was the result of Algeria's ambitious space program conducted by the Algerian

Space Agency, the Alcomsat-1 was also undoubtedly in response to Morocco's launch a month before, from Frenchman Arianespace's Kourou base in French Guiana, of its first high-performance observation satellite, the Mohammed VI A, a powerful surveillance military tool. Morocco's satellite worried not only Algeria but Spain, as well.[124] Alcomsat-1 and other satellites resulting from Sino-Algerian cooperation are used also for nonmilitary purposes, such as earth observation focused on the environment, regional planning, mining and agricultural resources, urban planning, transport, and prevention and management of major risks, as well as in the field of communication.[125] The cooperation in satellites has been rather successful and is part of the CSP the two countries had signed in 2014.

Because of the modernization and professionalization of the ANP, and in view of the colossal military budget ($10–12 billion annually), Algeria no longer wishes to buy inexpensive weapons or to acquire military hardware surplus that the Chinese army wishes to scrap. Quite the contrary; nowadays, the ANP buys high-tech and modern military equipment to transform the Armed Forces into one of the most modern in Africa.[126] Overall, China has progressively become an important military partner, which has helped Algeria reduce its dependency on Russia or on any other supplier for that matter. In 2018, for instance, it purchased the very sophisticated Chinese CX-1 cruise missile, which can travel a 280-kilometer distance and devastate with accuracy enemy warships at velocities of Mach 3.[127] The Algerian military chose the CX-1 instead of the Russian P-800, which is also a formidable missile. Nevertheless, despite this diversification of weapons procurement, Russia remains Algeria's main provider whose arms sales to Algeria had increased by 4.7 percent in 2012–16, compared to 2007–11. Currently, Russia accounts for 66 percent of Algerian arms imports, whereas imports from China and Germany account for 15 percent and 12 percent, respectively.[128] Algeria's military cooperation with China also includes military training; about 500 Algerian officers visit China annually to train in two or three Chinese academies.[129]

In the realm of security, China's cooperation with Algeria includes the fight against international terrorism, especially since Chinese multinational oil companies, such as Sinopec, are present in the Algerian oil extraction of hydrocarbons in the Sahara, where terrorist groups have remained active.[130] Because of the insecurity on its borders, resulting from the collapse of regimes following the Arab uprisings, Algeria has increased further its military cooperation with China, including the naval sector.[131] Notwithstanding this increased cooperation and Algeria's determination to diversify its supplies, the Chinese are not in a position today to provide Algeria with the equivalent sophisticated equipment that it can obtain from Russia, like the formidable *Iskander* missile, which Algeria displayed for the first time in November 2020, and other developed countries. Algeria is interested in acquiring advanced weapons systems, even requesting that Washington loosen its restrictions on Algeria's military imports from the United States.[132]

Culture, Cultural Cooperation, Student Exchanges, and Scientific Cooperation

China and Algeria signed numerous exchange and cooperation agreements on culture, education, sports, and media.[133] However, just like in the other parts of the MENA, China's cultural presence is limited. Occasionally, the Chinese embassy in Algiers or the Algerian Ministry of Culture organize cultural events, mainly opera, choreography, and celebrations of the Chinese New Year.

Despite the importance of economic relations, and unlike many African countries, including Morocco and Tunisia, China has been unable to open a Confucius Institute in Algeria. True, the teaching of the Chinese language is available at various universities across the country (Algiers, Constantine, Annaba, and Oran); there are a growing number of students in Chinese classes at universities. The Algerian Ministry of Foreign Affairs, the Ministry of Culture, and the Algerian Ministry of Higher Education have refused to open Confucius centers, although there exists a "Confucius Classroom" at the language center at the University of Algiers.[134] The Chinese language is also offered in private schools. Given the close ties between the two countries, some Algerian officials do not comprehend such opposition.[135] Some of them assert that this opposition emanates from religious figures, an assertion which a Chinese professor confirmed: "We were told that Confucius was referring to our religion. But in China, Confucius is the nation's first educator."[136] Regardless, students in Algeria continue to enroll in Chinese classes.

Hundreds of young Algerians study in China on scholarships from either the Chinese or Algerian governments.[137] Undoubtedly, because of the geographical distance, unlike the proximity and shared history with France, Algerians are still not too receptive to Chinese culture, preferring French, American, or Gulf Arab cultures. But, although there were some tensions with the Chinese community, like the incident in 2009 referred to earlier, things seem to have changed in the last decade; marriages between Chinese and Algerians are no longer an oddity.[138] The Chinese community, excluding the workers who come temporarily to build projects, by and large, has been able to integrate and be accepted in the country, although reports have highlighted the existence of stereotypes and xenophobic discourse about the Chinese.[139] This community is made up mainly of peddlers who hold individual shops or have stands in open markers; many of them had become immigrants by default once it proved almost impossible for them to continue their journey to Europe. While this community dominated the informal sector through the import of cheap products from China, they have now faced competition from Algerians in the informal sector who decided to travel to China to import those products.[140]

An important established sector in Sino-Algerian cooperation is the field of health. In May 2019, it was reported that a group of Chinese health practitioners would arrive in Algeria, the twenty-sixth such group since independence, the first dating back to 1963. The medical team was to intervene in various specialties, including gynecology-obstetrics, surgery, resuscitation, as well as ophthalmology.[141] Soon afterward, China's ambassador to Algeria, Li Lianhe, provided some figures regarding this long-standing medical assistance. He revealed that "since 1956, China has made available to Algeria 26 medical teams (81 doctors) with approximately 3,400 Chinese doctors, who have treated Algerian patients free of charge throughout the country" and "medical teams have managed to treat 23.7 million people and participate in the birth of some 1.6 million babies."[142]

Like other countries in the MENA, Algeria received assistance from China to fight the corona virus (Covid-19). China and Algeria seized this crisis not only to assist each other but also to reiterate the quality of their relations. In early February 2020, when China confronted the pandemic, Algeria was one of the first countries to send medical supplies (500,000 three-layer masks, 20,000 goggles, and 300,000 gloves) to Wuhan[143]; the Chinese government expressed its appreciation and reiterated the traditional friendship between the two countries.[144] When Algeria experienced its first infections in late February, it launched in March a distress appeal to China to provide it with aid and health equipment needed to combat the Covid-19 pandemic. Soon after that appeal, the Chinese government, as well as Chinese companies that operate in Algeria, was quick to send medical supplies the same month[145] and in early April.[146] In late March, China had already sent a medical team composed of thirteen doctors and eight virologists, who had fought Covid-19 in Wuhan.

Throughout the Covid-19 pandemic, the two governments made important political statements at the highest levels reiterating the bonds of friendship that hold the two countries. The Chinese embassy in Algiers used a slogan borrowed from the hirak to describe the brotherhood (*khawa*) with Algeria ("China-Algeria *khawa khawa*, always in solidarity and united in the struggle").[147] Faced with a political and socioeconomic crisis, Algeria will certainly need Chinese investment; because it has resisted borrowing from the IMF, Algeria will certainly rely on China for loans and greater cooperation. China, for its part, will certainly need countries like Algeria to enhance its image in the MENA region, especially when Western countries, the United States in particular, have decided to counter China's power.

In early October 2020, US Secretary of Defense Mark Esper came to Algeria during his tour of the Maghreb to increase military cooperation. While in Tunis, Esper warned Africans against China and Russia.[148] However, for Algerians, good relations with the United States did not signify sacrificing the excellent relations or the friendship with China. In fact, merely a week after Esper's visit, an important Chinese delegation, headed by Yang Jiechi, Director of the Foreign Affairs Commission of the Chinese Communist Party, came to Algiers and held meetings with the highest Algerian authorities, including President Tebboune. The communiqué issued after the meeting with the president is indicative of the prospects of cooperation between the two countries. Indeed, the communiqué stated that the objective of the meeting focused on

> cooperative relations between the two countries in various fields and to examine the possibilities of promoting and developing them, particularly in the economic sphere, including infrastructure, public works, transport,

trade and investment, in addition to areas related to higher education, scientific research and new technologies.[149]

Conclusion

For the last two decades, Algeria and China have strengthened their relations, and are likely to continue to do so, particularly within the framework of the BRI. While today the multifaceted nature of those relations is dominated by trade and commerce, the long-standing ties will probably translate into greater political understanding. Recent statements regarding the need to strengthen the CSP are an indication of the two sides' willingness to take relations to a higher level.

Already, cooperation between Algiers and Beijing extends to sensitive areas, such as armaments and civilian nuclear energy. However, China is only one actor among others seeking to develop more fruitful relations with China, an economic giant. So far, as with other countries in the Middle East, Africa, Asia, and elsewhere, bilateral trade is more favorable to China than to its partners. China's investment in Algeria is not significant and nor has there been any noteworthy technology transfer. Furthermore, most business is between the two countries' public sectors. The Chinese private business does not have a noteworthy presence in the country yet. Nevertheless, there exists substantial political understanding. This might prove to be an opportunity for the two countries to capitalize on their old ties to build upon their CSP to make it a real "win-win" cooperation. Algeria can gain a lot from China's experience, while China can contribute to Algeria's modernization efforts.

Undoubtedly, despite gigantic efforts to diversify its trade partners, Algeria is still dependent on Europe and, to a lesser degree, on the United States. It is thus doubtful whether China can, at least in the short term, supplant Europe in the region, Algeria being no exception, even if its economic relations with China have helped it reduce its dependency on the EU, which used to account for more than 50 percent of Algeria's trade. This is precisely why Europeans, France in particular, have worried about the evolution of Sino-Algerian ties. Indeed, the previous president of the European Parliament Antonio Tajani believes that China's influence in the continent, including in Algeria, is a menace to European interests.¹⁵⁰ Furthermore, despite France's endeavors to recapture its segment of the Algerian market, Chinese companies continue to acquire most of the major projects while China has remained the country's main trading partner and might remain so for in the longer term. Sino-Algerian close ties worry also the French; indeed, France's Senate report¹⁵¹ voiced alarm about China's commercial, economic, and even space ambitions in Algeria, as well as Algeria's participation in the BRI.¹⁵²

This Western concern is exaggerated because even if economic relations between China and Algeria are truly impressive, the EU remains Algeria's main economic partner; the volume of trade between Algeria and the EU exceeds $40 billion. Undoubtedly, internal developments in Algeria since February 2019, as well as the global context, will have a consequential impact on Algeria's relations with the outside world, particularly with the great powers. The post-Covid-19 will also create certainly both challenges and opportunities. Algeria can develop a mutually beneficial cooperation with China provided it delineates the parameters of that cooperation to make it really "win-win."

Because of the sharp drop in oil prices in April 2020, the depletion of its financial reserves, Algeria will certainly entice China to invest more in the country and to continue partaking in the major projects (port, phosphates, etc.). It will do so within the context of the CSP; this will be facilitated by Algeria's decision to create a better business environment, providing tax breaks/holidays, land concessions, and other financial incentives, including public–private partnerships with a Chinese promise for technology transfers. With its vast Sahara, Algeria has given indications that it would like China to invest in solar energy and other renewables, like its neighbors are doing. In view of the high cost of the Desertec project to produce electricity for the EU, Algeria might set up joint ventures with Chinese firms to partake in the project and thus offset European dominance.

To advance its interests and given the many construction contracts it granted the Chinese, Algeria will surely negotiate more persuasively with Chinese companies to employ a greater number of local workers and train them, thus limiting the import of Chinese workers and thus create more jobs in the country. There are other areas which can improve relations between the two countries. Both China and Algeria are still in need to acquire better understanding of the other's culture; they can do so through a multiplication of Chinese-language centers, exchange of students, cross-cultural studies, and learning about Chinese ways of doing business. Algeria can also integrate the study of Chinese in high school and university curricula, as Saudi Arabia and the UAE have done. Algeria's untapped tourism sector can be one other sector in which China and Algeria can cooperate like Tunisia and Morocco have done. Eco-tourism in the vast Algerian Sahara, for middle-class Chinese, could certainly contribute to people-to-people exchanges and better understanding between Algerians and Chinese. Given the long-standing cooperation in the health sector, especially in the post-Covid-19, the two countries will undoubtedly expand further their partnership; Algeria's health sector has shown many shortcomings during the Covid-19. It is almost certain that the two sides will expand scientific cooperation to the training of medical staff and the construction of hospitals, which are lacking in Algeria. Algiers is interested in China's ability to build hospitals in a speedy manner and such prospects have already been envisaged by the two.

Notes

1   On Algerian-Morocco rivalry see, Yahia H. Zoubir, "The Algerian-Moroccan Rivalry: Constructing the Imagined Enemy," in *Shocks and Rivalries in the Middle East and North Africa*, edited by Imad Mansour and William R. Thompson (Washington, DC: Georgetown University Press, 2020), Chapter 11.
2   Thierry Pairault, "La Chine au Maghreb: de l'esprit de Bandung à l'esprit du capitalisme" [China in the Maghreb: From the Spirit of Bandung to the Spirit of Capitalism] *Revue de la régulation: Capitalisme, institutions, pouvoirs* 21, no. 1 (2017), https://journals.openedition.org/regulation/12230
3   Ministry of Foreign Affairs of the People's Republic of China, "The Five Principles of Peaceful Coexistence—The Time-Tested Guideline of China's Policy with Neighbors," July 30, 2014, https://www.fmprc.gov.cn/mfa_eng/wjb_663304/zwjg_665342/zwbd_665378/t1179045.shtml
4   For an excellent account by one of the participants to the discussions, see, Commandant Azzedine, "Aux Origines de l'amitié algéro-chinoise-Des fellagas à Pékin," *Le soir d'Algérie*, February 27, 2019 (first part), https://www.lesoirdalgerie.com/articles/2017/02/27/article.php?sid=209968&cid=41. The author met Mao and recounted the visits and the FLN's meetings in China

5   Yahia H. Zoubir, "US and Soviet Policies toward France's Struggle with Anti-colonial Nationalism in North Africa," *Canadian Journal of History/Annales d'Histoire Canadiennes* 30, no. 3 (1995), pp. 439–66.
6   Ibid. See also, Mohammed Harbi, *Les Archives de la Révolution Algérienne* (Paris: Editions Jeune Afrique, 1980), p. 521. See also, Jeffrey James Byrne, *Mecca of Revolution. Algeria, Decolonization, and the Third World Order* (Oxford: Oxford University Press, 2016), p. 164.
7   Harbi, *Les Archives...*, p. 236.
8   Document 114, in ibid., p. 528.
9   John Copper, "China's Foreign aid program: an analysis of an instrument of Peking's foreign policy," PhD Dissertation in Political Science, University of South Carolina, International Law and Relations, 1975, p. 135.
10 Kyle Haddad-Fonda, "An Illusory Alliance: Revolutionary Legitimacy and Sino-Algerian Relations, 1958–1962," *The Journal of North African Studies* 19, no. 3 (2014), pp. 338–57.
11 Hisham Behbehani, *China's Foreign Policy in the Arab World, 1955–75: Three Case Studies* (London: Kegan Paul International, 1981), pp. 351–2. The Appendix lists the names and years of those agreements.
12 Jeremy Friedman, *Shadow Cold War: The Sino-Soviet Competition for the Third World* (Chapel Hill, NC: University of North Carolina Press, 2015).
13 The Yearbook of the United Nations- 1971, "Questions Relating to Asia and the Far East," https://www.unmultimedia.org/searchers/yearbook/page.jsp?volume=1971&page=139&srq=china%20resolution%20_2758&srstart=0&srvolumeFacet=1971&sroutline=false&searchType=advanced, pp. 129–130
14 John Calabrese, "Sino-Algerian Relations: On a Path to Realizing Their Full Potential?" *Middle East Institute*, October 31, 2017, http://www.mei.edu/content/map/sino-algerian-relations-path-realizing-their-full-potential
15 LI Anshan, "China's New Policy toward Africa," in *China into Africa: Trade, Aid, and Influence,* edited by Robert I. Rotberg (Washington, DC: Brookings Institution Press), pp. 21–47.
16 Stephan Halper, *The Beijing Consensus. Legitimizing Authoritarianism in Our Time* (New York: Basic Books, 2009), p. 336.
17 Degang Sun and Yahia H. Zoubir, "China's Participation in Conflict Resolution in the Middle East and North Africa: A Case of Quasi-Mediation Diplomacy?" *Journal of Contemporary China* 27, no. 110 (2018), pp. 224–243.

18 Chris Zambelis, "China's Inroads into North Africa: An Assessment of Sino-Algerian Relations," *China Brief* 10, no. 1, January 7, 2010, https://jamestown.org/program/chinas-inroads-into-north-africa-an-assessment-of-sino-algerian-relations/

19 Hongyi Harry Lai, "China's Oil Diplomacy: Is It a Global Security Threat?" *Third World Quarterly* 28, no. 3 (2007), pp. 519–37.

20 Faiza Kab, "Algerian-Chinese Relations through the Historic Visit of the Algerian Prime Minister (in Arabic)," *Arab Information Center*, 2015\PRS\4652, April 27, 2015, http://www.arabsino.com/articles/15-04-27/12348.htm

21 China Ministry of Foreign Affairs, "*China-Algeria Relations*," January 18, 2004, http://www.china.org.cn/english/features/phfnt/85069.htm

22 Ibid.

23 Tang Ying Xin Wang, "Algeria, China Strengthen Strategic partnership," *China Daily*, December 19, 2008, http://www.chinadaily.com.cn/cndy/2008-12/19/content_7320543.htm (access no longer available).

24 Author interview with Algerian Ambassador to China, November 8, 2016.

25 Xinhuanet (In Arabic), الجزائر والصين مثال يحتذى به في التعاون والصداقة الدائمة [Algeria and China are models of cooperation and lasting friendship], February 26, 2014, http://arabic.people.com.cn/31660/8547268.html

26 Hakim Darbouche et Yahia H. Zoubir, "The Algerian Crisis in European and US Foreign Policies: A Hindsight Analysis," *Journal of North African Studies* 14, no. 1 (2009), pp. 33–55.

27 Xinhuanet (In French), "Les pays en développement doivent renforcer leur solidarité pour mieux défendre leurs intérêts, déclare le président chinois" [Developing Countries Must Strengthen Their Solidarity to Better Defend Their Interests, says Chinese president], February 4, 2004. Retrieved from http://french.china.org.cn/french/100564.htm

28 Xinhuanet (In Arabic), الجزائر والصين مثال يحتذى به في التعاون والصداقة الدائمة [Algeria and China are models of cooperation and lasting friendship], February 26, 2014, http://arabic.people.com.cn/31660/8547268.html

29 "China, Algeria vow to boost comprehensive strategic partnership," *National Committee of the Chinese People's Political Consultative Conference*, November 3, 2014, http://www.cppcc.gov.cn/zxww/2014/11/04/ARTI1415071483256625.shtml

30 Degang Sun, "China's Partnership Diplomacy in the Middle East," unpublished paper, March 10, 2020 (personal documents). See also, Shan Jee Chua, "Understanding China's Strategic Partnership and Balance Diplomacy: The

Case of Sino-Iran Relations," *A thesis submitted to Peking University in partial fulfillment of the requirements of the PKU-LSE Double Master's Degree Program in International Affairs, School of International Studies Peking University*, June 2016 (personal documents).

31 "La Chine et l'Algérie établissent les relations de Partenariat Stratégique Global" [China and Algeria Establish Global Strategic Partnership Relations], Embassy of the People's Republic of China in the Democratic People's Republic of Algeria, February 25, 2014, http://dz.china-embassy.org/fra/xw/t1132178.htm

32 People's Democratic Republic of Algeria, *Ministry of Industry and Mines*, "Algeria, China Ink Several Agreements, MoUs," *APS*, April 28, 2015. Retrieved from http://www.andi.dz/index.php/en/presse/1212-algeria-china-ink-several-agreements-mous

33 "Xi Jinping Meets with Prime Minister Abdelmalek Sellal of Algeria," *Embassy of China in Croatia*, April 29, 2015, http://hr.china-embassy.org/eng/gnxw/t1260832.htm

34 Saïd Belguidoum, "Transnational Trade and New Types of Entrepreneurs in Algeria," in *The Politics of Algeria: Domestic Politics and International Relations*, edited by Yahia H. Zoubir (London & New York: Routledge, 2020), pp. 226–36.

35 Xinhua, "Xi Pledges Further Development of China-Algeria Strategic Partnership," December 20, 2018, http://www.xinhuanet.com/english/2018-12/20/c_137687090.htm

36 Ibid.

37 Imen Belhadj, Degang Sun, and Yahia H. Zoubir, "China in North Africa: A Strategic Partnership," in *North African Politics. Change and Continuity*, edited by Yahia H. Zoubir and Gregory White (London & New York: Routledge, 2016).

38 Yahia H. Zoubir, "'The Giant Afraid of Its Shadow': Algeria, the Reluctant Middle Power," in *Unfulfilled Aspirations: Middle Power Politics in the Middle East*, edited by Adham Saouli (Oxford: Oxford University Press/Hurst, 2020), pp. 67–90.

39 See Yahia H. Zoubir, "Algeria and the Sahelian Quandary: The Limits of Containment Security Policy," The Sahel: Europe's African Borders, Dalia Ghanem-Yazbeck (Ed), R. Barras Tejudo, G. Faleg, Y. Zoubir, *Euromesco Joint-Policy Paper*, 70–95, https://www.euromesco.net/wp-content/uploads/2018/03/EuroMeSCo-Joint-Policy-Study-8_The_Sahel_Europe_African_Border.pdf

40 While in China, the author noticed that Chinese TV, CGTN, showed only briefly the weekly protests of millions of Algerians throughout the country. Sudan, which had witnessed popular protests, too, obtained much lengthier coverage.

41. Chine Magazine, "Beijing se prononce sur la crise politique en Algérie" [Beijing Comments on the Political Crisis in Algeria], March 25, 2019, https://www.chine-magazine.com/beijing-se-prononce-sur-la-crise-politique-en-algerie/
42. EU Neighbors South, "European Parliament plenary debate on the situation of freedoms in Algeria," November 29, 2019, https://www.euneighbours.eu/en/south/stay-informed/news/european-parliament-plenary-debate-situation-freedoms-algeria
43. Iddir Nadir, "L'ambassadeur de Chine en Algérie: 'Nous nous opposerons à l'ingérence de toute puissance étrangère en Algérie'" [China's Ambassador to Algeria: "We will oppose the interference of any foreign power in Algeria"] *El Watan*, December 1, 2019, https://www.elwatan.com/edition/actualite/lambassadeur-de-chine-en-algerie-nous-nous-opposerons-a-lingerence-de-toute-puissance-etrangere-en-algerie-01-12-2019
44. Hang Zhou, "China's Balancing Act in the Western Sahara Conflict," *Africana Studia* 29 (2018), pp. 145–56.
45. Jillian Kestler-D'Amours, "US Recognised Morocco's Claim to Western Sahara. Now what?" *Aljazeera*, December 11, 2020, https://www.aljazeera.com/news/2020/12/11/us-recognised-moroccos-claim-to-western-sahara-now-what
46. Wu Wanjun and Pedro Sobral, "China's Non-interference Policy towards Western Sahara Conflict," *Africana Studia* 29 (2018), pp. 131–43.
47. Author interview (anonymous), Beijing, November 8, 2016.
48. Author interview (anonymous), Shanghai, September 16, 2018; see, also, Joseph Hammond, "Morocco: China's gateway to Africa?" *The Diplomat*, March 1, 2017, https://thediplomat.com/2017/03/morocco-chinas-gateway-to-africa/
49. Yahia H. Zoubir, "Expanding Sino–Maghreb Relations: Morocco and Tunisia," Research Paper, Chatham House, February 20, 2020, https://www.chathamhouse.org/search/site/zoubir
50. Rédéric Maury and Nadia Rabbaa, "Le Maroc, un pont d'or pour la Chine" [Morocco, a Golden Bridge for China], *Jeune Afrique*, December 29, 2015, https://www.jeuneafrique.com/mag/286294/economie/maroc-pont-dor-chine/
51. Youssef Hafti, "Moroccan-Chinese Relationship: The Interaction of 'Going East,'" in *The New Frontier of the Middle East Politics and Economy*, edited by Degang Sun and Zhongmin Liu (Beijing: World Affairs Press, 2017), pp. 211–44.
52. Author interview (anonymous), Shanghai, September 17, 2018.
53. Sefta Leïla, "S.E.M. LI Lianhe Ambassadeur de Chine en Algérie à propos des relations bilatérales: 'Inégalé': le développement de 70 années, 'Exemplaire':…" *Le Maghreb-Le Quotidien de l'économie*, October 1, 2019, https://www.lemaghrebdz.com/?page=detail_actualite&rubrique=Nation&id=95395

54 Akram Kharief, "Répression des Ouïghours: neuf pays arabes soutiennent la Chine" [Repression of the Uyghurs: Nine Arab Countries Support China], Middle East Eye, July 14, 2019, https://www.middleeasteye.net/fr/en-bref/repression-des-ouighours-neuf-pays-arabes-soutiennent-la-chine
55 Ministry of Foreign Affairs of the PRC, "China-Arab States Cooperation Forum Holds Ninth Ministerial Conference," July 6, 2020, ttps://www.fmprc.gov.cn/mfa_eng/zxxx_662805/t1795754.shtml
56 "Countries of the Belt and Road Initiative (BRI)," *Green Belt and Road Initiative Center*, https://green-bri.org/countries-of-the-belt-and-road-initiative-bri
57 Yahia H. Zoubir, "Les relations de la Chine avec les pays du Maghreb: la place prépondérante de l'Algérie" [China's Relations with the Maghreb Countries: The Predominance of Algeria], *Confluences Méditerranée* 109, no. 2 (2019), pp. 91–103.
58 "China Focus: Xi Unveils Plan to Make China 'Great Modern Socialist Country' by Mid-21st Century,'" *Xinhua*, October 18, 2017, http://www.xinhuanet.com//english/2017-10/18/c_136688933.htm
59 Tom Bayes, "China's Emerging Diplomatic and Economic Presence in North Africa," *The Atlantic Community*, February 27, 2019, https://atlantic-community.org/chinas-emerging-diplomatic-and-economic-presence-in-north-africa/
60 J. Xi, "Promoting the Silk Road Spirit and Deepening China-Arab Cooperation," speech at the opening ceremony of the 6th Ministerial Meeting of the China–Arab States Cooperation Forum, 2014, December 9, 2019, http://www.china.org.cn/report/2014-07/14/content_32941818.htm
61 Ministry of Foreign Affairs of the People's Republic of China, "China's Arab Policy Paper," 2016, November 8, 2017, https://www.fmprc.gov.cn/mfa_eng/zxxx_662805/t1331683.shtml
62 Xi, "Promoting the Silk Road Spirit and Deepening China-Arab Cooperation."
63 "Algeria Ratifies BRI Agreement with China," *Xinhua*, July 10, 2019, http://www.xinhuanet.com/english/2019-07/10/c_138212879.htm
64 "Route de la soie: l'Algérie ratifie le mémorandum d'entente avec la Chine" [Silk Road: Algeria Ratifies Memorandum of Understanding with China], *APS*, July 8, 2019, http://www.aps.dz/economie/91616-l-algerie-ratifie-le-memorandum-d-entente-relatif-a-l-initiative-de-la-ceinture-economique-de-la-route-de-la-soie
65 "Entretien téléphonique entre le Premier ministre et son homologue chinois" [Telephone Conversation between the Prime Minister and His Chinese Counterpart], *APS*, March 31, 2020, http://www.aps.dz/algerie/103576-entretien-telephonique-entre-le-premier-ministre-et-son-homologue-chinois

66 Yahia H. Zoubir, "The Dialectics of Algeria's Foreign Relations from 1990 to the Present," in *Algeria in Transition-Reforms and Development Prospects,* edited by Ahmed Aghrout (London & New York: Routledge, 2004), pp. 151–82.

67 For China's growing interest in the Mediterranean, see, Alice Ekman, "China and the Mediterranean: An Emerging Presence," *IFRI,* https://www.ifri.org/en/publications/notes-de-lifri/china-mediterranean-emerging-presence

68 Ministère des Finances-Direction Générale des Douanes, "Statistiques du Commerce Extérieur de l'Algérie-Période: onze mois de l'année 2019," https://douane.gov.dz/IMG/pdf/rapport_com_ext_2019_vf.pdf

69 Ibid., 17.

70 On the eve of the presidential election, six contenders withdrew because they became aware that the election would be rigged and that Bouteflika had already been chosen by the military to serve as president. See Rachid Tlemçani, "Policing Algeria under Bouteflika: From Police State to Civil State," in *The Politics of Algeria: Domestic Issues and International Relations*, edited by Yahia H. Zoubir (London & New York: Routledge, 2020), p. 66. There is evidence that Bouteflika was chosen by the military in 1999 to serve as president; it was also the military that removed him on April 2, 2019, after the protest movement hirak, refused to see him serve for a fifth term. See Yahia H. Zoubir, "Can Algeria Overcome Its Long-lasting Political Crisis?" *Brookings*, January 15, 2020, https://www.brookings.edu/blog/order-from-chaos/2020/01/15/can-algeria-overcome-its-long-lasting-political-crisis/

71 Xinhuanet, "Algerian PM Lauds Efficiency of Chinese Company in Highway Construction Project," April 30, 2017, http://www.xinhuanet.com//english/2017-04/30/c_136246926.htm

72 Xinhua, "Chinese Firm Supports Construction of Trans-Saharan Highway Project in Nigeria," November 12, 2019, http://www.china.org.cn/business/2019-11/12/content_75398522.htm

73 Farida Souiah, "La société algérienne au miroir des migrations chinoises," *Moyen Orient*, 7, August–September, https://www.pairault.fr/sinaf/doc_importes/fs2010.pdf, pp. 15–52.

74 Randa Lamara, "Algérie Telecom et ZTE, signent une convention afin d'assurer le très haut débit Internet" [Algérie Telecom and ZTE Sign an Agreement to Ensure Very High-speed Internet Access], *Algérie-Eco*, October 4, 2017, https://www.algerie-eco.com/2017/10/04/algerie-telecom-zte-signent-convention-afin-dassurer-tres-haut-debit-internet/

75 Amina Ahres, "10 étudiants algériens en formation en Chine" [10 Algerian Students in Training in China], *El Watan* 1, December 1, 2019, https://www.

elwatan.com/pages-hebdo/etudiant/10-etudiants-algeriens-en-formation-en-chine-11-12-2019

76 Ismain, "Grande Mosquee d'Alger: Le coût de la construction révélé" [Great Mosque of Algiers: Construction Cost Revealed], *Réflexion*, August 4, 2019. https://www.reflexiondz.net/GRANDE-MOSQUEE-D-ALGER-Le-cout-de-la-construction-revele_a56987.html. Although the government declared that the construction of the mosque cost $1.5 billion, multiple reports suggest that the actual cost is several times that figure.

77 Abdi Latif Dahir, "Africa's Largest Mosque Has Been Completed with Thanks to China," *Quartz Africa*, April 28, 2019, https://qz.com/africa/1606739/china-completes-africas-largest-mosque-in-algeria/; Alain Chémali, "Algérie: la Chine annonce la fin du chantier de la plus grande mosquée d'Afrique" [Algeria: China Announces the End of the Construction of the Largest Mosque in Africa], *FranceInfo*, May 4, 2019. https://www.francetvinfo.fr/culture/arts-expos/architecture/algerie-la-chine-annonce-la-fin-du-chantier-de-la-plus-grande-mosquee-d-afrique_3422171.html. The article said that the cost was $2 billion.

78 CSCEC Algérie, http://www.cscec.dz/fr/about/brief.html

79 Slimane Khalfa, "En Algérie, les Chinois raflent tous les contrats" [In Algeria, the Chinese Win All the Contracts], *Nouvel Observateur* (Paris), November 16, 2016. https://www.nouvelobs.com/rue89/rue89-chine/20111031.RUE5343/en-algerie-les-chinois-raflent-tous-les-contrats.html

80 Affrontements entre Algériens et Chinois: un cas isolé de sécurité publique (ambassadeur de Chine) [Confrontations between Algerians and Chinese: An Isolated Case of Public Security (Chinese Ambassador)], *China.org* (in French), August 7, 2009, http://french.china.org.cn/foreign/txt/2009-08/07/content_18295944.htm

81 Nasser Zerrouki, "Boudouaou: Bagarre dans un chantier chinois" [Boudouaou: Fight in a Chinese Construction Site], *Liberté*, February 10, 2016, https://www.liberte-algerie.com/actualite/bagarre-dans-un-chantier-chinois-241866

82 Thierry Pairault, "China's Economic Presence in Algeria," CCJ-Occasional-papers, 1, *HAL Archives Ouvertes*, 2015, https://halshs.archives-ouvertes.fr/halshs-01116295/document

83 "Algeria: Over 55,000 Visas Granted to Chinese Workers, Visitors in 2015," *All Africa*, July 12, 2016, https://allafrica.com/stories/201607120701.html

84 Author interview with Algerian ambassador to China, November 8, 2016.

85 François Simon, "Algeria: Africa's largest Chinese community," *The Dragon's Trail-China and International Affairs*, February 26, 2013, https://dragonstrail.wordpress.com/2013/02/26/algeria-china-community-affairs/

86 K. Sam, "Première communauté étrangère établie en Algérie: 20 000 chinois vivent à Alger" [First Foreign Community Established in Algeria: 20,000 Chinese Live in Algiers], *Les Echos d'Alger*, June 24, 2017, http://www.lesechosdalger.com/premiere-communaute-etrangere-etablie-algerie-20-000-chinois-vivent-a-alger/

87 Sefta Leïla, "S.E.M. LI Lianhe Ambassadeur de Chine en Algérie à propos des relations bilatérales: 'Inégalé': le développement de 70 années, 'Exemplaire':…" [Chinese Ambassador Lianhe to Algeria on Bilateral Relations: "Unequalled": The Development of 70 Years, "Exemplary"], *Le Maghreb-Le Quotidien de l'économie*, October 1, 2019, https://www.lemaghrebdz.com/?page=detail_actualite&rubrique=Nation&id=95395

88 There exist scant studies on the Chinese residents in Algeria; however, one can cite a study on the Chinese in Algiers, Jean-Pierre Taing, "L'immigration chinoise à Alger: l'émergence d'une place marchande à Bab Ezzouar?" [The Chinese Immigration in Algeria: The Emergency of a Marketplace in Bab Ezzouar?], *Les Cahiers d'EMAM* 26 (2015), https://journals.openedition.org/emam/934

89 "Algerian New Port of El Hamdania Construction to Be Completed by 2024," *PortSEurope*, July 3, 2017, https://www.portseurope.com/algerian-new-port-of-el-hamdania-construction-to-be-completed-by-2024/

90 "China Lends $3.3bn to Algeria to Build El Hamdania Port," *EcoFin Agency*, January 19, 2016, https://www.ecofinagency.com/finance/1901-33286-china-lends-3-3bn-to-algeria-to-build-el-hamdania-port; Antony Kiganda, "Algeria Approves US $3.3 Billion El Hamdania Port Construction," *Construction Review Online*, March 10, 2017, https://constructionreviewonline.com/2017/03/algeria-approves-us-3-3-billion-el-hamdania-port-construction/

91 "Algerian new port of El Hamdania…."

92 Ibid.

93 Jennifer Aguinaldo, "Exclusive: Work Yet to Start at Algeria's Planned Megaport," *MEED*, January 28, 2018, https://www.meed.com/exclusive-work-algerias-mega-port-project-yet-start/

94 Degang Sun and Yahia H. Zoubir, "Development First: China's Investment in Seaport Constructions and Operations along the Maritime Silk Road," *Asian Journal of Middle Eastern and Islamic Studies* 11, no. 3 (2017), pp. 35–47.

95 Romuald Ngueyap, "L'Algérie relance le mégaprojet du port Centre d'El Hamdania financé par la Chine" [Algeria Relaunches the Mega-project of El Hamdania's Central Port Financed by China], *Agence EcoFin*, July 2, 2020, https://www.agenceecofin.com/transports/0207-78104-l-algerie-relance-le-megaprojet-du-port-centre-d-el-hamdania-finance-par-la-chine

96 Naser al-Tamimi, "China-Algeria Relations: Growing Slowly but Surely," *Al-Arabiya*, March 26, 2014, https://english.alarabiya.net/en/views/business/economy/2014/03/26/China-Algeria-relations-growing-slowly-but-surely.html

97 "Le Chinois FAW assemblera ses autos en Algérie," *Challenges*, November 12, 2013, https://www.challenges.fr/automobile/actu-auto/le-chinois-faw-assemblera-ses-autos-en-algerie_180627

98 "Algeria's First Chinese Automobile Assembly Plant Open for Production," *People's Daily Online*, May 14, 2018, http://en.people.cn/n3/2018/0514/c90000-9459918.html

99 Abdou Semmar, "Sortie du premier camion Shacman 'made in Algérie' avec une remise de 2 millions de DA," *Algeriepart*, May 10, 2018, https://algeriepart.com/2018/05/10/photos-sortie-premier-camion-shacman-made-in-algerie-remise-de-2-millions-de-da/

100 "Algerian-Chinese Partnership on Manufacturing of Foton-Brand Trucks," *APS*, Thursday, April 20, 2017, http://www.aps.dz/en/economy/17914-algerian-chinese-partnership-on-manufacturing-of-foton-brand-trucks

101 US Energy Information Administration, Algeria's Key Energy Statistics 2018, https://www.eia.gov/beta/international/country.php?iso=DZA. According to this same source, in early 2018, Algeria held approximately 12.2 billion barrels of proved crude oil reserves.

102 Export. Gov., "Algeria—Oil and Gas—Hydrocarbons," January 31, 2019, https://www.export.gov/article?id=Algeria-Oil-and-Gas-Hydrocarbons

103 Organization of Petroleum Countries, "Algeria Facts and Figures," 2019, https://www.opec.org/opec_web/en/about_us/146.htm

104 In the 1980s, China had agreed to assist Algeria in building a nuclear research reactor in Aïn-Oussera, 150 kilometers south of Algiers. In 1991, the CIA revealed the construction suggesting that the small 15MW reactor (45MW according to the CIA) could also be part of a nuclear weapons program. Soon thereafter, Algeria signed the NPT (Non-Proliferation Treaty). See Nazir Kamal, "China's Arms Export Policy and Responses to Multilateral Restraints," *Contemporary Southeast Asia* 14, no. 2 (September 1992), pp. 122–23.

105 Author interviews with Algerian officials, Algiers, February 2–8, 2020.

106 Maria Gallucci, "Terror Attack on Algerian Gas Plant Raising Security Fears for North Africa's Oil and Gas Infrastructure," *International Business Times*, March 22, 2016, https://www.ibtimes.com/terror-attack-algerian-gas-plant-raising-security-fears-north-africas-oil-gas-2341217

107 Aylan Afir, "Algérie: British Petroleum veut quitter la base gazière de Tiguentourine" [Algeria: British Petroleum Wants to Leave the Tiguentourine

108 Tarek Hafid, "Algérie-Phosphate: Black-out sur un projet -presque- irréalisable," *Maghreb Émergent*, February 13, 2019, https://www.maghrebemergent.info/algerie-phosphate-black-out-sur-un-projet-presque-irealisable/

109 "Projet de phosphate: Sonatrach et CITIC signent un avenant à leur protocole d'accord" [Phosphate Project: Sonatrach and CITIC Sign an Amendment to Their Memorandum of Understanding], Algérie-Eco, January 9, 2020, https://www.algerie-eco.com/2020/01/09/projet-phosphate-sonatrach-citic-signent-avenant-protocole-accord/

110 "VIDÉO. Rencontre de Tebboune avec des médias: l'intégralité de l'interview," *TSA*, May 2, 2020, https://www.tsa-algerie.com/video-rencontre-de-tebboune-avec-des-medias-lintegralite-de-linterview/

111 American Enterprise Institute, "China Global Investment Tracker," February 12, 2020, https://www.aei.org/china-global-investment-tracker/

112 Sébastien Le Belzic, "'En Algérie, la Chine n'investit pas beaucoup, mais elle compte énormément,'" *Le Monde*, March 18, 2019, https://www.lemonde.fr/afrique/article/2019/03/18/en-algerie-la-chine-n-investit-pas-beaucoup-mais-elle-compte-enormement_5437927_3212.html

113 Yahia H. Zoubir, "Russia and Algeria: Reconciling contrasting interests," *The Maghreb Review* 36, no. 3 (2011), pp. 99–126.

114 Richard F. Grimmett, *Conventional Arms Transfers to Developing Countries 1994–2001* (Hauppage, NY: Novinka Books, 2003), p. 38, cited in, John Calabrese, "Sino-Algerian Relations: On a Path to Realizing Their Full Potential?" *Middle East Institute*, October 31, 2017, https://www.mei.edu/publications/sino-algerian-relations-path-realizing-their-full-potential

115 Cowburn Ashley, "Two-Thirds of African Countries Now Using Chinese Military Equipment, Report Reveals," *The Independent*, https://www.independent.co.uk/news/world/africa/two-thirds-of-african-countries-now-using-chinesemilitary-equipment-a6905286.html

116 Mediterranean Dialogue [MD] Staff, "Asia and the Middle East Lead Rising Trend in US Exports Grow Significantly," *Modern Diplomacy*, March 12, 2018, https://moderndiplomacy.eu/2018/03/12/asia-and-the-middle-east-lead-rising-trend-in-arms-imports-us-exports-grow-significantly/

117 "How Dominant Is China in the Global Arms Trade?" *ChinaPower-Center for Strategic & International Studies*, 2018, https://chinapower.csis.org/china-global-arms-trade/

118 "Algeria Receives Final Chinese Corvette," *DefenceWeb*, July 18, 2016, https://www.defenceweb.co.za/sea/sea-sea/algeria-receives-final-chinese-corvette/

119 Chris Alden, Abiodun Alao, Chun Zhang, and Laura Barber, *China and Africa: Building Peace and Security Cooperation on the Continent* (New York: Palgrave Macmillan, 2018), p. 337.

120 Adlène Badis, "Chine-Algérie: L'éloge d'un partenariat prometteur," *Reporters*, January 9, 2018, (Algeria), http://www.reporters.dz/index.php/item/90644-chine-algerie-l-eloge-d-unpartenariat-prometteur

121 "Algeria operating new UAV types," *DefenceWeb*, January 7, 2019, https://www.defenceweb.co.za/aerospace/unmanned-aerial-vehicles/algeria-operating-new-uav-types/; Jakob Reimann, "China is Flooding the Middle East with Cheap Drones," *Foreign Policy in Focus*, February 18, 2019, https://fpif.org/china-is-flooding-the-middle-east-with-cheap-drones/

122 Joseph Ibeh, "Alcomsat-1 Communications Satellite Clocks Two Years in Orbit," *Space in Africa*, December 11, 2019, https://africanews.space/alcomsat-1-communications-satellite-clocks-two-years-in-orbit/

123 Syrine Attia, "L'Algérie lance son premier satellite de télécommunications," December 11, 2017, https://www.jeuneafrique.com/501179/economie/lalgerie-lance-son-premier-satellite-de-telecommunications/

124 Ghalia Kadiri, "Satellite marocain en orbite: un lancement secret qui inquiète" [Moroccan Satellite in Orbit: A Secret Launch that causes Concern], *Le Monde*, November 19, 2017, https://www.lemonde.fr/afrique/article/2017/11/19/satellite-marocain-en-orbite-un-lancement-secret-qui-inquiete_5217299_3212.html

125 Adlène Badis, "Chine-Algérie: l'éloge d'un partenariat prometteur," *Reporters* (Algeria), January 9, 2018, https://www.reporters.dz/chine-algerie-l-eloge-d-un-partenariat-prometteur/

126 Thierry Pairault, "China's Economic Presence in Algeria," *ResearchGate*, February 2015 https://www.researchgate.net/publication/280793405_China-s_economic_presence_in_Algeria, p. 11.

127 "Algeria Acquires Lethal Mach 3 Ship Hunting Missies from China; How the CX-1 Allows Algiers to Close Off the Mediterranean," *Military Watch*, July 27, 2018, https://militarywatchmagazine.com/article/algeria-acquires-lethal-mach-3-ship-hunting-missies-from-china-how-the-cx-1-allows-algiers-to-close-off-the-mediterranean

128 Fleurant, Aude & Wezeman, Pieter D., Wezeman, Simon T, and Nan Tian, "Tendances des transferts internationaux d'armements 2016," in *Groupe de Recherche et d'information sur la Paix et La Sécurité (GRIP)*,

Dépenses militaires, production et transferts d'armes—Compendium 2017, 2017, https://www.grip.org/sites/grip, p. 34. org/files/RAPPORTS/2017/Rapport_2017-7.pdf

129 Author anonymous interview with high-level Algerian official, Beijing 2016.

130 China Ministry of Foreign Affairs, "China, Algeria Vow to Boost Counter-Terrorism Cooperation," July 12, 2016, http://english.www.gov.cn/news/international_exchanges/2016/07/12/content_281475391542866.htm

131 Zhao Lei, "China Delivers Warship to Algeria," *China Daily*, July 20, 2016, http://www.chinadaily.com.cn/world/2016-07-20/content_26155715.htm

132 Maggie Ybarra, "The Politics of Selling Weapons to Algeria-Algiers Looks to Shift Away from Its Dependence on Moscow," *The National Interest*, March 7, 2019, https://nationalinterest.org/feature/politics-selling-weapons-algeria-46362

133 China Ministry of Foreign Affairs, "China-Algeria Relations."

134 "China-Algeria Ties: Chinese Language Learning Increasingly Popular in Algeria," https://www.youtube.com/watch?v=SxaExh8RtA4

135 Author interview, high-level Algerian official, Beijing, November 2016.

136 Cited in Samir Azzoug, "Pour l'installation de l'institut Confucius en Algérie" [Establishing of the Confucius Institute in Algeria], *El Watan*, February 5, 2014, https://www.djazairess.com/fr/elwatan/444714

137 In December 2019, the Chinese government offered scholarships for up to 400 Euros monthly, in addition to housing, medical insurance, and registration fees; see, Ismain, "Etudiants Algeriens á l'etranger: La Chine propose une bourse de 400 Euros par mois," *ReflexionDZ*, December 22, 2019, https://www.reflexiondz.net/ETUDIANTS-ALGERIENS-A-L-ETRANGER-La-Chine-propose-une-bourse-de-400-euros-par-mois_a59556.html

138 Samy Abtroun, "Expatriés chinois en Algérie: l'amour au bout du voyage," *Paris Match*, September 14, 2018, https://www.parismatch.com/Actu/International/Expatries-chinois-en-Algerie-l-amour-au-bout-du-voyage-1574387

139 Farid Alilat, "Qui sont les Chinois d'Algérie?" [Who Are the Chinese in Algeria?] *Jeune Afrique*, June 2, 2015, https://www.jeuneafrique.com/233388/politique/qui-sont-les-chinois-d-alg-rie/; see, also, Taing, "L'immigration chinoise à Alger…," p. 2.

140 Belguidoum, "Transnational Trade and New Types of Entrepreneurs in Algeria," pp. 226–36.

141 "Santé: des équipes médicales chinoises prochainement en Algérie," *APS*, May 30, 2019, http://www.aps.dz/sante-science-technologie/90101-sante-des-equipes-medicales-chinoises-prochainement-en-algerie

142 "L'Ambassadeur de Chine: L'Algérie, 5e grand partenaire commercial africain de la Chine," *Le Maghreb*, June 20, 2019, https://lemaghreb.dz/?page=detail_actualite&rubrique=Nation&id=94319

143 "Contribution de l'ambassadeur de la république de chine à L'Expression-L'Algérie remportera la guerre du Covid-19" [Contribution of the Ambassador of the Republic of China to L'Expression-Algeria Will Win the Covid War-19] *L'Expression*, April 26, 2020, http://lexpressiondz.com/nationale/l-algerie-remportera-la-guerre-du-covid-19-329969

144 "Coronavirus: la Chine adresse ses remerciements à l'Algérie pour les aides médicales" [Coronavirus: China Thanks Algeria for Medical Assistance] *APS*, February 2, 2020. http://www.aps.dz/algerie/100995-coronavirus-la-chine-adresse-ses-remerciements-a-l-algerie-pour-les-aides-medicales-urgentes-fournies

145 "China Sends Medical Aid to Algeria to Help Combat COVID-19," *Xinhua*, March 28, 2020, https://english.sina.cn/news/2020-03-28/detail-iimxxsth2212857.d.html. CSCEC provided $450,000 worth of medical equipment, including, 500,000 medical surgical masks, 50,000 N95 masks, and 2,000 units of medical protective clothing and medical face masks as well as respirators for intensive care.

146 "China Sends 2nd Medical Donation to Help Algeria Combat COVID-19," *Market Watch News*, April 15, 2020 https://www.marketwatch.com/press-release/china-sends-2nd-medical-donation-to-help-algeria-combat-covid-19-2020-04-15?mod=mw_more_headlines&tesla=y. The medical donation included surgical masks, N95 masks, medical protective suits, face shields, test kits, and respirators for intensive care units.

147 Rafik Tadjer, "Chine-Algérie, khawa khawa: quand l'ambassade de Chine à Alger reprend un slogan du hirak" ["China-Algeria, Khawa Khawa": When the Chinese Embassy in Algiers Takes Up a Slogan from the Hirak] *Tout sur l'Algérie (TSA)*, April 22, 2020, https://www.tsa-algerie.com/chine-algerie-khawa-khawa-quand-lambassade-de-chine-a-alger-reprend-un-slogan-du-hirak/. The hirak, or protest movement, has used it to express the brotherhood with the Armed Forces [Djeich Chaâb Khawa Khawa].

148 Mark Esper, "Secretary Esper's Remarks at the North Africa American Cemetery in Carthage," Tunisia, September 30, 2020, https://www.defense.gov/Newsroom/Transcripts/Transcript/Article/2367437/secretary-espers-remarks-at-the-north-africa-american-cemetery-in-carthage-tuni/

149 Saïd Boucetta, "Un dirigeant du Parti communiste chinois à Alger-L'immense potentiel d'un partenariat," *L'Expression*, October 12, 2020, http://www.lexpressiondz.com/nationale/l-immense-potentiel-d-un-partenariat-336183

150 "L'Afrique risque de devenir une colonie chinoise' selon le président du Parlement européen," *Jeune Afrique*, March 29, 2017, https://www.jeuneafrique.com/422521/politique/lafrique-se-trouve-situation-dramatique-selon-president-parlement-europeen/

151 Pacal Allizard and Gisèle Jourda, *Sénat français, 520. Session Ordinaire de 20172018: Rapport d´information de la commission des affaires étrangères, de la défense et des forces armées (1), le groupe de travail sur les nouvelles routes de la soie (2)*, May 30, 2018, Retrieved from https://www.senat.fr/rap/r17-520/r17-5201.pdf

152 Mehenni Ouramdane, "Algérie-Chine: La France s'inquiète du rapprochement entre les deux pays." June 17, 2018, https://www.algerie-eco.com/2018/06/17/algerie-chine-la-france-sinquiete-du-rapprochement-entreles-deux-pays/

6

Sino-Moroccan Relations: A Partnership Seeking to Reach Its Full Potential

Anouar Boukhars

Five years, let alone a decade ago, Morocco had barely registered on the radar screen of China's Africa strategy. Nor had China featured prominently in Morocco's national economic development strategy or its calculus to attract foreign investors. It is, therefore, not surprising that Chinese investment and business activity in the kingdom were negligible, especially when compared with China's high degree of engagement in other African economies.

In May 2016, however, King Mohammed Vi's state visit to China injected new life into this desultory trajectory of Sino-Moroccan economic relationship. The significant increase in both the number of Chinese visitors to Morocco and a wide variety of cultural exchange activities points to the potential possibilities of a budding partnership. Perhaps the starkest demonstration of this people-to-people interaction occurred in 2019 when several Moroccan cities hosted several Chinese New Year celebration events. The most spectacular celebration was in the picturesque blue-walled city of Chefchaouen which saw its old medina decorated with 1,500 Chinese red lanterns. That year, the city also celebrated Chinese Spring Festival with dance performances by both Chinese and members of the Royal Moroccan Martial Arts Association.

Economic relations have also improved. After the kingdom's official accession to the Belt and Road Initiative (BRI) in 2017, Chinese-Moroccan business interactions have picked up steam. Several banking agreements, industrial partnerships, and memoranda of Understanding (MoUs) have been concluded. China's Citic Dicastal is investing 410 million dollars in building two aluminum car wheel factories in northern Morocco. The world's largest phosphate exporter, Morocco's Office Cherifien des Phosphate (OCP), is partnering with China's fertilizer additives supplier Hubei Forbon to develop eco-friendly fertilizers. Morocco's Attijariwafa Bank (AWB) is teaming up with state-owned Export-Import Bank of China (ExIm) to establish a $5 billion fund designed to spur its investment activities in the African countries where AWB is already well-established. In April 2019, Banque Marocaine du Commerce Exterieur (BMCE) African Bank signed an MoU with state-owned China Communications Construction Co (CCCC) and its subsidiary, China Road and Bridge Corp (CRBC), to develop a new industrial city in the north of Morocco.

The potential for the expansion of this nascent partnership is real, especially in promising sectors such as automobiles, agribusiness, renewable energy, seawater desalination, aeronautics, information communications technology and telecommunications, transport and logistics, and pharmaceuticals. For Chinese companies, Morocco can offer good market returns thanks to its political stability and relatively good infrastructure development. The kingdom's strategic geographic position and its economic and trade relations with Europe as well as its established economic footprint in several West African states make it a springboard for Chinese exports and investments into Europe and Francophone Africa. To leverage this attractiveness, however, necessitates that Morocco not only attracts Chinese investments but also generates returns in job creation and productivity. This requires the development of technology transfer agreements, the creation of joint educational programs, and the promotion of joint ventures between Moroccan and Chinese companies. To analyze these dynamics, this chapter examines the nascent partnership between Morocco and China with all that portends in terms of opportunities and challenges. It begins by providing a background on the relationship, then investigates the various socioeconomic, political, and security aspects of it, and concludes by providing a future outlook on the relationship.

A History of Unbalanced Relations

Sino-Moroccan relations have historically been low profile and mostly symbolic in nature. The few spaces of convergence were dominated by politics and diplomatic niceties. Morocco generally supported China's vital interests by recognizing People's Republic of China as early as 1958, endorsing the one-China principle, and in 1971 voting for the United Nations General Assembly resolution to re-assign the permanent seat in the Security Council to Beijing. For its part, China never recognized the self-proclaimed Saharan Arab Democratic Republic (SADR) or the Polisario Front, a Sahrawi rebel movement aiming to end Moroccan control of the Western Sahara. To be sure, stark political differences divided Morocco, which was allied with the capitalist West, and the socialist worlds that China aspired to lead. But by not crossing each other's territorial redlines, Morocco and China managed to retain cordial relations.

Politically, the two countries exchanged few high-profile diplomatic visits, notably by Premier Zhou Enlai in 1963. This visit came on the heels of an intensified rupture in the international communist movement. The Sino-Soviet split played out in the areas of economic development and foreign policy. Zhou Enlai's visit to Morocco and nine other African countries, and his announcement of the "Eight Principles of Foreign Economic and Technological Assistance" were designed to woo these states into the Chinese orbit.

China's limited capabilities, however, constrained its ambitions. Even in countries of socialist orientation, China's trade and aid lagged behind that of the Soviet Union and the West. In Morocco, the relationship was little more than a sideshow. The Moroccan OCP Group, which manages the country's vast reserves of phosphate, established in 1958 its first exchanges with the Chinese state-owned company Sinochem, the leading producer and distributor of fertilizers in China. In terms of aid, China sent a medical team in 1979 "to teach acupuncture in a Moroccan hospital" as well as operate "another hospital at Settat where acupuncture had been a popular success."[1] Since then, more than 1,700 Chinese doctors have volunteered in Morocco's remote areas. The Chinese also assisted Morocco in the cultivation of rice and tea as well as helped build and finance a large sports complex in Rabat that was used during the 1983 Mediterranean track and field games.[2]

In the early 1980s, there were efforts by both countries to upgrade relations. At the time, Morocco was embroiled in deadly battles with the Algerian-backed Polisario Front. The Saharan Guerillas' use of Soviet-made tanks and SAM-6 missiles strained Morocco's relations with Moscow whom King Hassan II accused of supporting the war that the Algerian-backed Polisario was waging on Morocco. As a warning to the Soviets, the kingdom decided to inch closer to Beijing, which was itself entangled in geopolitical competition with Moscow.[3] In February 1982, Moroccan prime minister Maati Bouabid became the first top government official to fly to China for a week-long official visit. In December, Chinese prime minister Zhao Ziyang had a three-day stopover in Morocco to help prop up the bilateral cooperation whose seeds were planted during a three-day visit in March 1975 by Moroccan foreign minister Ahmed Laraki to China. During the meetings of Premier Chou Enlai and Foreign Minister Chiao Kuanhua, a number of trade agreements and a protocol on medical cooperation were signed.[4]

China's links with Morocco were modestly upgraded after the end of the Cold War. In 1995, Prime Minister Li Peng visited Morocco, and in 1998 it was the turn of Prime Minister Abderrahmane Youssoufi to go to China. These diplomatic exchanges received a boost with President Jiang Zemin's visit to the kingdom in 1999. King Mohammed VI's visit to Beijing in 2002 illustrated Morocco's emerging interest in China's evolving "Going Global" strategy. By then, a number of Chinese companies had begun to venture into the African continent, seeking to expand their trade opportunities and scour for lucrative investments in energy, infrastructure, manufacturing, and services. Sino-Africa trade was growing annually by 20 percent. Chinese direct investment into the continent was also galloping ahead, growing by 40 percent yearly.[5] In some cases, this rapid speed of economic engagement allowed China to surpass the economic involvement of Africa's traditional partners. Obviously, the depth of China's engagement differed from one country to another. China's involvement was the strongest in countries endowed with natural resources as well as in those that developed a clear China strategy. In countries which lacked such strategic posture, Chinese presence was very modest.

At the turn of the millennium, the seeds of a Sino-Moroccan budding partnership started to be sown. BMCE, recently renamed BMCE Bank of Africa (BBOA), was the first to open a Beijing office in 2000, followed by AWB in 2005. In 2001, the Chinese tech giant, Huawei, began its penetration of the Moroccan market, supplying telecommunications equipment to its Moroccan counterpart, Maroc Telecom. In infrastructure, Chinese companies began competing for Morocco's ambitious infrastructure developments. In 2004, the Chinese construction company, Transtech Engineering Corporation

(TEC), built the Borj Moulay Omar railway tunnel and in 2005 expanded its penetration of the contracted construction market by building the Tangier-Ras R'mel rail link. During this same period, a small but growing number of Chinese cement manufacturers, power construction corporations, and water companies earned contracts to develop and run hydroelectric complexes (Tanafnit-El Borj and Tanafnit dam) and cement plants.[6] Other companies established their presence in the production of motorcycles, cables, steel, and molds. Chinese fishing fleets also began to take interest in Morocco's fisheries and aquaculture assets. In 2005, China's investments in Morocco's fishing industry amounted to $150 million. Sino-Moroccan joint ventures operated seventy vessels that employed more than 2,000 Moroccan employees.[7]

In terms of trade between the countries, Chinese exports had grown steadily to reach 695 million dollars in 2004, a 35 percent increase. Morocco's imports to China, however, stood at a paltry 46 million dollars. In 2005, that number improved when OCP signed an agreement with Sinochem to nearly quadruple the export of Moroccan phosphate fertilizers from 200,000 to 750,000 tons per year. But China's exports of goods and cheap wares grew substantially, with China exporting thirteen times as much as it imported from Morocco. To expand the trade links with Morocco and improve its image, China provided some official grants and concessionary loans. China delivered grants to the Ministry of Energy and Mines for the production of geochemical maps of the regions of Souss-Massa-Drâa, the Eastern Anti-Atlas, and Guelmim-Es-Semara in Western Sahara. Besides phosphate, some of these regions produce coveted minerals, namely, lead, zinc, tin, and copper. But the flows of aid and investments still paled in comparison with those provided by the kingdom's traditional partners.

Time for a Reset in Relations

In the second decade of the twenty-first century, Morocco had to readjust its posture to China. The Moroccan market was quite successful in attracting a steady flow of Western and Gulf direct investment but it was too closely connected to the European market, which had been reeling from the 2008 Global Financial Crisis (GFC). The imperative for the kingdom to reduce its dependence on the European market became greater as its trade relations with the European Union became entangled in court rulings and legal considerations over the Western Sahara dispute. In December 2011, EU lawmakers rejected an extension of the bloc's fisheries agreement with Morocco "because of fears the pact would strengthen Rabat's control of the disputed Western Sahara."[8] In 2013, a new pact was agreed but it was later torpedoed by the European Court which ruled in favor of the Polisario's legal case against the Moroccan-EU trade of agricultural products and fisheries.

This brought the bloc's relations with Morocco to a breaking point. The kingdom suspended contacts with the European Union and threatened to pivot away from Europe. As Aziz Akhannouch, Moroccan Minister of Agriculture, stated at the time, if Europe were to derail the fisheries and agricultural agreements with Morocco because of the situation in the Sahara, then the kingdom would have no choice but to "turn away from it in favor of an acceleration of partnerships initiated with various countries and regions, in particular Russia and China."[9] Russian trawlers were already fishing in the waters of the Moroccan-controlled Western Sahara.[10] The EU–Morocco relations would eventually return to normal when the European parliament conceded to Morocco's demands and "approved amendments to the EU-Morocco Association and fisheries agreements that resolved the dispute over the inclusion of Western Sahara in the scope of those accords."[11]

But despite the warming of relations, Morocco's strategic interests necessitated that the kingdom diversify its links beyond its traditional partners. On the Western Sahara dispute, the kingdom could no longer fully rely on the support of its allies. The failed attempt by the United States in April 2013 to extend the mandate of the United Nations Mission for the Referendum in the Western Sahara (MINURSO) to include human rights monitoring in the territory was a stern warning that Morocco needed more allies in the Security Council. For Rabat, handing the management of human rights to an international trusteeship system would have been the first step toward dismembering the country.

For the United States the move at the time was harmless as it did not contradict its official position in support of autonomy as the best framework for resolving the dispute (the United States would recognize Moroccan sovereignty later under the Trump Administration).[12] But for Morocco, and the Group of Friends of the Western Sahara (France, Russia, Spain, and the UK), the initiative was badly thought-out and ill-timed, especially at a time of great uncertainty in North Africa and the Sahel. "It was the wrong time, wrong strategy," said a senior French diplomat.[13] Concerned about setting a precedent for other territorial disputes, Russia had its own domestic reasons for opposing the US initiative, despite strong lobbying from Algeria, its closest political and economic ally in North Africa.

Despite the failure of the US initiative, the brief row between the United States and Morocco was another impetus for the kingdom to seek the support of other major powers, namely, China and Russia. This became even more urgent with the temporary deterioration of relations between Morocco and France, the kingdom's closest European ally and staunch supporter of its territorial integrity. In February 2014, Morocco suspended all judicial cooperation with France "following a diplomatic row over lawsuits in Paris that accuse the kingdom's intelligence chief of complicity in torture."[14] The relations between the countries became tense since François Hollande ascended to the presidency in 2012. Several in Morocco's hall of power suspected France's socialist president to be "pro Algeria."[15] This sentiment was intensified with Hollande's state visit to Algiers in December 2012 and the ensuing rapprochement between the two countries.

Several diplomatic incidents threatened to derail Moroccan-French ties, the most serious occurred when seven French policemen were dispatched to the Moroccan ambassador's residence to question the kingdom's powerful chief of secret services, Abdellatif Hammouchi, "over accusations his agency was involved in torture." This was enflamed when Moroccan foreign minister was searched in March 2014 while transiting at Paris's Charles de Gaulle airport. Then came revelations that the French ambassador to the UN reportedly described Morocco as "a mistress with whom we sleep every night, even if we are not particularly in love, but whom we must defend. In other words, we turn a blind eye."[16] To be sure, each of these incidences was followed by French apologies or denials. The countries' deep economic partnership and close security collaboration in the fight against terrorism also meant that the relations had to be mended, which they were in 2015.

Nonetheless, Morocco's spat with its closest ally reinforced the kingdom's desire to expand its partnerships. This was only accentuated few years later when former secretary-general Ban Ki-moon stirred controversy when he used the word "occupation" to describe Morocco's control of the Western Sahara. This led Morocco to expel dozens of UN staff and close a military liaison office for the MINURSO peacekeeping mission. This was "Morocco's worst dispute with the United Nations since 1991, when the U.N. brokered a ceasefire to end a war over Western Sahara and established a peacekeeping mission, known as MINURSO."[17]

Economically, Morocco had also to diversify its partnerships to fulfill its ambition to become a regional hub. In tourism, the drop in French and German tourists necessitated that Morocco tap the promising markets of Russia and China.[18] These two countries also presented opportunities for importing Moroccan agricultural products. China in particular presented the tantalizing possibility of investing billions in the kingdom.

In 2014, Morocco was falling behind a number of African countries when it came to attracting Chinese investments. Of the $11 billion that China invested in Africa, only $160 million was reserved for Morocco.[19] The China-Africa Development Fund, which had by then supported more than eighty investment projects of Chinese companies on the continent, had no presence in the kingdom.[20] When compared to its Algerian neighbor which had nearly 800 Chinese companies operating in the country, Morocco was home to only around 30 Chinese groups.[21] The French, by contrast, had more than 900 companies invested in the kingdom.[22]

The trade imbalance between the two countries was also steep. In 2013, China exported $3.13 billion to Morocco while its imports amounted to no more than $558 million.[23] China's exports to Morocco are made up mainly of textile products, household appliances, industrial equipment, and tea while phosphate fertilizers and seafood are the main Moroccan products exported to China. The challenge for Morocco has been how to transform the imbalanced economic relations between the two countries into a strategic partnership that transcended their basic clientelist relationship where Morocco was largely the customer of Chinese goods and products.

As the former president of the General Confederation of Moroccan Enterprises, Meriem Bensalah, put in 2014, Morocco wanted to transform the countries' business relations from "made in China" to "made by China in Morocco." In other words, the growth in trade relations between the two countries had to be accompanied by even faster growth in Chinese investments. To do so, Morocco had to step up its game to level the investment playing field. The country had already an integrated investment strategy that worked fairly well in attracting FDI. But it had to be put on the Chinese map. Naturally, it had also to be tailored to appeal and meet Chinese FDI objectives. But the essence of the kingdom's FDI-enabling framework made it ripe for Chinese investments.

The country's geographic position, its relatively good physical infrastructure, and the competitive positioning of some of its existing industry sectors make Morocco an attractive location for Chinese investors. Its generous tax incentives, booming free zones, and numerous free trade agreements are also tantalizing selling points for Chinese manufacturers looking to shift production to offshore. The kingdom's privileged political, cultural, and economic relations with a number of African countries are also a point of attraction. Moroccan companies play leading roles in the fields of banking, insurance, telecommunications, mining, renewable energy, agricultural sustainability, fishing, and infrastructure. Three Moroccan banks—AWB, Groupe Banque Centrale Populaire (BCP), and BMCE—for example dominate the sector in Francophone West Africa.[24] Through these corporations and the recent creation of the Casablanca Finance City (CFC), Morocco has positioned itself as a regional financial platform and gateway to Africa's fast-growing markets.[25] Indeed, part of the allure of Morocco is the prospects it offers of South–South triangular cooperation in which the kingdom uses its comparative advantages to mobilize the resources of its partners in the developed world to invest in Africa.

Morocco's infrastructure is also a major asset of attraction. The quality of the kingdom's expanding road network is higher than that of its many African peers. Likewise, the kingdom outperforms a number of African countries in terms of the connectivity of its transport subsectors (roads, ports, airports, and railroads). The (2017–18) Global Competitiveness Index ranked Morocco 38th out of 138 countries for the quality of its railroad infrastructure.[26] Morocco's ports were also ranked thirty-ninth in the world in terms of container capacity and flow. The mega Tanger Med was the biggest port in Africa in 2018, and was slated to surpass Spain's largest ports in the Mediterranean, Algeciras, and Valencia, in terms of container capacity.[27] Air transport has also expanded significantly, with Royal Air Maroc expanding its African network to more than thirty destinations on the continent in 2015.

These investments in infrastructure have been accompanied by important efforts by the kingdom to prop up its industrial base. As part of the sector strategy, the government has directed significant resources to speed the development of crucial economic sectors deemed to be strategic to growth. The trajectory and development path of the automotive industry constitutes a notable success story. Since the opening of Renault's Tangiers plant in 2012, Morocco has ascended to the top of the industry in Africa. In North Africa, it has outclassed all its competitors whose automotive sector is either limited to basic assembly (Egypt) or is just very small (Algeria) or lack the presence of a vehicle Original Equipment Manufacturers (Tunisia).[28] By contrast, Morocco's car industry has expanded beyond mere vehicle assembly and wiring into engine production. Its supplier base has also widened to include over thirty international auto component suppliers. This in turn attracted new car manufacturers such as the Spanish SEAT in 2016 and especially Groupe PSA Peugeot Citroen whose entry into Morocco enticed even more suppliers to support the ecosystem in the kingdom, including Chinese companies specializing in wheel rims, gearbox parts, cooling systems, and electric power steering.

The rising number of major car manufacturers has boosted Morocco's automobile ecosystems, increasing local sourcing from Moroccan suppliers and creating vital connections to other relevant industries such as lifting machines, iron springs, safety glass, and other rubber products.[29] As the country's value chain evolves, the kingdom has ramped up its vehicle output, making the country the largest producer of personal vehicles on the African continent.[30] Domestically, car exports have even surpassed phosphates. Moving forward the kingdom wants to capitalize on its successes to attract Chinese car manufacturers and suppliers that can help it boost production capacity, upgrade its ability to create higher value-added products, and better integrate local firms into supply chains. For the country to become competitive on global markets, it needs to create significant economies of scale and increase its productivity and value addition. It also needs to build up its capabilities through technology transfer and learning, including in more eco-friendly automotive technology. Hybrid vehicles, said Oussama Berrada Gouzi, Managing Director of automotive firm Global Engines, "have a significant integration potential in the market."³¹ This goal is no longer a pipe dream as the Chinese electric-car manufacturer BYD is set to become the third major automaker to enter the Moroccan market.

Another industry where Morocco has greater comparative advantage is fertilizer development and agricultural sustainability. The country has invested significantly in the development and use of tailored and context-specific fertilizer product as well as in improving soil management practices not only in the kingdom but also in several African countries. Africa boasts the largest share of arable land in the world (60 percent) but its agricultural productivity is more than four times lower than in high-yielding countries.³² Its fertilizer applications are inefficient and more often than not lack adaptability to local social conditions and crop requirements. "In Africa, only three types of fertilizer are used when at least thirty are needed," says Hind Kadiri.³³ This makes the rational use of fertilizers ten times lower than the low average of countries with high agricultural output.³⁴ The adaptation of African Agriculture (AAA) initiative, which Morocco launched during the 2016 Marrakesh Climate Change Conference (COP22), intends to raise agricultural productivity through the development of the most suitable management practices that help improve soil fertility and fertilizer use and optimize the productive use of water and energy in agriculture in fifteen African countries.³⁵ The initiative, which aims to adapt African agriculture to the mounting perils of climate change, is backed by more than two-thirds of African countries, the United Nations Framework Convention on Climate Change (UNFCCC) and the Food and Agriculture Organization of the United Nations (FAO). China can play a major role in boosting the Moroccan initiative as the country has its own 10–100–1000 initiative designed to implement "ten low-carbon development demonstration projects, one hundred climate mitigation and adaptation projects, and climate training programs for one thousand representatives from developing countries in the global south."³⁶

This creates opportunities for China and Morocco to cooperate in developing appropriate technologies and mobilizing more resources to boost the agricultural development of Morocco and the many African countries where the kingdom is investing in increasing smarter fertilizer use and higher yields. China, which has a proven track record in the smarter use of fertilizers and the extensive soil mapping to achieve higher agricultural productivity, has expressed interest in sharing its experiences and mobilizing more resources to bolster Morocco's agricultural expertise. Indeed, China's fertilizer additives supplier Hubei Forbon struck a deal with Morocco's OCP to build a new generation of eco-friendly fertilizers.

The Moroccan phosphates giant has played a major role in investing in physical infrastructure and the development and dissemination of smart technologies for agricultural development in Africa. Since 2008, the group has managed to triple fertilizer production from 3.6 million tons to 12 million tons.[37] The expansion of Jorf Lasfar chemical platform, located on the Moroccan Atlantic coast, transformed the complex into the largest fertilizer production hub in the world, with the capacity to produce 12 million tons of fertilizer per year and 6 million tons of phosphoric acid. Africa features prominently in the group's ambition to expand its export destinations. With 2.5 million tons exported to the continent in 2017, the group now controls more than two-thirds of the market of phosphate fertilizers in Africa.[38] In West and Central Africa, OCP has near-total dominance. In 2016, OCP added an African Fertilizer Complex to its industrial facilities at Jorf Lasfar. The plant includes a fertilizer unit that can produce more than 45 different blends as well as a sulfuric and a phosphoric acid unit.

OCP has also trained thousands of African farmers on how to apply fertilizers and prop up output of a range of crops.[39] The OCP School Lab program has offered around 300,000 farmers in twelve African countries free training and soil analysis data in local languages to be able to identify the nutrient needs of their soil and elevate agricultural productivity. "Every day we go to meet with the new communities, usually between 100 and 150 farmers. We do one day of training on good agricultural practices—not only on fertilizers but on the general use of seeds, which crops are the most efficient to grow and most importantly, we also offer soil analysis for free to farmers to raise awareness of the importance of knowing what the soil really needs," OCP Africa's head of business development, Jihane Ajijti, told *African Business*.[40]

Improving the productivity of farmers, however, is not enough. African farmers lack not only locally tailored farming products and agricultural training but also access to agriculture finance and insurance. In this regard, OCP launched in 2016 the Agribooster program, the objective of which has been to set up an ecosystem centered around the farmer to facilitate access not only to inputs, but also to insurance products. The goal for OCP is to act as "catalyst" rather than that of "financier."[41] In some cases OCP facilitated farmers' access to loans from micro-finance institutions. "We did this for 5,000 farmers," Ajijti said. "We proved," he added, "that this was possible and increased yields by 40 percent on average, on maize, and then we expanded from Nigeria, to Ghana and we are trying to do it in Côte d'Ivoire, and today we have 120,000 farmers who are benefitting from the program."[42]

OCP is also investing in logistics and distribution components to make sure the products are delivered in time. As Ajijti put it, OCP realized that "farmers lose an average 30 percent of the harvest just in their post-harvesting activities. Most of the time they are losing a lot of money because they don't maximize the value of their harvest." To redress this major deficiency, OCP, through the Agribooster program, works with "buyers and distributors to secure a market for the farmers at a certain price." In Nigeria, Ghana, and Côte d'Ivoire, "a warehousing receipt system was also put in place for farmers to store the produce until the market price was right."

OCP has also been trying to establish partnership agreements with countries that are ready to "co-invest."[43] An example of this South–South partnership is the pooling of the industrial assets of Morocco (phosphate) and Gabon (gas) to create one ammonia production unit and one phosphate fertilizer in Gabon as well as two phosphoric acid production units and one phosphate fertilizer in Morocco.[44] OCP estimates that this industrial project has the potential to cover more than 30 percent of the continent's total demand for adequate and affordable fertilizers. OCP is engaged in similar strategic partnerships to power agricultural sustainability and improve food security through the building of mega fertilizer plants adapted to local soils in several African countries, most notably Rwanda, Ethiopia, and Nigeria.

In 2016, OCP forged a position of strength in Ethiopia's agriculture sector, which accounts for 90 percent of its exports and 45 percent of its gross domestic product.[45] As the world's largest phosphate exporter, OCP sealed a major deal to build a $3.7bn fertilizer plant in Dire Dawa, 250 kilometers east of the capital Addis Ababa. Morocco's OCP will build a blending unit in Rwanda to produce fertilizers. Morocco is helping boost fertilizer production in Nigeria as well as exploring and upgrading phosphate reserves in the country. The group managing director (GMD) of the Nigerian National Petroleum Corporation (NNPC), Dr. Maikanti Kacalla Baru, noted that the supply of Moroccan phosphate to Nigeria is breathing new life into agriculture by making fertilizers available and affordable. "I am happy to inform you that this development has translated to the creation of about 50,000 jobs and led to the production of about 1.3 million tonnes of fertiliser in the country," Baru stated.[46]

Chinese firms can play an important role in accompanying OCP's important work in jumpstarting the agricultural transformation of a number of African countries. Like OCP, China runs many programs in the continent designed to both improve African farming and allow its agricultural companies a foothold in promising markets. It has also built agriculture technology demonstration centers (ATDC) on how African farmers can upgrade farming practices.

Morocco has *carved other niches* for itself to appeal to Chinese investors. The kingdom has emerged as one of Africa's most dynamic renewables markets, with clearly established regulatory framework that attracted major investors to develop its mega solar schemes and wind power projects. With the North African country set to become the first in the region to produce more than 50 percent of its energy requirements from clean energy by 2030, the next challenge is to ensure it can use the renewables drive to establish a local supply chain and secure jobs and skills for its citizens. This will require the continued growth of the supplier base which is critical to the creation of a virtuous circle to sustain the industry.

The aerospace industry is another attraction where Morocco has positioned itself "as a competitive subcontracting and aerospace supply chain destination, attracting major players in the field."[47] The main integrated capabilities of the industry are machining, surface treatment, aerostructure, aeronautic equipment, engineering, electrical wiring, MRO, and sheet metal work.

Contours of a Partnership

In the 2010s, Morocco became eager to market its vision for mutually beneficial cooperation with China. There was significant upside for Morocco to accelerate its catch-up strategy to attract more Chinese investments that can support the kingdom's industrial policy and efforts to create stable employment. As stated above, Chinese investors were already testing the waters in the kingdom. The 2011 Arab uprisings created further momentum, as Morocco emerged as the most stable country in North Africa. This stability, amplified by the kingdom's strategic geography, diversified economy, and business-friendly environment, made the country an attractive business destination for Chinese investors.

In 2012, the country launched a charm offensive to lay out the red carpet for Chinese investors. Dozens of Moroccan senior government officials, business leaders, and journalists started making regular trips to Beijing to highlight how the kingdom has diversified, developed its strategic sectors, and become a gateway to Europe and increasingly Africa. Until fairly recently, as acknowledged by the Chinese ambassador in Rabat, Chinese investors lacked awareness of Morocco as a strategic location for lucrative investments.[48] So it was critical for the kingdom to build up the image and brand of Morocco in China. The Forum on China-Africa Cooperation (FOCAC) was one platform to promote the relationship.

In 2014, Morocco and China created their own special Sino-Moroccan economic forum to better set priorities and focus areas. This provided an important framework for bilateral dialogue and practical cooperation on the best means to promote commercial interaction. The first gathering, held in Beijing in November 2014, was notable for the breadth and prominence of the political and business leaders who attended as well as the number of cooperation agreements, conventions, and MoUs that were signed. For example, the Moroccan company for energy investments and Ming Yang New Energy Investment Holding Group signed an agreement to reinforce Moroccan-Chinese partnership in renewable energies. Morocco's hydrocarbons office (ONHYM) struck an agreement with the Nerin Engineering Co-LTD in the fields of mining and hydrocarbons.[49] These agreements, which also covered infrastructure, tourism, finance, banking, and the automobile industry, signaled the willingness of the two countries to upgrade their bilateral relations.

Based on the promising results of the first Sino-Morocco forum, the kingdom intensified interactions with Chinese business leaders and investors via similar mechanisms. In 2015, Moulay Hafid Elalamy, Minister of Industry, Trade and Green and Digital Economy, lobbied for the kingdom to host the first Sino-African Entrepreneurs Summit (SAES). In it, Elalamy and others outlined the synergy between Morocco's strategic industrial acceleration plan and China's search for new offshoring opportunities. He also made the case for the relocation of Chinese factories to the kingdom. As stated by the economic and commercial advisor of the Chinese embassy in Rabat, there were sectors which were experiencing a certain overcapacity in China and which would benefit from relocating to Morocco which had numerous free trade agreements with markets as important as Europe, the United States, and Turkey. "I'm thinking in particular of the steel industry, consumer electronics, cars, boat building, cement and infrastructure," he said.[50] This was the same point hammered by Mamoune Bouhdoud, Minister Delegate to the Minister of Industry. "By producing textiles in Morocco, you can export without tax to the United States," Bouhdoud told the hundreds of Chinese investors present at SAES.[51]

The CEO of the BMCE Bank of Africa group, Othman Benjelloun, went further, calling for the establishment of a Sino-Moroccan-African alliance. "I am deeply convinced that the Sino-African partnership must be triangular," he stated, and Morocco, because of its geographic position and deep cultural and economic relations with Africa, "must be at the heart of this new paradigm for development."[52] Despite being a small market on a global scale, Morocco has managed to position itself as a privileged interlocutor and economic partner of European countries like France or Spain, but also for most of the French-speaking sub-Saharan countries; hence the idea, raised by Benjelloun, to develop a Sino-Moroccan-African platform.[53]

Such ambition was not a pipe dream as the Franco-Moroccan partnership has shown. The triangular cooperation constitutes one of the development axes of the Franco-Moroccan partnership. For French groups, Morocco has been a springboard for their investment strategy on the African continent. Morocco's cultural, political, and economic affinities with Francophone African countries have offered the French a more accessible entry into these markets.[54] Indeed, several French groups based in Morocco manage their African activities from their Casablanca base. CFC, which was transformed into a financial hub for investing in Africa, hosts dozens of French business groups (Accor, BNP, Essilor, Hopscotch Système Africa, Société Générale, Wendel, Tractafric Africa, just to name a few). Moroccan and French banks also cooperate in promoting trade and the development of French and Moroccan companies in sub-Saharan markets.[55] In 2014, the African Development Bank

(AfDB) chose CFC as the headquarters for the Africa50 fund, "an innovative financing vehicle" that African heads of states agreed to establish in 2012 at the eighteenth African Union Summit.

Morocco drummed support for its proposition as a hub for companies doing business in Africa in the several other economic forums it hosted. For the kingdom, these economic summits offered important business networking and information exchange platforms. They also laid the groundwork for institutionalizing the budding partnership between Moroccan and Chinese companies.

Morocco's engagement of China extended to the education, culture, and tourism spheres. Morocco became the first Arab country to host three Confucius Institutes in Rabat (2009), Casablanca (2012), and Tétouan (2017). The Chinese burgeoning appetite for international travel also created new opportunities for Morocco. In 2014, Moroccan National Tourist Office (ONMT) forged a partnership with the Beijing Tourist Office to develop a communication and marketing plan to promote the Moroccan destinations. ONMT also teamed up with the French Tourist Development Agency to develop a combined offer targeted at Chinese tourists. In 2014, Beijing supported the kingdom's bid to host the Summit of the World Tourism Cities Federation (WTCF), which offered an opportunity for Morocco to showcase its tourist attractions and charm Chinese tourists.

By 2016, Morocco's efforts to woo China had begun to pay off. The lure of investing in Morocco was indeed reflected in the spike of Chinese investments, which saw a 195 percent jump between 2011 and 2016. Chinese construction companies increased their participation in some of the kingdom's major infrastructural projects. The China Railway Major Bridge Engineering Group built the Mohammed VI Bridge, which connects the capital Rabat with the city of Salé. This is the longest cable-stayed bridge in Africa, and it took five years (2011–16) to complete.[56] In 2013, Dongfeng, the second-largest Chinese automaker, partnered with the Moroccan group Auto Hall to assemble and distribute light commercial vehicles in Morocco and in African countries.

In 2014, the Chinese manufacturer of railroad equipment, CSR Nanjing Puzhen Rolling Stock, partnered with The Cherifian Company of Industrial and Railway Equipment (SCIF) to prop up the kingdom's ambitions in developing a railway equipment manufacturing industry.[57] At the time, railway vehicles for the transport of phosphate, coal, and other chemicals were already manufactured in Morocco. SCIF was also exporting phosphate transport wagons to Tunisia and Mauritania. In 2014, the group won a €1 million contract for the renovation of twelve electric locomotives for ZNTK in Poland.[58]

In 2015, Dongfeng joined France PSA Peugeot Citroen in its plan to build and operate a $630 million Moroccan factory that assembles low-cost small and subcompact models for sale in Africa and the Middle East.[59] The car models would be built "on a new low-cost vehicle architecture," developed by PSA's "joint venture with Dongfeng for future models produced in China for the domestic market and South-East Asia."[60]

Chinese and Moroccan banks played an important role in this budding partnership. In May 2015, China Exim Bank opened in Rabat its second office on the continent to serve Chinese businesses present in twenty-six countries in North, Central, and West Africa. In December, Industrial and Commercial Bank of China (ICBC) signed a 171-million-dollar financing agreement with the Anouar Invest group to construct a cement plant with a production capacity of 2.2 million tons per year.[61] For their part, Moroccan banks also partnered with Chinese businesses operating in Morocco. In 2014, the AWB provided support to Shandong Shangang group to install a $150 million modern manufacturing plant for the production of steel pipelines in Tangier.[62] The bank also provided support to the joint venture between Haifen Fisheries and China National Fisheries Corporation (CNFC) and issued market guarantees to support Electric Power Construction Corporation (Sepco, a subsidiary of PowerChina) in building the Jerada thermal power plant.[63] The Moroccan Bank for Commerce and Industry (BMCI) also "granted loans to the Chinese equipment manufacturer Nanjing Xiezhong."[64]

Moroccan banks also stepped up collaboration with Chinese banks. In June 2013, AWB established a strategic partnership with Bank of China to facilitate trade between the two countries, jumpstart Sino-Moroccan investments in Africa, and promote the use of the Chinese currency renminbi (RMB) in African markets where the Moroccan bank has a solid presence. AWB also struck a partnership with China Development Bank to support Moroccan small and medium businesses (SMEs). In this regard, the Chinese development bank granted its Moroccan counterpart a financing line of $100 million to support SMEs in their investment adventures, including in Africa. For its part, the Moroccan BMCE bank of Africa consolidated its presence in China by partnering with China Development Bank Corporation.

These banking relations received an important boost with the visit of King Mohammed VI to China in May 2016 and the signing of a strategic partnership between the two countries. Symbolically, the visit started with the signing of a currency exchange agreement between the two countries. The objective was to provide banks with liquidity in yuan to finance Chinese investments in Morocco and in Africa.[65] The importance of banking stems from the fact that the major banking establishments in the kingdom dominate the scene in Francophone Africa.

Strategic Partnership

King Mohammed VI's visit to China in May 2016 breathed new life into Sino-Moroccan economic relations, which had steadily developed in a number of venues but they remained much below potential. The idea of establishing a win-win strategic partnership dates back to 2012 when the two countries pledged to strengthen their cooperation, through the establishment of "an institutionalized strategic partnership."[66] Some of the proposals that would later gain traction originated in that initial attempt to lay the groundwork for closer economic relations. For example, the idea of building a massive industrial park devoted to Chinese companies was first entertained in 2012. In 2016, it was put on the agenda in the form of developing an ambitious smart city with industrial zones beaming with Chinese companies.[67]

The king's visit gave birth to a series of initiatives, including a visa exemption for Chinese tourists traveling to Morocco, several industrial partnerships, and the planned construction of an industrial city near the port of Tanger-Med by a Chinese company.[68] All projects, fifteen in total, sought to capitalize on Morocco's most important strategic and economic assets, namely, its privileged commercial position between Europe and Africa, its competitive advantages in transportation and port-related infrastructure and its dynamic sectors in the automotive industry, agribusiness, renewable energy, aeronautics, and banking.

In 2017, Morocco became the first country in the Maghreb to officially sign up to China's BRI. This made sense, wrote Sébastien Le Belzic in the French daily, *Le Monde*.⁶⁹ The Mediterranean port of Tangier, he added, is the third most important strategic port in the world after Shanghai and Panama. It is an essential place for Beijing as it constitutes an entry point for Chinese products into both Europe and the fast-growing economies of West Africa. For Morocco, the hope is that joining the BRI will not only boost its major infrastructural projects in the kingdom but also advance its most ambitious goal of realizing mega infrastructural plans that connect west Africa with Europe, namely, through the trans-African route and the gas pipeline project extending from Nigeria to Morocco.⁷⁰ For Othman El Ferdaous, then Secretary of State to the Minister of Industry, Investment, Trade, and the Digital Economy, Morocco's strategic position on the Atlantic coast of Africa constitutes an essential link connecting ECOWAS, which Morocco formally applied to join in 2017, to European markets.⁷¹

To further explore these opportunities, the General Confederation of Moroccan Enterprises and the China Council for the Promotion of International Trade (CCPIT) signed in 2018 an MoU for the establishment of the Silk Road Business Council. The Council aims to be a platform for investors and businesses by providing them with information on investment opportunities and helping them to overcome the problems which hamper Sino-Moroccan cooperation through a better understanding of the legal and regulatory business environment.⁷²

The strategic partnership is bearing fruit. In 2017, Morocco received twice the number of Chinese investments than it did in 2015. Several Chinese companies also announced investments in Morocco, particularly in the industrial free zones and freed trade sites that Morocco established in proximity to Europe and other African markets. In 2018, China's Citic Dicastal translated the agreement it struck during the King's visit in 2016 into a $410 million investment in aluminum car wheel factories in northern Morocco in the Atlantic Free Zone in Kenitra and Tangier Tech city, respectively. Citic Dicastal's investment followed that of South Korea's Hands Corp, which was constructing an aluminum wheel plant in Tangier at a total cost of $472 million.⁷³ During the same year, Chinese Nexteer Automotive announced the building of its first African plant in Kenitra. The facility is manufacturing Electric Power Steering (EPS) systems and Driveline systems for the automotive French multinational

Group PSA. Chongqing Regal Automotive Parts, a medium-sized Chinese equipment supplier, specializing in the production of gearboxes, also opened its Moroccan subsidiary, Regal Automotive Morocco. Other new additions to Kenitra's automotive cluster included Chinese supplier Nanjing Xiezhong, which announced in July 2019 it would build a $15 million facility to supply Groupe PSA with air conditioners. In September 2019 Yazaki announced it would open its fourth plant in Kenitra.[74] The Chinese electric-car manufacturer BYD is also poised to open a factory near the Moroccan city of Tangiers to build battery-powered vehicles. This will become the third car manufacturer, after Renault and Peugeot of France, to build cars in the kingdom.

In the field of telecommunications, Huawei announced in September 2018 that it will set up a regional logistics center in the port of Tanger Med to cover markets in Morocco's neighboring countries.[75] As explained by Peng Zhongyang, Vice-President of Huawei, this was a rational and natural choice given Morocco's privileged geographic situation, its great political stability, its rich cultural diversity, and its adequate business environment.[76]

In the strategic area of agricultural sustainability, OCP struck in 2018 an ambitious deal with HUBEI FORBON Group ("FORBON") to develop a new generation of high added-value fertilizers. "FORBON is a world leader in coating for fertilizers and new products for smart agriculture," said Mr. Iliass El Fali, Executive Vice President of Industrial Operations at OCP Group. The partnership will allow OCP and FORBON to cooperate in developing custom solutions and fertilizers that are efficient and eco-friendly. As part of this endeavor, the two groups are planning a Joint R&D center to advance their goals in the use of digitalization technology to better optimize fertilizer consumption, improve water management, and reduce the industry's ecological footprint.[77]

In the promising field of renewable energy, China First Highway Engineering Co. (CFHEC) partnered in 2019 with Morocco's Platinum Power, a company in which American investment fund Brookstone Partners is a minority stakeholder, to finance, build, and run a $300 million hydropower plant in central Morocco. The two companies also agreed to partner on the development of renewable energy projects elsewhere in Africa, where Platinum Power has established a growing footprint, developing hydropower projects in Cameroon and Ivory Coast.[78]

In tourism, the number of Chinese tourists has multiplied by six in just two years since the entry into force of the visa exemption in June 2016.[79] The recent launch of a direct air link between China and Morocco and the organization of cultural events between the two countries foreshadow the arrival of more Chinese tourists.

Covid-19 and Prospects for Cooperation in Pharmaceuticals

Finally, Morocco has its sights set on attracting Chinese capital, technology, and expertise to boost its domestic pharmaceutical capabilities. The kingdom already has a dynamic industry that produces domestically around 70 percent of its demand for pharmaceutical and medical products as well as exports between 8 percent and 10 percent, mostly to other African countries.[80] The Covid-19 outbreak provided the country an opportunity to fulfill its ambition of becoming a regional hub for the production of generics and other affordable low-price drugs. In August 20, 2020, Morocco quickly jumped on the opportunity to participate in Chinese-led clinical trials of the Covid-19 vaccine.[81] Notably, the agreement that was struck by Rabat and Beijing provided for the possibility of technology transfer of the vaccine, so that if the coronavirus were to become endemic and require regular vaccination campaigns, Morocco would have the capacity to become a producer of the vaccine for parts of the African continent.[82] In this case, stated the minister of health, Tangier Tech city would be the site for the development of Moroccan expertise in the sustainable production of the vaccine.[83]

Importing a product, however, is one thing, manufacturing it is quite another.[84] Moroccan pharmaceutical companies like Pharma 5 and Sothema, which has been involved in the clinical trials of the Chinese Sinopharm vaccine, have the capability to produce generic drugs but not vaccines. As Sothema CEO Lamia Tazi stated, her company, which distinguished itself in 2019 by establishing one of the first medical industrial complexes in Africa capable of producing and exporting to the continent low-priced anti-cancer *drugs*, "can package the vaccine, but not—at least not yet—manufacture it."[85] Doing so requires significant financial investments.

This is where Sino-Moroccan collaboration in the pharmaceutical sector comes into play. "For the partnership to be a win-win," writes Nina Kozlowski in the French magazine *Jeune Afrique*, "China will have to invest in production units in the Kingdom and not just use Morocco to do packaging."[86] Such a possibility has a chance of realization if the Moroccan vaccination campaign proves to be a success, states Myriam Lahlou-Filali, Managing Director of Pharma 5 group, which has managed to domestically produce generics effective against hepatitis B and C. "Unlike China," asserts Lahlou-Filali, "Morocco has a strong presence in Africa where it has a number of pharmaceutical laboratories and enjoys strong partnerships with several distributors."[87] This positions Morocco well in its quest to become a regional manufacturing hub for vaccines.

Conclusion

Morocco is at the very beginning of developing a partnership with China. It is only in the last five years that Morocco has truly begun a determined effort to woo Chinese investors into its economic sectors primed for growth. The kingdom's automotive industry, aeronautics, and renewable energy have already attracted large foreign investors and created dynamic activity in these sectors. For China, Morocco holds important geo-economic value thanks to its strategic geographic location at the crossroads of continents, allowing access to European and African markets. The competitive advantages of some of its economic sectors and array of generous incentives to attract foreign direct investments are also important attractions to Chinese investors. So, there is considerable upside for Morocco and China to accelerate their economic engagement.

With continued and likely growing Chinese investment, it will become ever more urgent to address the gaps in the Morocco–China partnership. First, language and cultural differences still constitute a barrier to investments. As the Chinese ambassador to Morocco, Li Li, put it, both Chinese and Moroccan actors need to get out of their own comfort zones to take advantage of the manifold business opportunities.[88] Chinese companies have to adapt to working in an investment environment that differs from the African countries where they are active. In most economic sectors, French and European legal, fiscal, and normative standards prevail. As for Moroccan companies, Li Li said, they "are certainly used to working with their traditional partners, but they do not know or are not very motivated to explore the Chinese market." African countries such as Ethiopia that have made a concerted effort to learn the Chinese business landscape and language have had better success in attracting Chinese investments.[89] To be sure, both China and Morocco have made efforts to address these language and cultural challenges. An increasing number of Confucius Institutes are opening in Morocco. Mandarin is also becoming mandatory in certain professional training courses related to the tourism industry as well as in the programs of some of the sixty-six schools that the BMCE Bank Foundation for Education and Environment runs. BMCE Bank Foundation and the Confucius Institute in Casablanca have also piloted a number of projects that offer Mandarin in select primary schools.[90] The recent launch of direct flights between the countries and the organization of a series of high-profile cultural events multiply the possibilities for strengthening Sino-Moroccan bilateral relations.

The second challenge confronting Sino-Moroccan relations is to make their economic relationship more balanced. So far, the trade relationship is still lopsided and the economic relations still lack a framework for the development of technology transfer agreements and promotion of joint ventures. To transcend these hurdles, both governments and businesses need to ameliorate their models for collaboration. For example, Chinese investments in the kingdom need to be better linked to Morocco's national industrial policy and better tailored to local talent development. This necessitates the incorporation of local supplier firms and transfer of key technologies and skills. In Francophone Africa, the two countries can also step up their cooperation in lucrative sectors where they both have complementary strengths. Finally, the two countries can boost and balance their trade through an agricultural agreement that facilitates the entry of Morocco's products in China. In 2017, Morocco exported $2 billion in agricultural products, but only 0.2 percent of this value was exported to the Chinese market.

Notes

1. "Soixantième anniversaire de l'établissement des relations diplomatiques Chine-Maroc: huit grands moments" [Sixtieth Anniversary of the Establishment of China-Morocco Diplomatic Relations: Eight Great Moments] *Le Matin*, February 7, 2018, https://lematin.ma/journal/2018/soixantieme-anniversaire-letablissement-relations-diplomatiques-chine-maroc-huit-grands-moments/286794.html
2. "Visiting Chinese Prime Minister Zhao Ziyang and Moroccan Prime Minister," *United Press International*, December 27, 1982, https://www.upi.com/Archives/1982/12/27/Visiting-Chinese-Prime-Minister-Zhao-Ziyang-and-Moroccan-Prime/5101400898239/
3. Abdelkhaleq Berramdane, *Le Sahara occidental, enjeu maghrébin* (Paris: Karthala, 1992), p. 242.
4. Ibid., p. 243.
5. "Dance of the lions and dragons: How are Africa and China engaging, and how will the partnership evolve?" *Mckinsey report*, June 2017, https://www.mckinsey.com/~/media/McKinsey/Featured%20Insights/Middle%20East%20and%20Africa/The%20closest%20look%20yet%20at%20Chinese%20economic%20engagement%20in%20Africa/Dance-of-the-lions-and-dragons.ashx
6. Tandia Anthioumane and Mar Bassine Ndiaye, "Maroc-Chine: Des relations commerciales en forte progression," *La Gazette du Maroc*, April 24, 2006, https://www.maghress.com/fr/lagazette/9825
7. Ibid.
8. Aziz El Yaakoubi, "Morocco Suspends Contacts with EU Delegation over Trade Row," *Reuters*, January 28, 2016, https://www.reuters.com/article/uk-morocco-eu-westernsahara/morocco-suspends-contacts-with-eu-delegation-over-trade-row-idUKKCN0V6294
9. Jules Crétois et Jihâd Gillon, "Maghreb: comment la Russie est devenue un partenaire incontournable," *Jeune Afrique*, February 5, 2019, https://www.jeuneafrique.com/mag/728393/politique/maghreb-comment-la-russie-est-devenue-un-partenaire-incontournable/
10. "Pêche: Les Russes reviennent," *L'Economiste,* June 7, 2010, https://www.leconomiste.com/article/peche-les-russes-reviennent
11. James Moran, "EU-Morocco: Stage Set for a New Partnership," *EURACTIV*, October 11, 2019, https://www.euractiv.com/section/africa/opinion/eu-morocco-stage-set-for-a-new-partnership/

12 Jillian D'Amours, US Recognizes Morocco's Claim to the Western Sahara. Now What? *Al Jazeera*, December 11, 2020, https://www.aljazeera.com/news/2020/12/11/us-recognised-moroccos-claim-to-western-sahara-now-what
13 Anouar Boukhars, "Western Sahara: Beyond Complacency," *FRIDE*, October 4, 2013, https://carnegieendowment.org/2013/10/04/western-sahara-beyond-complacency-pub-53214
14 "Morocco-France Row over Hammouchi Torture Claims," *BBC*, February 26, 2014, https://www.bbc.com/news/world-europe-26360224
15 Laura Mousset, "France—Maroc: quelles relations diplomatiques?" *TV 5 Monde*, January 30, 2015, https://information.tv5monde.com/afrique/france-maroc-quelles-relations-diplomatiques-15273
16 Steve Tallantyre, "Javier Bardem Gaffe Sparks Diplomatic Row," *The Local*, February 26, 2014, https://www.thelocal.es/20140226/spanish-stars-joke-starts-france-morocco-diplomatic-row
17 Michelle Nichols, "U.N. Chief Regrets Morocco 'Misunderstanding' over Western Sahara Remark," *Reuters*, March 28, 2016, https://www.reuters.com/article/us-morocco-westernsahara-un-idUSKCN0WU1N9
18 Nadia Lamlili, "Maroc–Russie: Mohammed VI au pays des tsars," *Jeune Afrique*, March 16, 2016, https://www.jeuneafrique.com/309935/politique/maroc-russie-mohammed-vi-pays-tsars/
19 "Chine–Maroc: passer du commerce à l'investissement," *TelQuel*, December 2014, https://telquel.ma/2014/12/02/chine-maroc-passer-du-commerce-linvestissement_1424795
20 Frédéric Maury et Nadia Rabbaa, "Le Maroc, un pont d'or pour la Chine?" *Jeune Afrique*, December 29, 2015, https://www.jeuneafrique.com/mag/286294/economie/maroc-pont-dor-chine/
21 Sébastien Le Belzic, "Le Maroc fait les yeux doux à la Chine," *Le Monde*, May 16, 2016, https://www.lemonde.fr/afrique/article/2016/05/16/le-maroc-fait-les-yeux-doux-a-la-chine_4920195_3212.html
22 Janie Letrot Hadj Hamou and Eric Bonnel, "Le maroc et les nouvelles routes de la soie: un tournant Historique," *CNNNEF*, February 6, 2020, https://maroc.cnccef.org/wp-content/uploads/sites/108/2020/02/Lettre-Chine-hors-les-Murs-Maroc-et-NRS-janvier-20.pdf
23 Yahia H. Zoubir, Expanding Sino-Maghreb Relations: Morocco and Tunisia, Chatham House, February toto, https://www.chathamhouse.org/sites/default/files/CHHJ7839-SinoMaghreb-Relations-WEB.pdf

24 C. Guguen, "Enquete sur l'influence r eelle du soft-power de Mohammed VI en Afrique," *Le Desk*, 2016, https://mobile.ledesk.ma/grandangle/les-dessous-de-la-nouvelle-politique-africaine-de-mohammed-vi/
25 S. Jenkins, "Casablanca Hopes to Build the Gateway to Markets across Africa," *Financial Times*, 2015, https://www.ft.com/content/060570be-6e98-11e5-8171-ba1968cf791a
26 Klaus Schwab, "The Global Competitiveness Report 2017–2018," *World Economic Forum*, http://www3.weforum.org/docs/GCR2017-2018/05FullReport/TheGlobalCompetitivenessReport2017%E2%80%932018.pdf
27 "Morocco's Tangier Port to become Mediterranean's Largest," *Reuters*, June 26, 2019, https://www.reuters.com/article/us-morocco-economy-ports/tangier-port-to-become-mediterraneans-largest-idUSKCN1TR2G0
28 "Creating Markets in Morocco," *World Bank*, October 2019, https://www.ifc.org/wps/wcm/connect/d0c0f18c-26b7-4861-b4c5-14896aaba7f1/201910-CPSD-Morocco-EN.pdf?MOD=AJPERES&CVID=m-LGA3X
29 Ibid.
30 Ibid.
31 "Morocco Attracts Automotive Manufacturers and Suppliers," *Oxford Business Group*, https://oxfordbusinessgroup.com/analysis/driver%E2%80%99s-seat-automotive-manufacturers-and-suppliers-flock-kingdom
32 M. Soual, "L'Afrique a le potentiel pour nourrir le monde," *Jeune Afrique*, 2017, http://www.jeuneafrique.com/mag/485064/economie/lafrique-a-le-potentiel-pour-nourrir-le-monde/
33 Christophe Le Bec, "Le groupe OCP revoit sa stratégie en Afrique subsaharienne," *Jeune Afrique*, March 14, 2016, https://www.jeuneafrique.com/mag/307568/economie/groupe-ocp-revoit-strategie-afrique-subsaharienne/
34 Soual, "L'Afrique a le potentiel pour nourrir le monde," p. 102.
35 Anouar Boukhars, "Reassessing the Power of Regional Security providers: The Case of Algeria and Morocco," *Middle Eastern Studies* 55, no. 2 (2019), pp. 242–60, DOI: 10.1080/00263206.2018.1538968
36 Mohammed Tawfik MOULINE, "Sino-Moroccan Cooperation and The New Silk Road," *Shanghai Institutes for International Studies (SIIS)*, June 29, 2018, http://www.ires.ma/wp-content/uploads/2018/07/Finale-Overview-of-Sino-Moroccan-Cooperation.pdf
37 Julien Wagner, "Morocco's OCP—A Big, Green Mining Machine," *The Africa Report*, January 18, 2019, https://www.theafricareport.com/413/mining-a-big-green-mining-machine/

38 Julien Wagner, "Engrais: OCP, quelle stratégie en Afrique?" *Jeune Afrique*, April 17, 2018, https://www.jeuneafrique.com/mag/549143/economie/engrais-ocp-quelle-strategie-en-afrique/
39 Morocco expands use of fertilizers in agriculture, https://oxfordbusinessgroup.com/analysis/morocco-expands-use-fertilisers-agriculture
40 "Starting Africa's agricultural revolution," *African Business Magazine*, https://africanbusinessmagazine.com/company-profile/african-green-revolution-forum-agrf/starting-africas-agricultural-revolution/
41 Wagner, "Engrais: OCP, quelle stratégie en Afrique?"
42 Ibid.
43 This and the next paragraph are based on material found in Anouar Boukhars (2019), "Reassessing the power of regional security providers: the case of Algeria and Morocco," *Middle Eastern Studies* 55, no. 2, pp. 242–260, DOI: 10.1080/00263206.2018.1538968
44 'A South-South Partnership Project Between Morocco and Gabon'. http://www.ocpgroup.ma/media/corporatenews/south-south-partnership-project-between-morocco-and-gabon
45 J. Aglionby, "OCP Seals Deal to Build $3.7bn Fertiliser Plant in Ethiopia," *Financial Times* 2016, https://www. ft.com/content/469b5cd0-af27-11e6-a37c-f4a01f1b0fa1
46 Creating Markets in Morocco, World Bank Group, October 2019,https://www.ifc.org/wps/wcm/connect/d0c0f18c-26b7-4861-b4c5-14896aaba7f1/201910-CPSD-Morocco-EN.pdf?MOD=AJPERES&CVID=m-LGA3X
47 "Creating Markets in Morocco."
48 Fahd Iraqi, "Li Li: Jamais les relations entre la Chine et le Maroc n'ont été aussi bonnes," *Jenue Afrique*, February 7, 2019, https://www.jeuneafrique.com/mag/728406/politique/li-li-jamais-les-relations-de-la-chine-avec-le-maroc-nont-ete-aussi-bonnes/
49 "Morocco Eyes 'Mutually Beneficial' Partnership with China, FM," November 28, 2014, http://www.maroc.ma/en/news/moroccan-chinese-business-forum
50 "Au cœur du business avec la Chine," December 2016, https://www.challenge.ma/au-coeur-du-business-avec-la-chine-40786/
51 Maury and Rabbaa, "Le Maroc, un pont d'or pour la Chine?"
52 Frédéric Maury, "Le 1er sommet sino-africain des entrepreneurs s'ouvre à Marrakech," *Jenue Afrique*, November 26, 2015, https://www.jeuneafrique.com/281737/economie/le-1er-sommet-sino-africain-des-entrepreneurs-souvre-a-marrakech/
53 Maury and Rabbaa, "Le Maroc, un pont d'or pour la Chine?".

54 "Maroc-France: Ces nouvelles pistes de partenariat," https://leconomiste.com/article/950141-maroc-france-ces-nouvelles-pistes-de-partenariat
55 Aziza El Fass, "Maroc-France L'approche triangulaire prend forme," *L'Economiste*, May 19, 2015, https://www.leconomiste.com/article/971599-maroc-francel-approche-triangulaire-prend-forme
56 "The New Mohammed VI Bridge Brightens Morocco with Dazzling Light Display," *AFP*, July 21, 2016, https://www.yahoo.com/news/mohammed-vi-bridge-brightens-morocco-dazzling-light-display-200415184.html
57 "Light at End of Tunnel for Trains 'Made in Morocco,'" *The North Africa Post*, September 24, 2017, http://northafricapost.com/19970-light-end-tunnel-trains-made-morocco.html
58 Adama Sylla, "Au cœur du business avec la Chine," *Challenge*, December 2, 2014, https://www.challenge.ma/au-coeur-du-business-avec-la-chine-40786/
59 Laurence Frost, Gilles Guillaume, "Peugeot to Build Morocco Plant to Cut Costs, Lift Emerging-Market Sales," June 19, 2015, https://www.reuters.com/article/peugeot-morocco-plant/peugeot-to-build-morocco-plant-to-cut-costs-lift-emerging-market-sales-idUSL5N0Z52YV20150619
60 Ibid.
61 Nadia Rabbaa, "Maroc-Chine: les banques en première ligne," *Jenue Afrique*, December 27, 2015, https://www.jeuneafrique.com/mag/286260/economie/maroc-chine-banques-premiere-ligne/
62 Fumnanya Agbugah, "Chinese Manufacturing Group Invests $150 million in Morocco Steel industry," *Ventures*, July 24, 2014, http://venturesafrica.com/chinese-manufacturing-group-invests-150m-in-morocco-steel-industry/
63 Rabbaa, "Maroc-Chine: les banques en première ligne."
64 Ndeye Magatte Kebe, "Morocco: BMCI Unblocks 13 Million Euros to Finance Chinese Nanjing Xiezhong Plant," *Kapital Afrik*, July 6, 2018, https://www.kapitalafrik.com/2018/07/06/morocco-bmci-unblocks-13-million-euros-to-finance-chinese-nanjing-xiezhong-plant/
65 Le Belzic, "Le Maroc fait les yeux doux à la Chine."
66 Rachid Rhattat, "La relation économique et commerciale sino-marocaine: De la coopération au partenariat stratégique," *L'Année du Maghreb*, IX | 2013, http://journals.openedition.org/anneemaghreb/1922; DOI: https://doi.org/10.4000/anneemaghreb.1922
67 Joseph Hammond, "Morocco Wants to Build a New City from Scratch—with China's Help," *Quartz Africa*, November 22, 2016, https://qz.com/africa/841803/morocco-wants-to-build-a-new-city-from-scratch-with-chinas-help/

68. François Jurd De Girancourt, "Maroc—Chine: où en est-on dans le partenariat?" *Tel Quel*, May 22, 2019, https://telquel.ma/2019/05/22/maroc-chine-ou-en-est-on-dans-le-partenariat_1639269/?utm_source=tq&utm_medium=normal_post
69. Sébastien Le Belzic, "Le Maroc et les nouvelles routes de la soie: la troisième voie," *Le Monde*, December 4, 2017, https://www.lemonde.fr/afrique/article/2017/12/04/le-maroc-et-les-nouvelles-routes-de-la-soie-la-troisieme-voie_5224379_3212.html
70. "Le Maroc: Route de la Soie martime," https://fr.hibapress.com/news-10158.html
71. "Pékin: El Ferdaous fait le point sur la coopération sino-africaine," *Hepress*, June 26, 2019, https://fr.hespress.com/80562-pekin-el-ferdaous-fait-le-point-sur-la-cooperation-sino-africaine.html
72. "Maroc-Chine: la CGEM se positionne sur la route de la soie," *Challenge*, March 27, 2018, https://www.challenge.ma/maroc-chine-la-cgem-se-positionne-sur-la-route-de-la-soie-94741/
73. Ahmed Eljechtimi, "China's Citic Dicastal to produce aluminum car wheels in Morocco,"*Reuters*, July 26, 2018, https://www.reuters.com/article/us-citicdicastal-morocco/chinas-citic-dicastal-to-produce-aluminum-car-wheels-in-morocco-idUSKBN1KG33R
74. "Morocco Attracts Automotive Manufacturers and Suppliers."
75. "Huawei to Set up Regional Logistics Centre in Tanger Med Port," *PortsEurope*, September 7, 2018, https://www.portseurope.com/huawei-to-set-up-regional-logistics-centre-in-tanger-med-port/
76. "Morocco: Huawei to Build a Regional Logistics Hub in Tanger Med," September 7 2018 https://www.ecofinagency.com/public-management/0709-38933-morocco-huawei-to-build-a-regional-logistics-hub-in-tanger-med
77. "OCP Group and Hubei Forbon Group Build up an R&D Partnership in the New Generation of Fertilizers and Smart Agriculture," September 24, 2018, https://www.ocpgroup.ma/en/ocp-group-and-hubei-forbon-group-build-rd-partnership-new-generation-fertilizers-and-smart
78. "Morocco's Platinum Power Partners with China's CFHEC on $300 mln Hydropower Project," *Reuters*, July 10, 2019, https://www.reuters.com/article/us-morocco-power-hydropower/moroccos-platinum-power-partners-with-chinas-cfhec-on-300-mln-hydropower-project-idUSKCN1U5lO9
79. Jules Crétois, "À l'offensive, le Maroc a séduit un nombre croissant de visiteurs internationaux en 2019," *Jeune Afrique*, February 5, 2020, https://www.jeuneafrique.com/892177/economie/a-loffensive-le-maroc-a-seduit-un-nombre-croissant-de-visiteurs-internationaux-en-2019/

80 Sandrine Berthaud-Clair, "Covid-19: le Maroc aussi veut son vaccin," *Le Monde*, November 13, 2020, https://www.lemonde.fr/afrique/article/2020/11/13/la-maroc-dans-la-course-au-vaccin-anti-covid-19_6059679_3212.html
81 "Morocco to Take Part in Covid-19 Vaccine Clinical Trials Following Two Agreements Signed with Chinese Group CNBG," *MAP* August 2020, https://www.mapnews.ma/en/actualites/general/morocco-take-part-covid-19-vaccine-clinical-trials-following-two-agreements
82 Nina Kozlowski, "Vaccins contre le Covid-19: le Maroc peut-il devenir un hub pour l'Afrique?" *Jenue Afrique*, December 4, 2020, https://www.jeuneafrique.com/1086055/societe/vaccins-contre-le-covid-19-le-maroc-peut-il-devenir-un-hub-pour-lafrique/
83 Berthaud-Clair, "Covid-19: le Maroc aussi veut son vaccin."
84 Kozlowski, "Vaccins contre le Covid-19: le Maroc peut-il devenir un hub pour l'Afrique?"
85 Ibid.
86 Ibid.
87 Ibid.
88 Iraqi, "Li Li: Jamais les relations entre la Chine et le Maroc n'ont été aussi bonnes."
89 "Dance of the Lions and Dragons."
90 "Primary School near Tangier to Pilot Mandarin Chinese Classes," *Morocco World News*, December 5, 2019, https://www.moroccoworldnews.com/2019/12/288238/primary-school-mandarin-chinese-classes/

Conclusion

China's global rise will have major consequences over the twenty-first century. For its detractors in the West, this rise has to be carefully managed and restrained. For some developing nations, China's rise is a welcomed change as it provides another alternative to a Western-dominated global order.[1] It is unlikely that the tension between these two approaches to China will be reconciled anytime soon, and will manifest itself strongly across the Middle East and North Africa (MENA) region as governments, elites, and the public engage with China.

A crucial question is how much China is willing to commit to grow its power and influence across the MENA region. To date, China's primary interests in the region have focused on expanding its commercial reach and locking in energy supplies, all the while avoiding greater security entanglement. While US commentators forever predict that China cannot avoid a greater security role in the region, these predictions have been proven wrong time and again—a limited military deployment to evacuate workers from Libya in 2011 remains the high watermark of Chinese military operations in the area. Vague gestures toward an expanded role in the region are taken as evidence of greater security engagement despite evidence to the contrary.[2]

To be sure, some Chinese commentators have periodically advocated a foreign policy more focused on security concerns in the Middle East/West Asia such as Wang Jisi's "Marching Westward" position paper that garnered considerable attention in 2012–13. But this reflects a minority view within a Chinese state that may be interested in somewhat more security coordination in the Middle East yet has little desire to play the kind of intense militarized goal that the United States does. China's strategy is instead predicated on ensuring access to lucrative markets for its commercial products and productive sites of investment for capital generated by other activities.[3]

Altogether, the geostrategic location of the five North African countries along the southern shores of the Mediterranean represents one of the key motivations behind China's growing footprint there. Proximity to essential waterways, infrastructure, and markets makes North Africa an integral component of the ever-expanding Belt and Road Initiative (BRI). However, the region is also home to three major non-NATO allies: Morocco, Tunisia, and Egypt. All these countries are positioned within the European Neighborhood Policy. The West's political, economic, and security ties with these states will pose challenges for their burgeoning relations with China. North African policy makers are well aware of the global dynamics of the US–China rivalry, and have used China as a leverage in their dealings with the United States and Europe.

Challenges with China's Model

While China's growing presence in North Africa has seen many successes, it also has problematic aspects. Notable among these is the exploitation of cheap Chinese labor to build Chinese-funded construction projects. Chinese projects have been criticized over "questionable labor practices,"[4] and questions have been raised as to how much these construction projects actually support local labor markets or promote shared economic prosperity. These labor practices have already provoked resentment in various countries and are likely to amplify criticisms of the China-centric nature of many of these projects, as well as their lack of transparency and regulation.[5] As Sarah Yerkes highlights in her chapter, relying on Chinese, rather than local, labor alienates local populations.

Accusations regarding China's "debtbook diplomacy" and neocolonialism in South Asia, Africa, and Latin America have also become commonplace.[6] The cases of Pakistan,[7] Sri Lanka,[8] and Ecuador[9] have been cited as particularly disastrous in terms of Chinese debt and failed projects. While each of these countries has its own unique economic challenges, Chinese debt has given Beijing oversized influence in all of them, sometimes with disastrous consequences. In Ecuador, for example, the case of the $19 billion Coca Codo Sinclair dam, financed by China, has become a national scandal. The dam faced structural and operational issues before it even opened, environmental impact studies were woefully inadequate, and top Ecuadorian officials who signed the deal have been imprisoned on bribery charges.[10]

In a 2018 report on BRI debt, researchers from the Center for Global Development warned that eight countries were at risk for "above-average debt," including Djibouti, Tajikistan, Kyrgyzstan, Laos, the Maldives, Mongolia, Pakistan, and Montenegro.[11] High levels of debt with opaque terms undermine, rather than advance, developing economies. Countries like Morocco,[12] Egypt,[13] and Tunisia[14] are already struggling to reduce their external debt. According to the SAIS China-Africa research initiative, Chinese loans to North African governments from 2000 to 2017 totaled $4,607 million. Of the North African countries on the list, Egypt ranked the highest for total amount borrowed from China between 2000 and 2017 ($3,421.60 million), followed by Morocco ($1,030.55 million), Tunisia ($145.39 million), Algeria ($9 million), and Libya ($0).[15]

Although North African countries have not yet borrowed as much as other countries in Africa, South Asia, or Latin America, debt is rising in countries such as Morocco and Egypt, and will likely continue to do so. The region should thus be cautious not to replicate the negative experiences of other countries with Chinese debt and interference.

Furthermore, as the authors highlight in their respective chapters, the pressing issue of China's treatment of its Muslim minority the Uyghurs remains an issue that clouds people's perception of China. While North African governments have turned a blind eye, reports of human rights violations perpetrated against them in so-called re-education camps in the Xianjang province, in the long term will hurt perceptions of China amongst the populations of North Africa.

Covid-19 and Chinese Pandemic Diplomacy

China has worked to offset any negative perceptions of it in the region. Covid-19 presented opportunity to increase its influence and its outreach to North African governments and their public through pandemic diplomacy in response to the virus. By April 2020 China had largely contained the pandemic in its territory; however, it had proven to be a global public relations disaster.

The previous US administration had labeled it the "China virus" or the "Wuhan virus," and global powers began calling for a UN enquiry on how the virus originated. Regardless of how the virus originated, Chinese diplomacy shifted gears and began engaging with its partners across the world, including in North Africa sending tons of medical supplies, as well as Chinese doctors to help combat the virus.

In North Africa, China sent a number of shipments of medical supplies to Egypt, and the Chinese ambassador there stated that China would provide technical information to help tackle the coronavirus, which included a number of teleconferences between Chinese and Egyptian experts to exchange information about China's experience in dealing with the virus.[16] China also sent extensive supplies to Algeria to help combat the virus there.[17] Chinese medical aid to Algeria came also via state-owned China State Construction Engineering Corporation (CSCEC) which has extensive operation in Algeria, reflecting the intersection of commercial and diplomatic interests. China sent medical supplies to both Morocco[18] and Tunisia,[19] while also organizing scientific and research cooperation about Covid-19. Overall, through this pandemic diplomacy, China sought to shift the discourse from China being the origin of the problem, to being part of the solution.

China's "Health Silk Road Diplomacy" is becoming an even more important element of Chinese soft power, in many ways out of necessity. China must fix much of the damage done to its international image due to the global spread of Covid-19. China has sent aid to more than 150 countries and four international organizations. The government has shared medical expertise and support with 170 countries through video conferences and sent medical teams to 24 countries.[20] Some experts argue that "China is winning the vaccine race."[21] Even though US, European, Russian, and Chinese vaccines are now available, China is aiming to take the lead in vaccinating a significant amount of the global population, while the US government has no plans yet to support the global distribution of vaccines.[22] As Covid-19 rates continue to rise across the world, countries are anxious to get access to vaccines as soon as possible. At the time of writing this chapter, countries including Bahrain, United Arab Emirates, Egypt, Pakistan, Turkey, Morocco, Saudi Arabia, Bangladesh, Indonesia, and Russia have hosted final-phase trials of Chinese Covid-19 experimental vaccines,[23] and have begun their roll out.

While Chinese distributors face problems with regulation challenges in the US, European, and Japanese markets, these same hurdles are not present across the developing world. Moreover, China has promised billions in loans and subsidies to facilitate access to the Chinese vaccines. As Eyck Freymann and Justin Stebbing argue, "In the vast emerging markets of Asia, Africa, the Middle East, and Latin America, where more than half the global population lives and many governments can barely afford vaccines, Chinese producers are poised to dominate."[24]

As the Biden Administration slowly attempts to repair much of the damage done to US international engagement and diplomacy during the Trump era, China has already made strong headway in its pandemic diplomacy. At the time of writing in early 2021, The United States is facing an uphill battle to fight Covid-19 domestically, and it's unclear how significant of a role the new US administration will play in the global arena. China has by and large gotten the situation under control domestically and is focusing its attention on the global situation; the United States doesn't have this luxury. China is already poised as the main supplier across the developing world, creating another integral avenue for Chinese soft power to thrive.

China in North Africa: The Path Forward

As the chapters in this volume demonstrated, China's security and diplomatic cooperation with North Africa is beginning to reflect its economic priorities. If countries such as Morocco, Egypt, and Algeria remain stable and increase their economic and diplomatic engagement with China, the BRI will continue to expand in North Africa. While the Chinese are cautiously observing the political situation in Tunisia and the conflict in Libya, there is no doubt that they also aim to integrate these countries into the BRI.

Morocco appears to be the most open and ready BRI participant, given its ambitious industrialization strategy, growing infrastructure, and substantive emphasis on attracting foreign investment. In the 2019 Ease of Doing Business survey, Morocco ranks the highest in North Africa (60th out of 190 countries), followed by Tunisia (80th), Egypt (120th), Algeria (157th), and Libya (186th).[25] In Egypt and Algeria, on the other hand, there are still major obstacles to foreign investment. Military-owned companies still dominate most projects in Egypt, even as President al-Sissi has publicly expressed a desire to attract more foreign investment. Meanwhile, Chinese officials have expressed concern about the increasing level of red tape in Egypt and how this hurts investment projects. While the new 2017 investment law was a positive step, much work remains to be done in Egypt to ease the challenges of doing business.

Corruption scandals have also hurt the reputation of Chinese companies in Algeria, where there is a general lack of transparency surrounding construction deals. The China Railway Construction Corporation (CRCC) faced criticism after allegations of withholding wages valued at around $4.2 million. Megaprojects such as the East-West Highway have also been marred by various corruption scandals and delayed by needed repairs.[26]

Despite these challenges, it is very clear that there is potential for immense expansion in China–North Africa relations, but these growing ties could put other alliances at risks—notably the historical economic and political ties with Europe and the United States. Furthermore, much needs to change about China's current economic relationship with these countries. Perhaps, first and foremost is the importance of cultivating a more balanced trade relationship in the future. Moreover, regional security problems such as the Western Sahara conflict and the Libyan war could further destabilize region, and China may not be able to sit on the sidelines of these issues anymore if it hopes to be taken seriously as a major power in the MENA region, and in the Mediterranean.

Notes

1   This conclusion draws on the editor's previously published papers Adel Abdel Ghafar & Anna Jacobs, *Beijing Calling: Assessing China's Growing Footprint in North Africa*, Brookings Doha Center Policy Briefing, September 2019 and Adel Abdel Ghafar & Anna Jacobs, "China in the Mediterranean: Implications of Expanding Sino-North Africa Relations," *Brookings Institution Global China Project*, July 2020.
2   Fraihat, Ibrahim, and Andrew Leber. "China and the Middle East after the Arab Spring: From Status-Quo Observing to Proactive Engagement," *Asian Journal of Middle Eastern and Islamic Studies* 13, no. 1 (2019), pp. 1–17.

3   Camille Lons et al., "*China's Great Game in the Middle East*," Policy Brief (European Council on Foreign Relations, October 2019).

4   Emily Feng, "China's Global Construction Boom Puts Spotlight on Questionable Labor Practices," *National Public Radio*, March 30, 2019, https://www.npr.org/2019/03/30/707949897/chinas-global-construction-boom-puts-spotlight-on-questionable-labor-practices

5   Jonathan E. Hillman, "China's Belt and Road Initiative: Five Years Later," *Center for Strategic and International Studies*, Testimony, January 25, 2018, https://www.csis.org/analysis/chinas-belt-and-road-initiative-five-years-later-0."

6   See Sam Parker and Gabrielle Chefitz, "Debtbook Diplomacy: China's Strategic Leveraging of Its Newfound Economic Influence and the Consequences for U.S. Foreign Policy," *Belfer Center for Science and International Affairs, Policy Analysis Exercise*, May 2018, https://www.belfercenter.org/sites/default/files/files/publication/Debtbook%20Diplomacy%20PDF.pdf; John Hurley, Scott Morris, and Gailyn Portelance, "Examining the Debt Implications of the Belt and Road Initiative from a Policy Perspective," *Center for Global Development, Policy Paper* 121, March 2018, https://www.cgdev.org/sites/default/files/examining-debt-implications-belt-and-road-initiative-policy-perspective.pdf; Yun Sun, "China's 2018 Financial Commitments to Africa: Adjustment and Recalibration," *Brookings Institution*, Africa in Focus, September 5, 2018, https://www.brookings.edu/blog/africa-in-focus/2018/09/05/chinas-2018-financial-commitments-to-africa-adjustment-and-recalibration/; Matina Stevis-Gridneff, "More of Africa Finds Itself in China's Debt," *The Wall Street Journal*, July 25, 2018, https://www.wsj.com/articles/more-of-africa-finds-itself-in-chinas-debt-1532549741; and Tanner Greer, "One Belt, One Road, One Big Mistake," *Foreign Policy*, December 6, 2018, https://foreignpolicy.com/2018/12/06/bri-china-belt-road-initiative-blunder/

7   Anthony B. Kim, "Is Pakistan about to Be Caught in China's 'Debt-Trap Diplomacy'?" *The Heritage Foundation*, Commentary, August 8, 2018, https://www.heritage.org/international-economies/commentary/pakistan-about-be-caught-chinas-debt-trap-diplomacy

8   Mario Esteban, "Sri Lanka and Great-Power Competition in the Indo-Pacific: A Belt and Road Failure?" *Elcano Royal Institute*, November 28, 2018, http://www.realinstitutoelcano.org/wps/wcm/connect/6f0582c6-24d9-414a-b51e-7f63fa6e2b5b/ARI129-2018-Esteban-Sri-Lanka-great-power-competition-Indo-Pacific-Belt-and-Road-failure.pdf?MOD=AJPERES&CACHEID=6f0582c6-24d9-414a-b51e-7f63fa6e2b5b

9. Nicholas Casey and Clifford Krauss, "It Doesn't Matter If Ecuador Can Afford This Dam. China Still Gets Paid," *New York Times*, December 24, 2018, https://www.nytimes.com/2018/12/24/world/americas/ecuador-china-dam.html.
10. Ibid.; María Cristina Vallejo et al., "Evading Sustainable Development Standards: Case Studies on Hydroelectric Projects in Ecuador," Boston University Global Development Policy Center, Working Paper 19, October 2018, http://www.bu.edu/gdp/files/2018/10/GEGI_GDP-Ecuador-WP.pdf
11. Tim Fernholz, "Eight Countries in Danger of Falling into China's 'Debt Trap,'" *Quartz*, March 7, 2018, https://qz.com/1223768/china-debt-trap-these-eight-countries-are-in-danger-of-debt-overloads-from-chinas-belt-and-road-plans/
12. Souhail Karam, "Morocco Chief Planner Warns on State Companies' Debt Spree," *Bloomberg*, July 26, 2018, https://www.bloomberg.com/news/articles/2018-07-26/morocco-chief-planner-warns-on-state-companies-borrowing-spree
13. Reuters, "Egypt's foreign debt rises to $92.64 bln at end-June, PM tells paper," September 9, 2018, https://www.reuters.com/article/egypt-economy-debt/egypts-foreign-debt-rises-to-92-64-bln-at-end-june-pm-tells-paper-idUSL5N1VV035
14. See Eliza Volkmann, "Tunisia: An Economy Drowning in Debt," *Arab News*, January 31, 2018, http://www.arabnews.com/node/1237021/middle-east; Juan Pablo Bohoslavsky, "A Human Rights Approach to Debt, Structural Adjustment and Corruption in Tunisia: Report of the United Nations Independent Expert on Foreign Debt and Human Rights on His Mission to Tunisia," Observatoire Tunisien de l'Economie, Policy Brief, no. 4, April 11, 2018, pp. 5–6, https://www.economie-tunisie.org/sites/default/files/20180411-pb-ohchr-bap_0.pdf
15. China Africa Research Initiative Database, "Chinese Loans to African Governments, Country by Country, 2000–2017," August 25, 2019, http://www.sais-cari.org/data-chinese-loans-to-africa. It is important to note that the CARI loan data "represents amounts *borrowed* since 2000. These totals should be reported as amounts borrowed and should *not* be reported as current *debt* figures since many countries have been servicing their debts promptly and have made substantial payments on these loans."
16. Egypt Independent, Egypt Receives Medical Supplies from China to Combat Coronavirus, April 16, 2020, https://egyptindependent.com/egypt-receives-medical-supplies-from-china-to-combat-coronavirus/
17. AFP, China a True Friend as Algeria Battles Coronavirus Outbreak, *SCMP*, 5 April, 2020. https://www.scmp.com/news/world/africa/article/3078482/china-true-friend-algeria-battles-coronavirus-outbreak

18 The North Africa Post, "China Sends Morocco Medical Aid to Fight Coronavirus," March 23, 2020, https://northafricapost.com/39269-china-sends-morocco-medical-aid-to-fight-coronavirus.html
19 Xinhua, "Interview: Tunisia Satisfied with Tunisia-China Cooperation in Fighting COVID-19: Health Minister," May 8, 2020, http://www.xinhuanet.com/english/2020-05/08/c_139038916.htm
20 Yahia Zoubir, "China's 'Health Silk Road' Diplomacy in the MENA, Konrad Adenauer Stiftung," *Mediterranean Dialogue Series*, July 2020, https://www.kas.de/documents/282499/282548/MDS_China+Health+Silk+Road+Diplomacy.pdf/3b0af715-8671-cb10-5022-5e4a94eec086?t=1595341252822
21 EykcFreymann and Justin Stebbing, China is Winning the Vaccine Race, Foreign Affairs, November 5, 2020. https://www.foreignaffairs.com/articles/united-states/2020-11-05/china-winning-vaccine-race
22 Ibid.
23 Simone McCarthy, Coronavirus: More Countries Host Final Trial of Chinese - Made Vaccines, South China Morning Post, 29 September, 2020. https://www.scmp.com/news/china/science/article/3103459/coronavirus-more-countries-host-final-trials-chinese-made
24 Eyck Freymann and Justin Stebbing, China is Winning the Vaccine Race, *Foreign Affairs*, November 5, 2020, https://www.foreignaffairs.com/articles/united-states/2020-11-05/china-winning-vaccine-race
25 World Bank Group, "Doing Business 2019: Training for Reform," *Flagship Report*, 2019, 5, http://www.worldbank.org/content/dam/doingBusiness/media/Annual-Reports/English/DB2019-report_web-version.pdf
26 See Dalia Ghanem and Lina Benabdallah, "The China Syndrome," *Carnegie Middle East Center, Diwan*, November 18, 2016, https://carnegie-mec.org/diwan/66145 and Ahmed Marwane, "Fighting Corruption in Algeria: Turning Words into Action," *The Washington Institute, Fikra Forum*, December 12, 2018, https://www.washingtoninstitute.org/fikraforum/view/fighting-corruption-in-algeria-turning-words-into-action

Bibliography

Abdel Ghafar, Adel and Anna Jacobs. "Beijing Calling: Assessing China's Growing Footprint in North Africa," *Policy Briefing Brookings Doha Center*, September 2019, https://www.brookings.edu/research/beijing-calling-assessing-chinas-growing-footprint-in-north-africa/

Abdel Ghafar, Adel and Anna Jacobs. "China in the Mediterranean: Implications of Expanding Sino-North Africa Relations," *Brookings Institution Global China Project*, July 2020.

Abdel-Alim, Wessam. "Text of President El Sisi's Speech at the Opening Session of the Belt and Road Forum Summit," *Al-Ahram*, April 26, 2019, http://gate.ahram.org.eg/News/2148829.aspx

Abtroun, Samy. "Expatriés chinois en Algérie: l'amour au bout du voyage," *Paris Match*, September 14, 2018, https://www.parismatch.com/Actu/International/Expatries-chinois-en-Algerie-l-amour-au-bout-du-voyage–1574387

Abu El-Gheit, Ahmed. 2013. *My Testimony: Egyptian Foreign Policy, 2004–2011*. Cairo: Nahdet Misr.

Abu Hatab, Assem. 2015. "Economically Aggressive, Politically Soft: Understanding China's Policy toward the Arab World," https://poseidon01.ssrn.com/delivery.php?ID=666112089118088010103089088107107066019041046044086035108099076122066102025087096113031012096001011007032118003115085098068120121055070011022073025106115006067093019046039010121027031077112064000065018025113016093030019109028084118006019073009119086105&EXT=pdf

Abu Hatab, Assem, Nada Shoumann and Huo Xuexi. "Exploring Egypt-China Bilateral Trade: Dynamics and Prospects," *Journal of Economic Studies* 39.3 (2012): 314–26.

Afir, Aylan. "Algérie: British Petroleum veut quitter la base gazière de Tiguentourine" [Algeria: British Petroleum Wants to Leave the Tiguentourine Gas Base], *ObservAlgerie*, February 6, 2020, https://www.observalgerie.com/algerie-british-petroleum-veut-ceder-ses-parts-dans-lusine-de-tiguentourine/2020/

Africa Infrastructure Knowledge Program. 2019. "Africa Infrastructure Development Index (AIDI), 2019," http://infrastructureafrica.opendataforafrica.org/rscznob/africa-infrastructure-development-index-aidi–2019.

Afrobarometer. "Data," n.d. https://www.afrobarometer.org/data.

Agbugah, Fumnanya. "Chinese Manufacturing Group Invests $150 million in Morocco Steel Industry," *Ventures*, July 24, 2014, http://venturesafrica.com/chinese-manufacturing-group-invests-150m-in-morocco-steel-industry/

Aglionby, J. "OCP Seals Deal to Build $3.7bn Fertiliser Plant in Ethiopia," *Financial Times* 2016, https://www.ft.com/content/469b5cd0-af27-11e6-a37c-f4a01f1b0fa1

Aguinaldo, Jennifer. "Exclusive: Work Yet to Start at Algeria's Planned Mega-port," *MEED*, January 28, 2018, https://www.meed.com/exclusive-work-algerias-mega-port-project-yet-start/

Ahram Online. "Egypt, China to Cooperate on First Industrial Zone in New Alamein," May 30, 2018, http://english.ahram.org.eg/NewsContent/3/0/301451/Business/0/Egypt,-China-to-cooperate-on-first-industrial-zone.aspx

Ahram Online. "Egypt Signs $3 Billion Loan Deal with Chinese Commercial Bank to Build Business Zone in New Capital," April 28, 2019, http://english.ahram.org.eg/NewsContent/3/12/330776/Business/Economy/Egypt-signs–billion-loan-dealwith-Chinese-commer.aspx

Ahram Online. "Egypt, China Naval Forces Carry out Joint Military Drills off Egypt's Mediterranean," August 21, 2019, http://english.ahram.org.eg/NewsContent/1/64/344171/Egypt/Politics-/Egypt,-China-naval-forces-carry-out-joint-military.aspx

Ahres, Amina. "10 étudiants algériens en formation en Chine" [10 Algerian Students in Training in China], *El Watan*, December 11, 2019, https://www.elwatan.com/pages-hebdo/etudiant/10-etudiants-algeriens-en-formation-en-chine-11-12–2019

AidData. "China's Public Diplomacy Dashboard," 2019, http://china-dashboard.aiddata.org

Al-Aees, Shaimaa. "Egypt-China Economic Cooperation Will Further Grow Post-COVID-19: Chinese Ambassador," *Daily News Egypt*, July 28, 2020, https://dailynewsegypt.com/2020/07/28/egypt-china-economic-cooperation-will-further-grow-post-covid-19-chinese-ambassador/.

Al Ahram Online. "Egypt-China Trade Hits $7.5 Bln in 7 Months: Chinese Customs," August 26, 2018, http://english.ahram.org.eg/NewsContent/3/12/310274/Business/Economy/EgyptChina-trade-hits—bln-in–months-Chinese-cus.aspx

Albert, Eleanor. "China's Big Bet on Soft Power," *Council on Foreign Relations*, Backgrounder, February 9, 2018, https://www.cfr.org/backgrounder/chinas-big-bet-soft-power

Alden, Chris and Faten Aggad-Clerx. "Chinese Investments and Employment Creation in Algeria and Egypt," Economic Brief. *African Development Bank (AfDB)*, 2012, https://www.afdb.org/fileadmin/uploads/afdb/Documents/Publications/Brochure%20China%20Anglais.pdf

Alden, Chris, Abiodun Alao, Chun Zhang, and Laura Barber. 2018. *China and Africa: Building Peace and Security Cooperation on the Continent.* New York: Palgrave Macmillan, 337.

"Algeria Acquires Lethal Mach 3 Ship Hunting Missies from China: How the CX-1 Allows Algiers to Close Off the Mediterranean," *Military Watch*, July 27, 2018, https://militarywatchmagazine.com/article/algeria-acquires-lethal-mach-3-ship-hunting-missies-from-china-how-the-cx-1-allows-algiers-to-close-off-the-mediterranean

"Algeria Operating New UAV Types," *DefenceWeb*, January 7, 2019, https://www.defenceweb.co.za/aerospace/unmanned-aerial-vehicles/algeria-operating-new-uav-types/

"Algeria: Over 55,000 Visas Granted to Chinese Workers, Visitors in 2015," *All Africa*, July 12, 2016, https://allafrica.com/stories/201607120701.html

"Algeria Ratifies BRI Agreement with China," *Xinhua*, July 10, 2019, http://www.xinhuanet.com/english/2019-07/10/c_138212879.htm

"Algeria Receives Final Chinese Corvette" *DefenceWeb*, July 18, 2016, https://www.defenceweb.co.za/sea/sea-sea/algeria-receives-final-chinese-corvette/

"Algerian-Chinese Partnership on Manufacturing of Foton-Brand Trucks," *APS*, Thursday, April 20, 2017, http://www.aps.dz/en/economy/17914-algerian-chinese-partnership-on-manufacturing-of-foton-brand-trucks

"Algerian New Port of El Hamdania Construction to Be Completed by 2024," *PortSEurope*, July 3, 2017, https://www.portseurope.com/algerian-new-port-of-el-hamdania-construction-to-be-completed-by-2024/

"Algeria's First Chinese Automobile Assembly Plant Open for Production," *People's Daily Online*, May 14, 2018, http://en.people.cn/n3/2018/0514/c90000-9459918.html

Algerie Presse Service. "Commerce extérieur: un déficit de plus de 6 milliards de dollars en 2019," February 15, 2020, http://www.aps.dz/economie/101654-commerce-exterieur-un-deficit-de-plus-de-6-milliards-de-dollars-en-2019

alHarathy, Safa. "Libyan Foreign Ministry Calls on Beijing to Act against the Use of Chinese-Made Drones in Killing Libyans," *Libya Observer*, November 20, 2019, https://www.libyaobserver.ly/inbrief/libyan-foreign-ministry-calls-beijing-act-against-use-chinese-made-drones-killing-libyans

Alilat, Farid. "Qui sont les Chinois d'Algérie? " [Who Are the Chinese in Algeria?] *Jeune Afrique*, June 2, 2015, https://www.jeuneafrique.com/233388/politique/qui-sont-les-chinois-d-alg-rie/; see, also, Taing, "L'immigration chinoise à Alger …, "

Alkoutami, Sandy and Frederic Wehrey. "China's Balancing Act in Libya," *Lawfare* May 10, 2020, https://www.lawfareblog.com/chinas-balancing-act-libya

Allizard, Pacal and Gisèle Jourda. *Sénat français, 520. Session Ordinaire de 20172018: Rapport d´information de la commission des affaires étrangères, de la défense et des forces armées (1), le groupe de travail sur les nouvelles routes de la soie (2)*. May 30, 2018. Retrieved from https://www.senat.fr/rap/r17-520/r17-5201.pdf

Al-Quds Al-Arabi. "Egyptian Diplomat: China Has Decided to Stand beside Egypt in Any Discussions at the Security Council," August 28, 2013, https://www.alquds.co.uk/%D8%AF%D8%A8%D9%84%D9%88%D9%85%D8%A7%D8%B3%D9%8A-%D9%85%D8%B5%D8%B1%D9%8A-%D8%A7%D9%84%D8%B5%D9%8A%D9%86-%D8%AA%D9%82%D8%B1%D8%B1-%D8%A7%D9%84%D9%88%D9%82%D9%88%D9%81-%D8%A8%D8%AC%D8%A7%D9%86%D8%A8/

Al-Tahrir. "Agreement between Abdel-Ghaffar and China's Deputy Security Minister on Combatting Terrorism," June 19, 2017, https://www.eltahrer.com/Story/789836/اتفاق-بين-عبد-الغفار-ونائب-وزير-الأمن-بالصين-على-مكافحة-الإرهاب

Al-tamimi, Naser. "China-Algeria Relations: Growing Slowly but Surely," *Al-Arabiya*, March 26, 2014, https://english.alarabiya.net/en/views/business/economy/2014/03/26/China-Algeria-relations-growing-slowly-but-surely.html

Alterman, Jon, Doug Paal, Sulmaan Khan and Evan Medeiros. "China in the Middle East: Part One," *Babel: Translating the Middle East*. February 5, 2020, https://www.csis.org/podcasts/babel-translating-middle-east

Alterman, Jon, et al. "China in the Middle East: Part Two," *Babel: Translating the Middle East*. February 5, 2020, https://www.csis.org/podcasts/babel-translating-middle-east.

Alwasat. "GNA Interior Minister Bashagha Affirms Libya's Desire for Security Cooperation with China," January 9, 2019, http://en.alwasat.ly/news/libya/232190

American Enterprise Institute (2020). "China Global Investment Tracker." February 12, 2020, https://www.aei.org/china-global-investment-tracker/.

American University. 1979. *Libya: A Country Study*. Washington, DC.

Anshan, Li. 2008. "China's New Policy toward Africa," in *China into Africa: Trade, Aid, and Influence*, edited by Robert I. Rotberg. Washington, DC: Brookings Institution Press, 21–47.

Anthioumane, Tandia and Mar Bassine Ndiaye. "Maroc-Chine: Des relations commerciales en forte progression," *La Gazette du Maroc*, April 24, 2006, https://www.maghress.com/fr/lagazette/9825

Aoun, Elena and Thierry Kellner. "The Crises in the Middle East: A Window of Opportunity for Rising China," *European Journal of East Asian Studies* 14 (2015): 189–224.

AP News Wire. "Russia, China Block Release of UN Report Criticizing Russia," *The Independent,* September 26, 2020, https://www.independent.co.uk/news/russia-china-block-release-un-report-criticizing-russia-un-diplomats-security-council-parties-libya-b612738.html

Arab Barometer. "Data Analysis Tool," n.d. https://www.arabbarometer.org/survey-data/data-analysis-tool/

Arab Republic of Egypt, Ministry of Communications and Information Technology. "Egypt Vision 2030," http://mcit.gov.eg/Upcont/Documents/Reports%20and%20Documents_492016000_English_Booklet_2030_compressed_4_9_16.pdf

Arabian Aerospace Online News Service. "Egypt Inducts Chinese Armed Drones," April 29, 2019, https://www.arabianaerospace.aero/egypt-inducts-armed-chinese-drones.html

Arita, Shawn, Sumner La Croix and James Mak. "How China's Approved Destination Status Policy Spurs and Hinders Chinese Travel Abroad," Working Paper. University of Hawai'i at Manoa: The Economic Research Organization at the University of Hawai'i, October 19, 2012.

Ashley, Cowburn. "Two-thirds of African Countries Now Using Chinese Military Equipment, Report Reveals," *The Independent*, https://www.independent.co.uk/news/world/africa/two-thirds-of-african-countries-now-using-chinesemilitary-equipment-a6905286.html

Assad, Abdulkader. "Libya's NOC Mulls Cooperation with Chinese Oil Firms," *Libya Observer*, July 25, 2018, https://www.libyaobserver.ly/economy/libyas-noc-mulls-cooperation-chinas-oil-firms

Assad, Abdulkader. "China Vows to Probe Use of Its Drones by Haftar's Forces in Libya," *Libya Observer*, October 16, 2019, https://www.libyaobserver.ly/news/china-vows-probe-use-its-drones-haftars-forces-libya

Attia, Syrine. "L'Algérie lance son premier satellite de télécommunications," December 11, 2017, https://www.jeuneafrique.com/501179/economie/lalgerie-lance-son-premier-satellite-de-telecommunications/

"Au cœur du business avec la Chine," December 2016, https://www.challenge.ma/au-coeur-du-business-avec-la-chine–40786/

Author's interview with a High-level Algerian Official, Beijing, November 2016.

Author's interview with Algerian Ambassador to China, November 8, 2016.
Author's discussions with Pentagon officials, 2019.
Author's interview with a US State Department Official, January 2019.
Author's interview with a Tunisian Diplomat, 2019.
Author's interview with a US Official, January 2020.
Author's interviews with Algerian officials, Algiers, February 2–8, 2020.
Azzoug, Samir. "Pour l'installation de l'institut Confucius en Algérie," *El Watan*, February 5, 2014, https://www.djazairess.com/fr/elwatan/444714
B. Kim, Anthony. "Is Pakistan about to Be Caught in China's 'Debt-Trap Diplomacy'?" *The Heritage Foundation*, Commentary, August 8, 2018. https://www.heritage.org/international-economies/commentary/pakistan-about-be-caught-chinas-debt-trap-diplomacy
Badis, Adlène. "Chine-Algérie: l'éloge d'un partenariat prometteur," *Reporters* (Algeria), January 9, 2018, https://www.reporters.dz/chine-algerie-l-eloge-d-un-partenariat-prometteur/
"Banque Misr Signs $100 Million Loan with China Development Bank," https://www.banquemisr.com/en/about-us/press/china-development-bank
Bayes, Tom. "China's Emerging Diplomatic and Economic Presence in North Africa," *The Atlantic Community*, February 27, 2019, https://atlantic-community.org/chinas-emerging-diplomatic-and-economic-presence-in-north-africa/
Baynes, Chris. "Muslim Women 'Forced to Share Beds' with Male Chinese Officials after Husbands Detained in Internment Camps," *The Independent*, November 5, 2019 https://www.independent.co.uk/news/world/asia/muslim-china-uighur-forced-share-beds-male-officials-detention-camps-a9185861.html
BBC. "Data Leak Reveals How China 'Brainwashes' Uighurs in Prison Camps," November 24, 2019, https://www.bbc.com/news/world-asia-china–50511063
Behbehani, Hisham. 1981. *China's Foreign Policy in the Arab World, 1955–75: Three Case Studies.* London: Kegan Paul International, 351–2.
Belguidoum, Saïd. "Transnational Trade and New Types of Entrepreneurs in Algeria," in *The Politics of Algeria: Domestic Politics and International Relations*, edited by Yahia H. Zoubir. London & New York: Routledge, 2020, 226.
Belhadj, Imen, Degang Sun, and Yahia H. Zoubir. "China in North Africa: A Strategic Partnership," in *North African Politics. Change and Continuity*, edited by Yahia H. Zoubir and Gregory White. London & New York: Routledge, 2016.
Belmekki, Hasnae. "Derb Omar, Stronghold of the Chinese Traders of Casablanca," University of the Witwatersrand Africa-China Reporting Project, Francophone Africa and China Series, May 4, 2018, http://africachinareporting.co.za/2018/05/derb-omar-stronghold-of-the-chinese-traders-of-casablanca-francophone-africa-china-series/

Ben Salah, Nizar. "The Construction of the Community with a Shared Future for Mankind: Chinese Investment in Africa, The Maghreb and Tunisia," Economy & Finance. MEF Reflections. *Maghreb Economic Forum* (MEF), 2019, https://www.slideshare.net/MAGEF/chinese-investment-in-africa-the-maghreb-and-tunisia

Bennis, Samir. "Moroccan Pragmatism: A New Chapter for Western Sahara," *Aljazeera English*, February 13, 2017, https://www.aljazeera.com/indepth/opinion/2017/02/moroccan-pragmatism-chapter-western-sahara-170213074116469.html

Berramdane, Abdelkhaleq. 1992. *Le Sahara occidental, enjeu maghrébin*. Paris: Karthala, 242.

Berthaud-Clair, Sandrine. "Covid-19: le Maroc aussi veut son vaccin," *Le Monde*, November 13, 2020, https://www.lemonde.fr/afrique/article/2020/11/13/la-maroc-dans-la-course-au-vaccin-anti-covid-19_6059679_3212.html

Blair, Robert A, Robert Marty and Phillip Roessler. "Foreign Aid and Soft Power," Working Paper. *AidData*, August 2019.

Bloomberg Markets and Finance. "China's Belt and Road Initiative: 5 Years Later," February 3, 2019, https://www.youtube.com/watch?v=Z0iMgoFPnDw

Bohoslavsky, Juan Pablo. "A Human Rights Approach to Debt, Structural Adjustment and Corruption in Tunisia: Report of the United Nations Independent Expert on Foreign Debt and Human Rights on His Mission to Tunisia," *Observatoire Tunisien de l'Economie*, Policy Brief no. 4, April 11, 2018, 5–6, https://www.economie-tunisie.org/sites/default/files/20180411-pb-ohchr-bap_0.pdf

Boucetta, Saïd. "Un dirigeant du Parti communiste chinois à Alger-L'immense potentiel d'un partenariat," *L'Expression*, October 12, 2020, http://www.lexpressiondz.com/nationale/l-immense-potentiel-d-un-partenariat-336183

Boukhars, Anouar. "Western Sahara: Beyond Complacency," *FRIDE*, October 4, 2013, https://carnegieendowment.org/2013/10/04/western-sahara-beyond-complacency-pub-53214

Boukhars, Anouar (2019). "Reassessing the Power of Regional Security Providers: The Case of Algeria and Morocco," *Middle Eastern Studies* 55, 2: 242–60, DOI: 10.1080/00263206.2018.1538968

Braut-Hegghammer, Malfrid. 2016. *Unclear Physics: Why Iraq and Libya Failed to Build Nuclear Weapons*. New York: Cornell University Press.

Brautigam, Deborah. 2009. *The Dragon's Gift: The Real Story of China in Africa*. Oxford: Oxford University Press, New York.

Bruce-Lockhart, Anna. "Why Is China Building a New Silk Road?" *World Economic Forum*, June 26, 2016, https://www.weforum.org/agenda/2016/06/why-china-is-building-a-new-silk-road/

Buckley, Chris. "China Defends Syria Veto, Doubts Wests Intentions," *Reuters*, February 6, 2012, https://www.reuters.com/article/us-china-syria-un/china-defends-syria-veto-doubts-wests-intentions-idUSTRE8150NY20120206

Burton, Guy. "What Protests in Algeria and Sudan Mean for China," *The Diplomat*, March 8, 2019, https://thediplomat.com/2019/03/what-protests-in-algeria-and-sudan-mean-for-china/

Business Reporting Desk. "Here's the Real Reason China Isn't Taking Sides in Libya," *Belt & Road News*, January 29, 2020, https://www.beltandroad.news/2020/01/29/heres-the-real-reason-china-isnt-taking-sides-in-libya/

Cafiero, George. "The Geopolitics of China's Libya Foreign Policy," August 4, 2020, https://www.chinamed.it/publications/the-geopolitics-of-chinas-libya-foreign-policy

Calabrese, John. "The Risks and Rewards of China's Deepening Ties with the Middle East," *China Brief* 5, 2 (May 24, 2005), https://jamestown.org/program/the-risks-and-rewards-of-chinas-deepening-ties-with-the-middle-east/

Calabrese, John. "Sino-Algerian Relations: On a Path to Realizing Their Full Potential?" *Middle East Institute*, "All About China" Series Essay, October 31, 2017, https://www.mei.edu/publications/sino-algerian-relations-path-realizing-their-full-potential

Calabrese, John. "Towering Ambitions: Egypt and China Building for the Future," *Middle East Institute*, October 6, 2020, https://www.mei.eu/publications/towering-ambitions-egypt-and-china-building-future

Casey, Nicholas and Clifford Krauss. "It Doesn't Matter if Ecuador Can Afford This Dam. China Still Gets Paid," *New York Times*, December 24, 2018, https://www.nytimes.com/2018/12/24/world/americas/ecuador-china-dam.html

CBS News. "Trump Administration Cuts, Delays $300M in Aid to Egypt," August 22, 2017, https://www.cbsnews.com/news/egypt-united-states-delays-military-economic-aid/

Central Bank of Egypt. "Foreign Direct Investment (FDI) in Egypt by Country," https://www.cbe.org.eg/_layouts/15/WopiFrame.aspx?sourcedoc={554C10B8-7EA4-4514-9670-AF1068A22148}&file=External%20Sector%20Data%20271.xlsx&action=default

Centre for International Trade and Security (CITS). "Export Control's in the People's Republic of China," University of Georgia (February 2005).

Chaziza, Mordechai. "China in the Middle East: Tourism as a Stealth Weapon," *Middle East Quarterly* 26. 4 (Fall 2019), https://www.meforum.org/59293/mordechai-chaziza-china-in-the-middle-east

Chémali, Alain. "Algérie: la Chine annonce la fin du chantier de la plus grande mosquée d'Afrique" [Algeria: China Announces the End of the Construction of the Largest Mosque in Africa], *FranceInfo*, May 4, 2019 https://www.francetvinfo.fr/culture/arts-expos/architecture/algerie-la-chine-annonce-la-fin-du-chantier-de-la-plus-grande-mosquee-d-afrique_3422171.html. The article says that the cost was $2 billion

Chen, John. "Re-orientation: The Chinese Azharites between Umma and Third World, 1938–55," *Comparative Studies of South Asia, Africa and the Middle East* 34, 1 (2014): 24–51.

Chen, Juan. "Strategic Synergy between Egypt 'Vision 2030' and China's 'Belt and Road' Initiative," *Outlines of Global Transformations: Politics, Economics, Law* 11, 5 (2018): 219–35.

China Africa Research Initiative Database. "Chinese Loans to African Governments, Country by Country, 2000–2017." August 25, 2019, http://www.sais-cari.org/data-chinese-loans-to-africa.

China Daily. "Sisi's Attendance of Parade in Beijing Highlights Egypt-China Close Ties," September 2, 2015, http://www.chinadaily.com.cn/world/2015victoryanniv/2015-09/02/content_21774686.htm

China Daily. "Egyptian, Chinese Banks Sign Loan Deals to Enhance Financial Cooperation," September 18, 2017, http://www.chinadaily.com.cn/business/2017-09/18/content_32147872.htm

China Daily. "Egypt, China Join Hands to Build Up Egypt's New Capital," July 10, 2018, https://www.chinadaily.com.cn/a/201807/10/WS5b445cada3103349141e1e00.html

China Daily. "Cultural Exchange Builds a Bridge for Tunisia and China," September 27, 2019, //www.chinadaily.com.cn/a/201909/27/WS5d8da36ea310cf3e3556ddf3.html

"China Focus: Xi Unveils Plan to Make China 'Great Modern Socialist Country' by Mid-21st Century," *Xinhua,* October 18, 2017, http://www.xinhuanet.com//english/2017-10/18/c_136688933.htm

"China Lends $3.3bn to Algeria to Build El Hamdania Port," *EcoFin Agency*, January 19, 2016, https://www.ecofinagency.com/finance/1901-33286-china-lends-3-3bn-to-algeria-to-build-el-hamdania-port

China Med Project. https://www.chinamed.it/chinamed-data/north-africa/libya

China Military Online. "Chinese Naval Ships Visit Algeria," *China Military Online*, January 9, 2018, http://eng.chinamil.com.cn/view/2018-01/09/content_7901306.htm

China Ministry of Foreign Affairs. "China-Algeria Relations," January 18, 2004, http://www.china.org.cn/english/features/phfnt/85069.htm

China Ministry of Foreign Affairs. "China, Algeria Vow to Boost Counter-terrorism Cooperation," July 12, 2016, http://english.www.gov.cn/news/international_exchanges/2016/07/12/content_281475391542866.htm

China Railway Construction Corporation, Vice-president in charge of production, Li Chongyang (interview with the authors), September 2019, Beijing.

"China Sends 2nd Medical Donation to Help Algeria Combat COVID-19," *Market Watch News*, April 15, 2020, https://www.marketwatch.com/press-release/china-sends-2nd-medical-donation-to-help-algeria-combat-covid-19-2020-04-15?mod=mw_more_headlines&tesla=y

"China Sends Medical Aid to Algeria to Help Combat COVID-19," *Xinhua*, March 28, 2020, https://english.sina.cn/news/2020-03-28/detail-iimxxsth2212857.d.html

"China-Algeria Ties: Chinese Language Learning Increasingly Popular in Algeria," https://www.youtube.com/watch?v=SxaExh8RtA4

Chine Magazine. "Beijing se prononce sur la crise politique en Algérie" [Beijing Comments on the Political Crisis in Algeria], March 25, 2019 https://www.chinemagazine.com/beijing-se-prononce-sur-la-crise-politique-en-algerie/

"Chine – Maroc: passer du commerce à l'investissement," *TelQuel*, December 2014, https://telquel.ma/2014/12/02/chine-maroc-passer-du-commerce-linvestissement_1424795

Chinese Diplomat, Interview with the Authors, Cairo, Egypt, January 2019.

Chinese Diplomats, Interviews with the Authors, Cairo, Egypt, and Rabat, Morocco, January 2019

Chinese Diplomats, Interviews with the Authors, Rabat, Morocco, and Cairo, Egypt, January 2019.

Chinese Foreign Ministry. "Tunisia," China.org.cn, October 10, 2006, http://sars.china.com.cn/english/features/focac/183413.htm

Commandant Azzedine. "Aux Origines de l'amitié algéro-chinoise-Des fellagas à Pékin," *Le soir d'Algérie*, February 27, 2019, https://www.lesoirdalgerie.com/articles/2017/02/27/article.php?sid=209968&cid=41

"Contribution de l'ambassadeur de la république de chine à L'Expression-L'Algérie remportera la guerre du Covid-19" [Contribution of the Ambassador of the Republic of China to L'Expression-Algeria Will Win the Covid War-19], *L'Expression*, April 26, 2020, http://lexpressiondz.com/nationale/l-algerie-remportera-la-guerre-du-covid–19–329969

Copper, John. "China's Foreign Aid Program: An Analysis of an Instrument of Peking's Foreign Policy." PhD Dissertation in Political Science, University of South Carolina, International Law and Relations, 1975.

"Coronavirus: la Chine adresse ses remerciements à l'Algérie pour les aides médicales" [Coronavirus: China Thanks Algeria for Medical Assistance], *APS*, February 2, 2020, http://www.aps.dz/algerie/100995-coronavirus-la-chine-adresse-ses-remerciements-a-l-algerie-pour-les-aides-medicales-urgentes-fournies

"Countries of the Belt and Road Initiative (BRI)," *Green Belt and Road Initiative Center*, https://green-bri.org/countries-of-the-belt-and-road-initiative-bri

"Creating Markets in Morocco," *World Bank Group*, October 2019, https://www.ifc.org/wps/wcm/connect/d0c0f18c-26b7-4861-b4c5-14896aaba7f1/201910-CPSD-Morocco-EN.pdf?MOD=AJPERES&CVID=m-LGA3X

Crétois, Jules. "À l'offensive, le Maroc a séduit un nombre croissant de visiteurs internationaux en 2019," *Jeune Afrique*, February 5, 2020, https://www.jeuneafrique.com/892177/economie/a-loffensive-le-maroc-a-seduit-un-nombre-croissant-de-visiteurs-internationaux-en-2019/

Crétois, Jules, et Jihâd Gillon. "Maghreb: comment la Russie est devenue un partenaire incontournable," *Jeune Afrique*, Febraury 5, 2019, https://www.jeuneafrique.com/mag/728393/politique/maghreb-comment-la-russie-est-devenue-un-partenaire-incontournable/

CSCEC. "China State Construction Signs a 9.6 Billion US Dollar EPC Contract with Egypt," September 2, 2018, https://english.cscec.com/CompanyNews/CorporateNews/201811/2892383.html

CSCEC Algérie, http://www.cscec.dz/fr/about/brief.html

Cumming-Bruce, Nick. "More Than 35 Countries Defend China over Mass Detention of Uighur Muslims in UN Letter," *The Independent*, July 13, 2019, https://www.independent.co.uk/news/world/asia/china-mass-detentions-uighur-muslims-un-letter-human-rights-a9003281.html

Curran, Enda. "These Could Be the World's Biggest Economies by 2030," *Bloomberg*, January 8, 2019, https://www.bloomberg.com/news/articles/2019-01-08/world-s-biggest-economies-seen-dominated-by-asian-ems-by-2030

Dahir, Abdi Latif. "Africa's Largest Mosque Has Been Completed with Thanks to China," *Quartz Africa*, April 28, 2019, https://qz.com/africa/1606739/china-completes-africas-largest-mosque-in-algeria/

"Dance of the Lions and Dragons: How Are Africa and China Engaging, and How Will the Partnership Evolve?" *Mckinsey Report*, June 2017, https://www.mckinsey.com/~/media/McKinsey/Featured%20Insights/Middle%20East%20and%20Africa/The%20closest%20look%20yet%20at%20Chinese%20economic%20engagement%20in%20Africa/Dance-of-the-lions-and-dragons.ashx

Darbouche, Hakim and Yahia H. Zoubir. "The Algerian Crisis in European and US Foreign Policies: A Hindsight Analysis," *Journal of North African Studies* 14, 1 (2009): 33–55.

Davis, Leslye, A.J. Chavar, Abe Sater and David Frank. "Exclusive Interview: Obama on the World," *New York Times*, August 9, 2014, https://www.nytimes.

com/video/opinion/100000003048414/obama-on-the-world.html?playlist Id=1194811622299

De Girancourt, François Jurd. "Maroc – Chine: où en est-on dans le partenariat ?" *Tel Quel*, May 22, 2019, https://telquel.ma/2019/05/22/maroc-chine-ou-en-est-on-dans-le-partenariat_1639269/?utm_source=tq&utm_medium=normal_post

Dessouki, Ali Hillal. "The Primacy of Economics: The Foreign Policy of Egypt," in *The Foreign Policies of Arab States: The Challenge of Change*. 2nd Edition, edited by Bahgat Korany and Ali Hillal Dessouki. Boulder, CO: Westview Press, 1991, 156–85.

Diab, Mahmoud Saad. "'Belt and Road' Puts Egypt at Forefront of China's New Renewable Energy Projects," *Ahram Online*, March 23, 2019, http://english.ahram.org.eg/NewsContent/1/64/328705/Egypt/Politics-/Belt-and-Road-puts-Egypt-at-forefront-of-Chinas-ne.aspx

Diawara, Barassou and Kobena Hanson. "What Does the Evidence Say About Contemporary China-Africa Relations," in *Innovating South-South Cooperation: Policies, Challenges, and Prospects*, edited by Hany Besada, Evren Tok and Leah Polonenko. Ottawa: University of Ottawa Press, 2019, 217–42.

Dorsey, James. "Fall of Gaddafi: Policy Challenge for China and Russia," *RSIS Commentaries*, September 5, 2011, https://dr.ntu.edu.sg/bitstream/10356/94773/1/RSIS1262011.pdf

Dreher, Axel, Andreas Fuchs, Bradley Parks, Austin M. Strange and Michael J. Tierney. "Aid, China, and Growth: Evidence from a New Global Development Finance Dataset," Working Paper. *AidData*, October 2017, https://www.ssrn.com/abstract=3051044

Egypt Independent. "Chinese Fleet Arrives in Egypt for 5-Day Visit," September 3, 2015, https://ww.egyptindependent.com/chinese-fleet-arrives-egypt-5-day-visit/

Egypt Oil and Gas Newspaper. "The Far East and Near East Are Meeting Somewhere in the Middle: An In-Depth Look at the Recent Sino-Egyptian Rig Agreement," December 29, 2014, https://egyptoil-gas.com/features/the-far-east-and-near-east-are-meeting-somewhere-in-the-middle-an-in-depth-look-at-the-recent-sino-egyptian-rig-agreement/11423/

Egypt Today. "New Agreement to Develop Sokhna Port Sees China Cooperation," May 12, 2017, https://www.egypttoday.com/Article/3/5021/New-agreement-to-develop-Sokhna-Port-sees-China-cooperation

Egypt Today. "Egypt, China to Establish Electric Train Project Worth $1.2B," July 24, 2017, https://www.egypttoday.com/Article/3/13432/Egypt-China-to-establishelectric-train-project-worth-1-2B

Egypt Today. "Trade Exchange Bet. Egypt, China Hits $13.8B in 2018," June 17, 2019, https://www.egypttoday.com/Article/3/71681/Trade-exchange-bet-Egypt-China-hits-13-8B-in–2018

Egypt Today. "Egypt Sends Medical Supplies to China to Help Face Coronavirus Spread," January 31, 2020, https://www.egypttoday.com/Article/1/81158/Egypt-sends-medical-supplies-to-China-to-help-face-coronavirus.

Egypt Today. "3rd Chinese Medical Aid to Egypt Weighing 30 Tons Arrives amid COVID-19 Crisis," May 16, 2020, https://www.egypttoday.com/Article/1/86799/3rd-Chinese-medical-aid-to-Egypt-weighing-30-tons-arrives

Egypt Today. "Trade Exchange Bet. Egypt, China Reaches $5.2B in 7 Months," August 26, 2020. https://www.egypttoday.com/Article/3/91279/Trade-exchange-bet-Egypt-China-reaches-5-2B-in–7

Ehteshami, Anoushiravan and Niv Horesh. 2019. *How China's Rise Is Changing the Middle East*. Abingdon and New York: Routledge.

Eisenmann, Joshua. 2007. *China and the Developing World: Beijing's Strategy for the Twenty First Century*. New York: M.E Sharpe.

Ekman, Alice. "China's Regional Forum Diplomacy," European Union Institute for Security Studies (EUISS), November 2016, 1, https://www.iss.europa.eu/sites/default/files/EUISSFiles/Alert_44_China_diplomacy.pdf

Ekman, Alice. "China and the Mediterranean: An Emerging Presence," *IFRI*, https://www.ifri.org/en/publications/notes-de-lifri/china-mediterranean-emerging-presence

El Fass, Aziza. "Maroc-France L'approche triangulaire prend forme," *L'Economiste*, May 19, 2015, https://www.leconomiste.com/article/971599-maroc-francel-approche-triangulaire-prend-forme

El Yaakoubi, Aziz. "Morocco Suspends Contacts with EU Delegation over Trade Row," *Reuters*, January 28, 2016, https://www.reuters.com/article/uk-morocco-eu-westernsahara/morocco-suspends-contacts-with-eu-delegation-over-trade-row-idUKKCN0V6294.

Eljechtimi, Ahmed. "China's Citic Dicastal to Produce Aluminum Car Wheels in Morocco," *Reuters*, July 26, 2018, https://www.reuters.com/article/us-citicdicastal-morocco/chinas-citic-dicastal-to-produce-aluminum-car-wheels-in-morocco-idUSKBN1KG33R

El-Sayed Al-Naggar, Ahmed. "Developing Egyptian-Chinese Relations," *Ahram Online*, January 24, 2016, http://english.ahram.org.eg/NewsContentP/4/185697/Opinion/developing-egyptianchinese-relations.aspx

El-Sayed Al-Naggar, Ahmed. "Egypt and China: The Potential for Stronger Economic Ties," *Ahram Online*, October 21, 2016, http://english.ahram.org.eg/

NewsContentP/4/246289/Opinion/Egypt-and-China-The-potential-for-stronger-economi.aspx

elWardany, Salma and Laura Hurst. "PetroChina Is Said to Agree to 2018 Deal to Lift Libya Oil," *Bloomberg*, March 1, 2018, https://www.bloomberg.com/news/articles/2018-03-01/libya-crude-output-is-said-to-be-stable-despite-key-field-s-halt

Embassy of the PRC in Libya. "The Economic Cooperation between China and Libya," 2012, http://ly.china-embassy.org/eng/jmgx/t297043.htm

Embassy of the PRC in the Democratic People's Republic of Algeria "La Chine et l'Algérie établissent les relations de Partenariat Stratégique Global" [China and Algeria Establish Global Strategic Partnership Relations], February 25, 2014, http://dz.china-embassy.org/fra/xw/t1132178.htm

Embassy of PRC in Croatia. "Xi Jinping Meets with Prime Minister Abdelmalek Sellal of Algeria," April 29, 2015, http://hr.china-embassy.org/eng/gnxw/t1260832.htm

Energy Egypt. "Chinese Consortium Wins Contract for Hamrawein Coal-Fired Plant," June 26, 2018, https://energyegypt.net/chinese-consortium-wins-contract-for-egypts-hamrawein-coal-fired-power-plant/

Enterprise. "China, Egypt Sign USD 571 mn in Contracts for Electric Train Project," October 14, 2019. https://enterprise.press/stories/2019/10/14/china-egypt-sign-usd-571-mn-in-contracts-for-electric-train-project/

Enterprise. "Egypt Is Africa's Number One Investment Destination, Says RMB Report," September 19, 2019. https://enterprise.press/stories/2019/09/19/egypt-is-africas-number-one-investment-destination-says-rmb-report/

Enterprise. "Egyptian-Chinese Consortium Wins Ain Sokhna–Alamein High-Speed Rail Contract," September 6, 2020, https://enterprise.press/stories/2020/09/06/egyptian-chinese-consortium-wins-ain-sokhna-alamein-high-speed-rail-contract–21245/

"Entretien téléphonique entre le Premier ministre et son homologue chinois" [Telephone Conversation between the Prime Minister and His Chinese Counterpart], *APS*, March 31, 2020, http://www.aps.dz/algerie/103576-entretientelephonique-entre-le-premier-ministre-et-son-homologue-chinois

Erian, Stephanie. "China at the Libyan Endgame," *Policy magazine* 28, 1 (Autumn 2012): 49.

Escobar, Pepe. "China's Interests in Gaddafi," *Aljazeera*, April 14, 2011, https://www.aljazeera.com/indepth/opinion/2011/04/201141195046788263.html

Esper, Mark. "Secretary Esper's Remarks at the North Africa American Cemetery in Carthage," Tunisia, September 30, 2020, https://www.defense.gov/Newsroom/

Transcripts/Transcript/Article/2367437/secretary-espers-remarks-at-the-north-africa-american-cemetery-in-carthage-tuni/

Esteban, Mario. "Sri Lanka and Great-Power Competition in the Indo-Pacific: A Belt and Road Failure?" *Elcano Royal Institute*, November 28, 2018, http://www.realinstitutoelcano.org/wps/wcm/connect/6f0582c6-24d9-414a-b51e-7f63fa6e2b5b/ARI129-2018-Esteban-Sri-Lanka-great-power-competition-Indo-Pacific-Belt-and-Road-failure.pdf?MOD=AJPERES&CACHEID=6f0582c6-24d9-414a-b51e-7f63fa6e2b5b

EU Neighbors South. "European Parliament Plenary Debate on the Situation of Freedoms in Algeria," November 29, 2019, https://www.euneighbours.eu/en/south/stay-informed/news/european-parliament-plenary-debate-situation-freedoms-algeria

Export. Gov. "Algeria—Oil and Gas—Hydrocarbons," January 31, 2019, https://www.export.gov/article?id=Algeria-Oil-and-Gas-Hydrocarbons

Fabiani, Riccardo. "Morocco's Difficult Path to ECOWAS Membership," *Carnegie Endowment for International Peace, Sada Journal*, March 28, 2018, https://carnegieendowment.org/sada/75926

Farid, Farid. "Nightmare as Egypt Aided China to Detain Uighurs," *AFP*, August 18, 2019. https://news.yahoo.com/nightmare-egypt-aided-china-detain-uighurs-024625386.html

Fayed, Hassan. "Egypt Should Teach Mandarin at School and Build a Chinese Temple," *Egyptian Streets*, January 18, 2016, https://egyptianstreets.com/2016/01/18/egypt-should-teach-mandarin-at-school-and-build-a-chinese-temple/

Feng, Emily. "China's Global Construction Boom Puts Spotlight on Questionable Labor Practices," *National Public Radio*, March 30, 2019, https://www.npr.org/2019/03/30/707949897/chinas-global-construction-boom-puts-spotlight-on-questionable-labor-practices

Fernholz, Tim. "Eight Countries in Danger of Falling into China's 'Debt Trap'," *Quartz*, March 7, 2018, https://qz.com/1223768/china-debt-trap-these-eight-countries-are-in-danger-of-debt-overloads-from-chinas-belt-and-road-plans/

Fleurant, Aude, Wezeman, Pieter D., Wezeman, Simon T. and Nan Tian (2017). "Tendances des transferts internationaux d'armements 2016," in *Groupe de Recherche et d'information sur la Paix et La Sécurité (GRIP)*, Dépenses militaires, production et transferts d'armes – Compendium 2017. 34, https://www.grip.org/sites/grip.org/files/RAPPORTS/2017/Rapport_2017-7.pdf

Fouly, Mahmoud. "Suez Canal University Model of Fruitful Educational Cooperation between Egypt, China: University Chief," *Xinhua*, September 21, 2018, http://www.xinhuanet.com/english/2018-09/21/c_137484410.htm

Fraihat, Ibrahim and Andrew Leber. "China and the Middle East after the Arab Spring: From Status-Quo Observing to Proactive Engagement," *Asian Journal of Middle Eastern and Islamic Studies* 13, 1 (January 2, 2019): 1–17. DOI: https://doi.org/10.1080/25765949.2019.1586177

Fraser, Christian. "China's Chequebook Draws African Nations," *BBC*, November 9, 2009, http://news.bbc.co.uk/2/hi/8350228.stm

Frédéric, Maury and Nadia Rabbaa. "Le Maroc, un pont d'or pour la Chine?" *Jeune Afrique*, December 2015, https://www.jeuneafrique.com/mag/286294/economie/maroc-pont-dor-chine/

Friedman, Jeremy. 2015. *Shadow Cold War: The Sino-Soviet Competition for the Third World*. Chapel Hill: University of North Carolina Press.

Frost, Laurence and Gilles Guillaume. "Peugeot to Build Morocco Plant to Cut Costs, Lift Emerging-Market Sales," June 19, 2015, https://www.reuters.com/article/peugeot-morocco-plant/peugeot-to-build-morocco-plant-to-cut-costs-lift-emerging-market-sales-idUSL5N0Z52YV20150619

Fulton, Jonathan. "Friends with Benefits: China's Partnership Diplomacy in the Gulf," 2019, *POMEPS Studies 34: Shifting Global Politics and the Middle East*, 34, https://www.academia.edu/38580068/Friends_with_Benefits_Chinas_Partnership_Diplomacy_in_the_Gulf

Gadallah, Yasser. "An Analysis of the Evolution of Sino-Egyptian Economic Relations," in *Toward Well-Oiled Relations? China's Presence in the Middle East following the Arab Spring*, edited by Niv Horesh. London: Palgrave Macmillan, 2016, 94–114.

Galal, Shaimaa. "The Alliance of the Seven: How Egypt Handles the File of Military Production," *Al-Dostour*, March 6, 2018, https://www.dostor.org/2081187

Gallucci, Maria. "Terror Attack on Algerian Gas Plant Raising Security Fears for North Africa's Oil and Gas Infrastructure," *International Business Times*, March 22, 2016, https://www.ibtimes.com/terror-attack-algerian-gas-plant-raising-security-fears-north-africas-oil-gas–2341217

Gamal, Mahmoud. "Egypt: Policies of Military Armament, 2018," *Egyptian Institute for Studies*, April 5, 2019, https://eipss-eg.org/-العسكري-التسليح-سياسات-مصر/2018

Ghanem, Dalia and Lina Benabdallah. "The China Syndrome," *Carnegie Middle East Center, Diwan*, November 18, 2016, https://carnegie-mec.org/diwan/66145

Ghanmi, Lamine. "Algeria Draws Europe's Ire by Cutting Imports, Boosting Trade with China," *The Arab Weekly*, April 22, 2018, https://thearabweekly.com/algeria-draws-europes-ire-cutting-imports-boosting-trade-china

Global Times. "West Should Feel Guilty for Resumed Fighting in Libya," April 8, 2019, https://www.globaltimes.cn/content/1145108.shtml

Government of the People's Republic of China. "China's Arab Policy Paper," *Embassy of the People's Republic of China in the Kingdom of Saudi Arabia*, January 2016, http://sa.china-embassy.org/eng/xwdt/t1331633.htm

Greer, Tanner. "One Belt, One Road, One Big Mistake," *Foreign Policy*, December 6, 2018, https://foreignpolicy.com/2018/12/06/bri-china-belt-road-initiative-blunder/

Grimmett, Richard F. 2003. *Conventional Arms Transfers to Developing Countries 1994–2001.* Hauppage, NY: Novinka Books, 38, cited in, John Calabrese, "Sino-Algerian Relations: On a Path to Realizing Their Full Potential?" *Middle East Institute*, October 31, 2017, https://www.mei.edu/publications/sino-algerian-relations-path-realizing-their-full-potential

Guguen, C. "Enquete sur l'influence r eelle du soft-power de Mohammed VI en Afrique," *Le Desk* (2016) https://mobile.ledesk.ma/grandangle/les-dessous-de-la-nouvelle-politique-africaine-de-mohammed-vi/

Haddad-Fonda, Kyle. "The Domestic Significance of China's Policy toward Egypt, 1955–1957," *The Chinese Historical Review* 21, 1 (May 2014): 45–64.

Haddad-Fonda, Kyle. "An Illusory Alliance: Revolutionary Legitimacy and Sino-Algerian Relations, 1958–1962," *The Journal of North African Studies* 19, 3 (2014): 338–57.

Haddad-Fonda, Kyle. "The Rhetoric of 'Civilization' in Chinese-Egyptian Relations," *Middle East Institute*, August 1, 2017, https://www.mei.edu/publications/rhetoric-civilization-chinese-egyptian-relations.

Hafid, Tarek. "Algérie-Phosphate: Black-out sur un projet -presque- irréalisable," *Maghreb Émergent*, February 13, 2019, https://www.maghrebemergent.info/algerie-phosphate-black-out-sur-un-projet-presque-irrealisable/

Hafti, Youssef. "Moroccan-Chinese Relationship: The Interaction of 'Going East,'" in *The New Frontier of the Middle East Politics and Economy*, edited by Degang Sun and Zhongmin Liu. Beijing: World Affairs Press, 2017, 211–44.

Halime, Farah. "Chinese Firms Brave Uncertainty in Egypt to Gain a Foothold in Middle East," *New York Times*, August 29, 2012, https://www.nytimes.com/2012/08/30/world/middleeast/chinese-firms-brave-uncertainty-in-egypt.html

Halper, Stephan. 2009. *The Beijing Consensus. Legitimizing Authoritarianism in Our Time*. New York: Basic Books, 336.

Hammond, Joseph. "Morocco Wants to Build a New City from Scratch—With China's Help," *Quartz Africa*, November 22, 2016, https://qz.com/africa/841803/morocco-wants-to-build-a-new-city-from-scratch-with-chinas-help/

Hammond, Joseph. "Morocco: China's Gateway to Africa?" *The Diplomat*, March 1, 2017, https://thediplomat.com/2017/03/morocco-chinas-gateway-to-africa/

Harbi, Mohammed. 1980. *Les Archives de la Révolution Algérienne*. Paris: Editions Jeune Afrique, 521. See, also, Jeffrey James Byrne, 2016. *Mecca of Revolution. Algeria, Decolonization, and the Third World Order*. Oxford: Oxford University Press.

Hamshi, Mohamed. "The Political Economy of Arab-Chinese Relations: Challenges and Strategic Opportunities," *Al-Mustaqbal Al-Arabi* 2017: 111–34.

Harris, Lillian Craig. "China's Relations with the PLO," *Journal of Palestine Studies* 7, 1 (1977): 123–54.

Harry Lai, Hongyi. "China's Oil Diplomacy: Is It a Global Security Threat?" *Third World Quarterly*, 28, 3 (2007): 519–37.

Hassanein, Haisam. "Arab States Give China a Pass on Uyghur Crackdown," *Policy Watch* 3169 (The Washington Institute for Near East Policy), August 26, 2019, https://www.washingtoninstitute.org/policy-analysis/view/arab-states-give-china-a-pass-on-uyghur-crackdown

Holland, Christopher. "Chinese Attitudes to International Law: China, the Security Council, Sovereignty, and Intervention," *NYU Journal of International Law and Politics Online Forum*, July 2012.

Hong'e, Mo. "Cultural Exchange Builds a Bridge for Tunisia and China," *China Daily*, September 27, 2019, http://www.ecns.cn/news/2019-09-27/detail-ifzpknpx2078795.shtml

Hook, Leslie. "China's Future in Africa, after Libya," *Financial Times*, March 4, 2011, http://blogs.ft.com/beyond-brics/2011/03/04/chinas-future-in-africa-after-libya/

Hook, Leslie and Geoff Dyer. "Chinese Oil Interests Attacked in Libya," *Financial Times*, February 24, 2011, https://www.ft.com/content/eef58d52-3fe2-11e0-811f-00144feabdc0

"How Dominant Is China in the Global Arms Trade?" *Center for Strategic and International Studies, China Power Project*, April 26, 2018. March 6, 2019, https://chinapower.csis.org/china-global-arms-trade/

"Huawei to Set up Regional Logistics Centre in Tanger Med Port," *PortSEurope*, September 7, 2018, https://www.portseurope.com/huawei-to-set-up-regional-logistics-centre-in-tanger-med-port/

Hurley, John, Scott Morris and Gailyn Portelance. "Examining the Debt Implications of the Belt and Road Initiative from a Policy Perspective," *Center for Global Development*, Policy Paper 121, March 2018, https://www.cgdev.org/sites/default/files/examining-debt-implications-belt-and-road-initiative-policy-perspective.pdf

Ibeh, Joseph. "Alcomsat-1 Communications Satellite Clocks Two Years in Orbit," *Space in Africa*, December 11, 2019, https://africanews.space/alcomsat-1-communications-satellite-clocks-two-years-in-orbit/

Idir, Ali. "Grand port du centre: le projet fortement compromise," *Le Soir d'Algérie*, February 23, 2020, https://www.tsa-algerie.com/grand-port-du-centre-le-projet-fortement-compromis/

International Monetary Fund. "World Economic Outlook Database, October 2019," 2019, https://tinyurl.com/y6xvstrs

Iraqi, Fahd. "Li Li: Jamais les relations entre la Chine et le Maroc n'ont été aussi bonnes," *Jenue Afrique*, February 7, 2019, https://www.jeuneafrique.com/mag/728406/politique/li-li-jamais-les-relations-de-la-chine-avec-le-maroc-nont-ete-aussi-bonnes/

Ismain. "Grande Mosquee d'Alger: Le coût de la construction révélé" [Great Mosque of Algiers: Construction Cost Revealed], *Réflexion*, August 4, 2019 https://www.reflexiondz.net/GRANDE-MOSQUEE-D-ALGER-Le-cout-de-la-construction-revele_a56987.html

Ismain. "Etudiants Algeriens á l'etranger: La Chine propose une bourse de 400 Euros par mois" [Algerian Students Abroad: China Offers a Scholarship of 400 Euros Per Month], *ReflexionDZ*, December 22, 2019, https://www.reflexiondz.net/ETUDIANTS-ALGERIENS-A-L-ETRANGER-La-Chine-propose-une-bourse-de-400-euros-par-mois_a59556.html

Jacobs, Andrew. "China Urges Quick End to Airstrikes in Libya," March 22, 2011, https://www.nytimes.com/2011/03/23/world/asia/23beiijing.html

Jee Chua, Shan. "Understanding China's Strategic Partnership and Balance Diplomacy: The Case of Sino-Iran Relations," *A Thesis Submitted to Peking University in Partial Fulfillment of the Requirements of the PKU-LSE Double Master's Degree Program in International Affairs, School of International Studies Peking University*, June 2016 (personal documents).

Jenkins, S. "Casablanca Hopes to Build the Gateway to Markets Across Africa," *Financial Times* (2015). https://www.ft.com/content/060570be-6e98-11e5-8171-ba1968cf791a

Jin, Wang. "Selective Engagement: China's Middle East Policy after the Arab Spring," *Strategic Assessment* 19, 2 (July 2016): 105–17.

June Teufel Dreyer. "China's Vulnerability to Minority Separatism," *Asian Affairs: An American Review* 32, 2 (Summer 2005): 69–85, https://www.jstor.org/stable/30172869

Kab, Faiza. "Algerian-Chinese Relations through the Historic Visit of the Algerian Prime Minister" (in Arabic)," *Arab Information Center*, 2015\PRS\4652, April 27, 2015, http://www.arabsino.com/articles/15-04-27/12348.htm

Kadiri, Ghalia. "Satellite marocain en orbite: un lancement secret qui inquiète" [Moroccan Satellite in Orbit: A Secret Launch that Causes Concern], *Le Monde*,

November 19, 2017, https://www.lemonde.fr/afrique/article/2017/11/19/satellite-marocain-en-orbite-un-lancement-secret-qui-inquiete_5217299_3212.html

Kamal, Nazir. "China's Arms Export Policy and Responses to Multilateral Restraints," *Contemporary Southeast Asia* 14, 2 (September 1992): 122–3.

Karam, Souhail. "Morocco Chief Planner Warns on State Companies' Debt Spree," *Bloomberg*, July 26, 2018, https://www.bloomberg.com/news/articles/2018-07-26/morocco-chief-planner-warns-on-state-companies-borrowing-spree

Kavalski, Emilian. *China and the Global Politics of Regionalization*. Routledge, 2016. DOI: https://doi.org/10.4324/9781315571638

Kemboi, Linus. "Morocco Begins Construction of New Tech City in Tangier," *Construction Review Online*, July 9, 2019, https://constructionreviewonline.com/2019/07/morocco-begins-construction-of-new-tech-city-in-tangier/

Khalfa, Slimane. "En Algérie, les Chinois raflent tous les contrat" [In Algeria, the Chinese Win All the Contracts], *Nouvel Observateur* (Paris), November 16, 2016, https://www.nouvelobs.com/rue89/rue89-chine/20111031.RUE5343/en-algerie-les-chinois-raflent-tous-les-contrats.html

Khalili, Joseph. "Communist China and the United Arab Republic," *Asian Survey* 10, 4 (April 1970): 308–19.

Kharief, Akram. "Répression des Ouïghours: neuf pays arabes soutiennent la Chine" [Repression of the Uyghurs: Nine Arab Countries Support China], *Middle East Eye*, July 14, 2019, https://www.middleeasteye.net/fr/en-bref/repression-des-ouighours-neuf-pays-arabes-soutiennent-la-chine

Khechib, Djallel. "One Belt, Different Aims: Beyond China's Increasing Leverage in the Grand Maghreb," *IHH Humanitarian and Social Research Center*, October 4, 2018, http://insamer.com/en/one-belt-different-aims-beyond-chinas-increasing-leverage-in-the-grand-maghreb_1665.html

Kiganda, Antony. "Algeria Approves US $3.3 Billion El Hamdania Port Construction," Construction Review Online, March 10, 2017, https://constructionreviewonline.com/2017/03/algeria-approves-us-3-3-billion-el-hamdania-port-construction/

Kington, Tom. "UAE Allegedly Using Chinese Drones for Deadly Airstrikes in Libya," *DefenseNews*, May 2, 2019, https://www.defensenews.com/unmanned/2019/05/02/uae-allegedly-using-chinese-drones-for-deadly-airstrikes-in-libya/

Kozlowski, Nina. "Vaccins contre le Covid-19: le Maroc peut-il devenir un hub pour l'Afrique?" *Jenue Afrique*, December 4, 2020, https://www.jeuneafrique.com/1086055/societe/vaccins-contre-le-covid-19-le-maroc-peut-il-devenir-un-hub-pour-lafrique/

"L'Afrique risque de devenir une colonie chinoise' selon le président du Parlement européen," *Jeune Afrique*, March 29, 2017, https://www.jeuneafrique.com/422521/politique/lafrique-se-trouve-situation-dramatique-selon-president-parlement-europeen/

Lamara, Randa. "Algérie Telecom et ZTE, signent une convention afin d'assurer le très haut débit Internet" [Algérie Telecom and ZTE Sign an Agreement to Ensure Very High-Speed Internet Access], *Algérie-Eco*, October 4, 2017, https://www.algerieeco.com/2017/10/04/algerie-telecom-zte-signent-convention-afin-dassurer-treshaut-debit-internet/

"L'Ambassadeur de Chine: L'Algérie, 5e grand partenaire commercial africain de la Chine," *El Moudjahid*, February 24, 2020, http://www.elmoudjahid.com/fr/actualites/138308

Lamlili, Nadia. "Maroc–Russie: Mohammed VI au pays des tsars," *Jenue Afrique*, March 16, 2016, https://www.jeuneafrique.com/309935/politique/maroc-russie-mohammed-vi-pays-tsars/

Larkin, Bruce D. "China and Africa 1949–1970: The Foreign Policy of the People's Republic of China. No. 5," University of California Press, 1973.

Le Bec, Christophe. "Le groupe OCP revoit sa stratégie en Afrique subsaharienne," *Jeune Afrique*, March 14, 2016, https://www.jeuneafrique.com/mag/307568/economie/groupe-ocp-revoit-strategie-afrique-subsaharienne/

Le Belzic, Sébastien. "Le Maroc fait les yeux doux à la Chine," *Le Monde*, May 16, 2016, https://www.lemonde.fr/afrique/article/2016/05/16/le-maroc-fait-les-yeux-doux-a-la-chine_4920195_3212.html

Le Belzic, Sébastien. "Le Maroc et les nouvelles routes de la soie: la troisième voie," *Le Monde*, December 4, 2017, https://www.lemonde.fr/afrique/article/2017/12/04/le-maroc-et-les-nouvelles-routes-de-la-soie-la-troisieme-voie_5224379_3212.html

Le Belzic, Sébastien. "En Algérie, la Chine n'investit pas beaucoup, mais elle compte énormément," *Le Monde*, March 18, 2019, https://www.lemonde.fr/afrique/article/2019/03/18/en-algerie-la-chine-n-investit-pas-beaucoup-mais-elle-compte-enormement_5437927_3212.html

"Le Chinois FAW assemblera ses autos en Algérie," *Challenges*, November 12, 2013, https://www.challenges.fr/automobile/actu-auto/le-chinois-faw-assemblera-ses-autos-en-algerie_180627

"Le Maroc: Route de la Soie martime," https://fr.hibapress.com/news-10158.html

Lei, Zhao. "China Delivers Warship to Algeria," *China Daily*, July 20, 2016, http://www.chinadaily.com.cn/world/2016-07/20/content_26155715.htm

Leïla, Sefta. "S.E.M. LI Lianhe Ambassadeur de Chine en Algérie à propos des relations bilatérales: 'Inégalé': le développement de 70 années, 'Exemplaire': … " *Le

Maghreb-Le Quotidien de l'économie, October 1, 2019, https://www.lemaghrebdz.com/?page=detail_actualite&rubrique=Nation&id=95395

Letrot, Janie, Hadj Hamou and Eric Bonnel. "Le maroc et les nouvelles routes de la soie: un tournant Historique," *CNNNEF*, February 6, 2020, https://maroc.cnccef.org/wp-content/uploads/sites/108/2020/02/Lettre-Chine-hors-les-Murs-Maroc-et-NRS-janvier-20.pdf

Lewis, Aidan and Mohamed Abdellah. "Egypt's New Desert Capital Faces Delays as It Battles for Funds," *Reuters*, May 13, 2019, https://www.reuters.com/article/us-egypt-new-capital/egypts-new-desert-capital-faces-delays-as-it-battles-for-funds-idUSKCN1SJ10I.

"Libya's Oil Exports to China More Than Double in 2018 – NOC," *Reuters*, November 30, 2018, https://www.reuters.com/article/libya-china-oil/libyas-oil-exports-to-china-more-than-double-in-2018-noc-idUSL8N1Y46TN

"Light at End of Tunnel for Trains 'Made in Morocco,'" *The North Africa Post*, September 24, 2017, http://northafricapost.com/19970-light-end-tunnel-trains-made-morocco.html

Lihan, Zhu. *Deputy Director of the Bureau of West Asia and North Africa, International Department of the Central Committee*, Communist Party of China (interview with the Authors, September 2019), Beijing, China.

Liste, Janvier, Jacob Kolster and Nono Matondo-Fundani. "Chinese Investments and Employment Creation in Algeria and Egypt," *African Development Bank*, 2012, https://ecdpm.org/wp-content/uploads/2013/10/Chinese-Investments-Employment-Creation-Algeria-Egypt-2012.pdf

Liu, Zhongmin. "On Political Unrest in the Middle East and China's Diplomacy," *Journal of Middle Eastern and Islamic Studies (in Asia)* 6, 1 (March 1, 2012): 1–18. DOI: https://doi.org/10.1080/19370679.2012.12023195

Lons, Camille, Jonathan Fulton, Degang Sun and Naser Al-Tamimi. "China's Great Game in the Middle East," Policy Brief. *European Council on Foreign Relations*, October 2019.

Magdy, Mirette. "China's $20 Billion New Egypt Capital Project Talks Fall Through," *Bloomberg*, December 16, 2018, https://www.bloomberg.com/news/articles/2018-12-16/china-s-20-billion-new-egypt-capital-project-talks-fallthrough

Magdy, Mirette "Emaar's Talks with Egypt over New Capital City Project Stall," *Bloomberg*, December 30, 2018, https://www.bloomberg.com/news/articles/2018-12-30/emaar-s-talks-with-egypt-over-new-capital-city-project-stall

Mansour, Imad. "A GCC-China Security 'Strategic Partnership': Its Potential and Contours," in *The Arab States of the Gulf and BRICS: New Strategic Partnerships in Politics and Economics* (Frankfurt: Gerlach Press, 2016).

Mansour, Muhammad. "Egypt Set to Mass Produce China-Developed COVID-19 Vaccine," *Chinafrica*, September 3, 2020, http://www.chinafrica.cn/Homepage/202009/t20200904_800219713.html

Marefa. "Chinese-Egyptian Relations," (https://www.marefa.org/العلاقات_الصينية_المصرية/).

"Maroc-Chine. De la culture pour faire du business," *LesEchos.ma*, January 17, 2020, https://leseco.ma/maroc-chine-de-la-culture-pour-faire-du-business/

"Maroc-Chine: la CGEM se positionne sur la route de la soie," *Challenge*, March 27, 2018, https://www.challenge.ma/maroc-chine-la-cgem-se-positionne-sur-la-route-de-la-soie–94741/

"Maroc-France: Ces nouvelles pistes de partenariat," https://leconomiste.com/article/950141-maroc-france-ces-nouvelles-pistes-de-partenariat

Marwane, Ahmed. "Fighting Corruption in Algeria: Turning Words into Action," The Washington Institute, *Fikra Forum*, December 12, 2018, https://www.washingtoninstitute.org/fikraforum/view/fighting-corruption-in-algeria-turning-words-into-action

Matambo, Emmanuel. "Sino-Egyptian Industrial and Infrastructure Cooperation: Determinants and Outcomes," *UJ Centre for Africa-China Studies*, May 2019, http://confucius-institute.joburg/wp-content/uploads/2019/06/Belt-Road-Policy-Brief-No-1-desktop.pdf

Maury, Frédéric. "Le 1er sommet sino-africain des entrepreneurs s'ouvre à Marrakech," *Jenue Afrique*, November 26, 2015, https://www.jeuneafrique.com/281737/economie/le-1er-sommet-sino-africain-des-entrepreneurs-souvre-a-marrakech/

Maury, Rédéric and Nadia Rabbaa. "Le Maroc, un pont d'or pour la Chine" [Morocco, a Golden Bridge for China], *Jeune Afrique*, December 29, 2015, https://www.jeuneafrique.com/mag/286294/economie/maroc-pont-dor-chine/

McTague, Tom. "Britain and the United States Have a China Problem," *The Atlantic* (blog), January 30, 2020, https://www.theatlantic.com/international/archive/2020/01/britain-us-huawei-china-mike-pompeo-dominic-raab/605806/

Mediterranean Dialogue [MD] Staff. "Asia and the Middle East Lead Rising Trend in US Exports Grow Significantly," *Modern Diplomacy*, March 12, 2018, https://moderndiplomacy.eu/2018/03/12/asia-and-the-middle-east-lead-rising-trend-in-arms-imports-us-exports-grow-significantly/

Micallef, Joseph V. R. "A Nuclear Bomb for Libya?" *Bulletin of the Atomic Scientists* (August 1981).

Ministère des Finances-Direction Générale des Douanes "Statistiques du Commerce Extérieur de l'Algérie-Période: onze mois de l'année 2019," https://douane.gov.dz/IMG/pdf/rapport_com_ext_2019_vf.pdf

Ministry of Foreign Affairs of the PRC. "The Five Principles of Peaceful Coexistence—The Time-Tested Guideline of China's Policy with Neighbors," July 30, 2014, https://www.fmprc.gov.cn/mfa_eng/wjb_663304/zwjg_665342/zwbd_665378/t1179045.shtml

Ministry of Foreign Affairs of the PRC. "China's Arab Policy Paper," January 13, 2016, https://www.fmprc.gov.cn/mfa_eng/zxxx_662805/t1331683.shtml

Ministry of Foreign Affairs of the PRC. "China's Arab Policy Paper." November 8, 2016, https://www.fmprc.gov.cn/mfa_eng/zxxx_662805/t1331683.shtml

Ministry of Foreign Affairs of the PRC. "China-Arab States Cooperation Forum Holds Ninth Ministerial Conference, July 6, 2020, https://www.fmprc.gov.cn/mfa_eng/zxxx_662805/t1795754.shtml

Ministry of Foreign Affairs of the PRC. "Written Interview with Asharq al-Awsat by State Councillor and Foreign Minister Wang Yi," November 19, 2020, https://www.fmprc.gov.cn/mfa_eng/zxxx_662805/t1833773.shtml

Mitchell, Tom. "Egypt Courts China for Suez Special Zone," *Financial Times*, March 2, 2010, https://www.ft.com/content/5a3445fa-2625-11df-aff3-00144feabdc0

Mizokami, Kyle. "For the First Time, Chinese UAVs Are Flying and Fighting in the Middle East," *Popular Mechanics*, December 22, 2015, https://www.popularmechanics.com/military/weapons/news/a18677/chinese-drones-are-flying-and-fighting-in-the-middle-east/

Mohamed, Sherifa Fadel. "Egyptian-Chinese Relations between Continuity and Change (2003–2013)," *Al-Mustaqbal Al-Arabi* 420 (February 2014): 36–52.

Moneim, Doaa. 2019. "Egyptian Investment Minister Hails China's Belt and Road Initiative," *Ahram Online*, October 22, http://english.ahram.org.eg/NewsContent/3/12/353403/Business/Economy/Egyptian-investment-minister-hails-China's-Belt-an.aspx

Moran, James. "EU-Morocco: Stage Set for a New Partnership," *EURACTIV*, October 11, 2019, https://www.euractiv.com/section/africa/opinion/eu-morocco-stage-set-for-a-new-partnership/

"Morocco Attracts Automotive Manufacturers and Suppliers," https://oxfordbusinessgroup.com/analysis/driver%E2%80%99s-seat-automotive-manufacturers-and-suppliers-flock-kingdom

"Morocco Eyes 'Mutually Beneficial' Partnership With China, FM," November 28, 2014, http://www.maroc.ma/en/news/moroccan-chinese-business-forum

"Morocco: Huawei to Build a Regional Logistics Hub in Tanger Med," September 7, 2018 https://www.ecofinagency.com/public-management/0709-38933-morocco-huawei-to-build-a-regional-logistics-hub-in-tanger-med

"Morocco's Platinum Power Partners with China's CFHEC on $300 Mln Hydropower Project," *Reuters*, July 10, 2019, https://www.reuters.com/article/us-morocco-power-hydropower/moroccos-platinum-power-partners-with-chinas-cfhec-on-300-mln-hydropower-project-idUSKCN1U51O9

"Morocco's Tangier Port to Become Mediterranean's Largest," June 26, 2019, https://www.reuters.com/article/us-morocco-economy-ports/tangier-port-to-become-mediterraneans-largest-idUSKCN1TR2G0

"Morocco to Take Part in Covid-19 Vaccine Clinical Trials Following Two Agreements Signed with Chinese Group CNBG," *MAP*, August 2020, https://www.mapnews.ma/en/actualites/general/morocco-take-part-covid-19-vaccine-clinical-trials-following-two-agreements

Mostafa, Mohamed and Mohamed Nagi. "'They Are Not Welcome': Report on the Uyghur Crisis in Egypt," *Association for Freedom of Thought and Expression and the Egyptian Commission for Rights and Freedoms*, https://afteegypt.org/en/academic_freedoms/2017/10/01/13468-afteegypt.html

Mouline, Mohammed Tawfik. "Sino-Moroccan Cooperation and the New Silk Road," *Shanghai Institutes for International Studies (SIIS)*, June 29, 2018, http://www.ires.ma/wp-content/uploads/2018/07/finale-overview-of-sino-moroccan-cooperation.pdf

Mousset, Laura. "France–Maroc: quelles relations diplomatiques?" *TV 5 Monde*, January 30, 2015, https://information.tv5monde.com/afrique/france-maroc-quelles-relations-diplomatiques–15273

Mustafa, Nada. "Cairo-Beijing Have Witnessed Obvious Growth since Sisi's Presidency: Chinese Official," *Sada Elbalad English*, July 9, 2019, https://see.news/egypt-enjoys-attractive-tourist-destinations-chinese-official/

Nadir, Iddir. "L'ambassadeur de Chine en Algérie: 'Nous nous opposerons à l'ingérence de toute puissance étrangère en Algérie'" [China's Ambassador to Algeria: "We Will Oppose the Interference of any Foreign Power in Algeria"], *El Watan*, December 1, 2019, https://www.elwatan.com/edition/actualite/lambassadeur-de-chine-en-algerie-nous-nous-opposerons-a-lingerence-de-toute-puissance-etrangere-en-algerie-01-12-2019

National Committee of the Chinese People's Political Consultative Conference. "China, Algeria Vow to Boost Comprehensive Strategic Partnership," November 3, 2014, http://www.cppcc.gov.cn/zxww/2014/11/04/ARTI1415071483256625.shtml

National Development and Reform Commission, Ministry of Foreign Affairs, and Ministry of Commerce of the PRC. "Vision and Proposed Actions Outlined on Jointly Building Silk Road Economic Belt and 21st-Century Maritime Silk Road,"

China Daily, March 30, 2015, http://language.chinadaily.com.cn/2015-03/30/content_19950951.htm

Ndeye Magatte Kebe. "Morocco: BMCI Unblocks 13 Million Euros to Finance Chinese Nanjing Xiezhong Plant," *Kapital Afrik*, July 6, 2018, https://www.kapitalafrik.com/2018/07/06/morocco-bmci-unblocks-13-million-euros-to-finance-chinese-nanjing-xiezhong-plant/

Ngueyap, Romuald. "L'Algérie relance le mégaprojet du port Centre d'El Hamdania financé par la Chine" [Algeria Relaunches the Mega-Project of El Hamdania's Central Port Financed by China], *Agence EcoFin*, July 2, 2020, https://www.agenceecofin.com/transports/0207-78104-l-algerie-relance-le-megaprojet-du-port-centre-d-el-hamdania-finance-par-la-chine

Nichols, Michelle. "U.N. Chief Regrets Morocco 'Misunderstanding' Over Western Sahara Remark," *Reuters*, March 28, 2016, https://www.reuters.com/article/us-morocco-westernsahara-un-idUSKCN0WU1N9

"OCP Group and Hubei Forbon Group Build Up an R&D Partnership in the New Generation of Fertilizers and Smart Agriculture," September 24, 2018, https://www.ocpgroup.ma/en/ocp-group-and-hubei-forbon-group-build-rd-partnership-new-generation-fertilizers-and-smart

OECD. "FDI in Figures," April 2018, http://www.oecd.org/daf/inv/investment-policy/FDI-in-Figures-April-2018.pdf

Olimat, Muhamad, 2014. *China and North Africa since World War II: A Bilateral Approach*. London: Lexington Books, 49 & 58.

Olimat, Muhamad S. 2012. *China and the Middle East: From Silk Road to Arab Spring*. 1st Edition. Milton Park, Abingdon, Oxon: Routledge.

Organization of Petroleum Countries. "Algeria Facts and Figures," 2019, https://www.opec.org/opec_web/en/about_us/146.htm

Ouramdane, Mehenni. "Algérie-Chine: La France s'inquiète du rapprochement entre les deux pays," June 17, 2018, https://www.algerie-eco.com/2018/06/17/algerie-chine-la-france-sinquiete-du-rapprochement-entreles-deux-pays/

Paal, Douglas H. "China: Mugged by Reality in Libya, Again," *Carnegie Endowment for International Peace*, April 11, 2011, https://carnegieendowment.org/2011/04/11/china-mugged-by-reality-in-libya-again-pub-43554

Pairault, Thierry. "China's Economic Presence in Algeria," CCJ-Occasional-papers, 1, *HAL Archives Ouvertes*, 2015, https://halshs.archives-ouvertes.fr/halshs-01116295/document

Pairault, Thierry. "China's Economic Presence in Algeria," *ResearchGate*, February 2015, 11, https://www.researchgate.net/publication/280793405_China's_economic_presence_in_Algeria

Pairault, Thierry. "Economic Relations between China and Maghreb Countries," in *China, the European Union and the Developing World: A Triangular Relationship*, edited by Jan Wouters, Jean-Christophe Defraigne, and Matthieu Burnay. Cheltenham: Edward Elgar Publishing, 2015, 312.

Pairault, Thierry. "La Chine au Maghreb: de l'esprit de Bandung à l'esprit du capitalisme" [China in the Maghreb: From the Spirit of Bandung to the Spirit of Capitalism], *Revue de la régulation: Capitalisme, institutions, pouvoirs*, 21.1 2017, https://journals.openedition.org/regulation/12230

Parker, Sam and Gabrielle Chefitz. "Debtbook Diplomacy: China's Strategic Leveraging of Its Newfound Economic Influence and the Consequences for U.S. Foreign Policy," *Belfer Center for Science and International Affairs*, Policy Analysis Exercise, May 2018, https://www.belfercenter.org/sites/default/files/files/publication/Debtbook%20Diplomacy%20PDF.pdf

"Pêche: Les Russes reviennent," *L'Economiste*, June 7, 2010, https://www.leconomiste.com/article/peche-les-russes-reviennent

"Pékin: El Ferdaous fait le point sur la coopération sino-africaine," *Hepress*, June 26, 2019, https://fr.hespress.com/80562-pekin-el-ferdaous-fait-le-point-sur-la-cooperation-sino-africaine.html

People's Democratic Republic of Algeria, *Ministry of Industry and Mines*. "Algeria, China Ink Several Agreements, MoUs," APS, April 28, 2015. Retrieved from http://www.andi.dz/index.php/en/presse/1212-algeria-china-ink-several-agreements-mous

Permanent Mission of the PRC to the UN. "Statement by Ambassador Wang Min, Deputy Permanent Representative of China to the United Nations, at the Security Council Briefing on the Impact of the Sahel Region Caused by the Libyan Conflict," January 26, 2012, http://www.china-un.org/eng/chinaandun/securitycouncil/regionalhotspots/africa/lib/t930690.htm

Permanent Mission of the PRC to the UN. "Libya," http://www.china-un.org/eng/chinaandun/securitycouncil/regionalhotspots/africa/lib/

"Primary School Near Tangier to Pilot Mandarin Chinese Classes," *Morocco World News*, December 5, 2019, https://www.moroccoworldnews.com/2019/12/288238/primary-school-mandarin-chinese-classes/

"Projet de phosphate: Sonatrach et CITIC signent un avenant à leur protocole d'accord" [Phosphate Project: Sonatrach and CITIC Sign an Amendment to Their Memorandum of Understanding], *Algérie-Eco*, January 9, 2020, https://www.algerie-eco.com/2020/01/09/projet-phosphate-sonatrach-citic-signent-avenant-protocole-accord/

Ports Europe. "CHEC Starts Construction of Second Container Terminal in Egypt's Ain Sokhna," September 5, 2018, https://www.portseurope.com/__trashed-13/

Putz, Catherine. "Which Countries Are for or Against China's Xinjiang Policies?" *The Diplomat*, July 15, 2019, https://thediplomat.com/2019/07/which-countries-are-for-or-against-chinas-xinjiang-policies/

Rabbaa, Nadia. "Maroc-Chine: les banques en première ligne," *Jenue Afrique*, December 27, 2015, https://www.jeuneafrique.com/mag/286260/economie/maroc-chine-banques-premiere-ligne/

Rahim, Zamira. "Prisoners in China's Xinjiang Concentration Camps Subjected to Gang Rape and Medical Experiments, Former Detainee Says," *The Independent*, October 22, 2019https://www.independent.co.uk/news/world/asia/china-xinjiang-uighur-muslim-detention-camps-xi-jinping-persecution-a9165896.html

Rakhmat, Muhammad Zulfikar. "China and Tunisia: A Quiet Partnership," *The Diplomat*, June 28, 2014 https://thediplomat.com/2014/06/china-and-tunisia-a-quiet-partnership/

Reimann, Jakob. "China Is Flooding the Middle East with Cheap Drones," *Foreign Policy in Focus*, February 18, 2019, https://fpif.org/china-is-flooding-the-middle-east-with-cheap-drones/

Reuters. "Russia, Libya Seal Debt Accord, Eye Arms Deal," 2008, https://www.reuters.com/article/us-russia-libya-idUSSHC61895920080417

Reuters. "Syria Protestors Hurl Rocks at China Embassy in Libya," February 6, 2012, http://english.ahram.org.eg/NewsContent/2/8/33848/World/Region/Syria-protesters-hurl-rocks-at-China-embassy-in-Li.aspx

Reuters. "Hutchison Port Holdings Buys Stake in Egyptian Ports Operator—Statement," March 7, 2016, https://www.reuters.com/article/aict-ma-ckh-holdings/hutchison-port-holdings-buys-stake-in-egyptian-ports-operator-statement-idUSL5N16F0R6

Reuters. "Egypt's Foreign Debt Rises to $92.64 Bln at End-June, PM Tells Paper," September 9, 2018, https://www.reuters.com/article/egypt-economy-debt/egypts-foreign-debt-rises-to-92-64-bln-at-end-june-pm-tells-paper-idUSL5N1VV035

Reuters. "Libyan Fighters Seize U.S and Chinese Missiles from Haftar's Forces," June 29, 2019, https://www.reuters.com/article/us-libya-security/libyan-fighters-seize-u-s-and-chinese-missiles-from-haftars-forces-idUSKCN1TU0W8

Rhattat, Rachid. "La relation économique et commerciale sino-marocaine: De la coopération au partenariat stratégique," *L'Année du Maghreb*, IX | 2013, http://journals.openedition.org/anneemaghreb/1922; DOI: https://doi.org/10.4000/anneemaghreb.1922

Ritter, Daniel. 2015. *The Iron Cage of Liberalism: International Politics and Unarmed Revolutions in the Middle East and North Africa*. Oxford: Oxford University Press.

Rolland, Nadège. 2017. *China's Eurasian Century?*," Belt and Road Initiative (BRI)," *European Bank for Reconstruction and Development*. August 14, 2019.

Rolland, Nadège, 2017. *China's Eurasian Century? Political and Strategic Implications of the Belt and Road Initiative*. Seattle and Washington, DC: The National Bureau of Asian Research, 3.

Rossabi, Morris (Ed.). 1983. *China among Equals: The Middle Kingdom and Its Neighbors, 10th–14th Centuries*. Berkeley: University of California Press.

"Route de la soie: l'Algérie ratifie le mémorandum d'entente avec la Chine" [Silk Road: Algeria Ratifies Memorandum of Understanding with China], *APS*, July 8, 2019, http://www.aps.dz/economie/91616-l-algerie-ratifie-le-memorandum-d-entente-relatif-a-l-initiative-de-la-ceinture-economique-de-la-route-de-la-soie

Saba, Yousef. "IMF Expects Egypt Economy to Grow 5.9% in Year to End of June," *Reuters*, October 15, 2019, https://www.reuters.com/article/us-egypt-economy-imf/imf-expects-egypt-economy-to-grow-5-9-in-year-to-end-of-june-idUSKBN1WU1TG

Safa alHarathy. "Libya Joins China's Belt and Road initiative," *Libya Observer*, July 13 2018, https://www.libyaobserver.ly/economy/libya-joins-china%E2%80%99s-belt-and-road-initiative

Said, Abdel Monem. "From Geopolitics to Geo-Economics: Egyptian National Security Perceptions," in *National Threat Perceptions in the Middle East*, edited by James Leonard, Shmuel Limone, Abdel Monem Said and Yezid Sayigh. New York and Geneva: United Nations, 1995, 17–30.

Saidi, Nasser and Aathira Prasad. "Trends in Trade and Investment Policies in the MENA Region," *Organisation for Economic Co-operation and Development*, Background Note, November 2018, http://www.oecd.org/mena/competitiveness/WGTI2018-trends-trade-investment-policies-MENA-nasser-saidi.pdf

Saleh, Heba. "Egypt Sees Chinese Investment, and Tourists as a 'Win-Win' Boost," *Financial Times*, October 30, 2018, https://www.ft.com/content/e490d960-7613-11e8-8cc4-59b7a8ef7d3d

Salem, Maha. "Get to Know the Most Important Milestones of Egyptian-Chinese Military Cooperation," *Al-Ahram*, September 3, 2017, http://gate.ahram.org.eg/News/1575795.aspx

Samir, Aya. "Egyptian-Chinese Relations: Historical Similarity and Political Support," *Akhbar El-Yom*, August 30, 2018, https://m.akhbarelyom.com/news/newdetails/2716881/1/العلاقات-المصرية-الصينية-تشابه-تاريخي-ودعم-دبلوماسي.

"Santé: des équipes médicales chinoises prochainement en Algérie," *APS*, May 30, 2019, http://www.aps.dz/sante-science-technologie/90101-sante-des-equipes-medicales-chinoises-prochainement-en-algerie

Schafer, Edward H. 1985. *The Golden Peaches of Samarkand: A Study of T'ang Exotics*. Berkeley: University of California Press.

Schwab, Klaus. "The Global Competitiveness Report 2017–2018x," *World Economic Forum*, http://www3.weforum.org/docs/GCR2017-2018/05FullReport/TheGlobal CompetitivenessReport2017%E2%80%932018.pdf

Scott, Emma. 2015. "China-Egypt Trade and Investment Ties: Seeking a Better Balance," *Policy Briefing* (Centre for Chinese Studies), June.

Scott, Emma. "Sino-Arab, Sino-Egyptian Relations: 60 Years On," *CCS Commentary* (Centre for Chinese Studies), April 4, 2016, http://www0.sun.ac.za/ccs/wp-content/uploads/2016/04/CCS_Commentary_Sino-Arab_60_Years_04APR2016.pdf

Sefta, Leïla. "S.E.M. LI Lianhe Ambassadeur de Chine en Algérie à propos des relations bilatérales: 'Inégalé': le développement de 70 années, 'Exemplaire': … " [Chinese Ambassador Lianhe to Algeria on Bilateral Relations: "Unequalled": The Development of 70 Years, "Exemplary"], *Le Maghreb-Le Quotidien de l'économie*, October 1, 2019, https://www.lemaghrebdz.com/?page=detail_actualite&rubrique=Nation&id=95395

Selim, Mohammed. 2000. "Egypt and the New Silk Road." *Executive Intelligence Review*, August 4, 2028–33.

Semmar, Abdou. "Sortie du premier camion Shacman 'made in Algérie' avec une remise de 2 millions de DA," *Algeriepart*, May 10, 2018, https://algeriepart.com/2018/05/10/photos-sortie-premier-camion-shacman-made-in-algerie-remise-de-2-millions-de-da/

Shaheen, Mai. "Ain Shams Univ. Opens 'Silk Road' Research, Studies Center," *Sada Elbalad English*, January 13, 2019, https://see.news/ain-shams-univ-opens-silk-road-research-studies-center/.

Shama, Nael. "Egypt and Obama: Turbulent Times, Bouncy Relations," in *The World Views of the Obama Era: From Hope to Disillusionment*, edited by Matthias Maass. London: Palgrave Macmillan, 2018, 65–85.

Shambaugh, David. 2013. *China Goes Global: The Partial Power*. 1st Edition. Oxford & New York: Oxford University Press.

Sharma, Anu. "An Analysis of 'Belt and Road' Initiative and the Middle East," *Asian Journal of Middle Eastern and Islamic Studies* 13, 1 (2019): 35–49.

Shichor, Yitzhak. 1979. *The Middle East in China's Foreign Policy, 1949–1977*. Cambridge: Cambridge University Press.

Shichor, Yitzhak. "Respected and Suspected: Middle Eastern Perceptions of China's Rise," in *Asian Thought on China's Changing International Relations*, edited by Niv Horesh and Emilian Kavalski. Basingstoke & New York: Palgrave Macmillan, 2014, 123–40.

Shinn, David H. "China's Approach to East, North and the Horn of Africa," Testimony before the U.S.-China Economic and Security Review Commission presented at the China's Global Influence: Objectives and Strategies, Dirksen Senate Office Building, July 21, 2005, https://www.uscc.gov/sites/default/files/7.21-22.05shinn_david_wrts.pdf

Shinn, David H. and Joshua Eisenman. 2012. *China and Africa: A Century of Engagement.* Philadelphia: University of Pennsylvania Press.

Shinn, David H. and Joshua Eisenman. "China's Relations with North Africa and the Sahel," in *China and Africa*, A Century of Engagement (University of Pennsylvania Press, 2012), 228–48, https://www.jstor.org/stable/j.ctt3fhwkz.12

Simon, François. "Algeria: Africa's Largest Chinese Community," *The Dragon's Trail-China and International Affairs*, February 26, 2013, https://dragonstrail.wordpress.com/2013/02/26/algeria-china-community-affairs/

Singh, Michael. "Chinese Policy in the Middle East in the Wake of the Arab Uprisings," in *Toward Well-Oiled Relations? China's Presence in the Middle East Following the Arab Spring* London: Palgrave Macmillan, 2016.

Sino-Arab Chemical Fertilizers Co., Ltd. "Index," February 5, 2020. http://www.sacf.com/en/index.aspx

Smith, Graeme. "China Offered Gadhafi Huge Stockpiles of Arms: Libyan Memos," *The Globe and Mail*, September 2, 2011, https://www.theglobeandmail.com/news/world/china-offered-gadhafi-huge-stockpiles-of-arms-libyan-memos/article1363316/

"Soixantième anniversaire de l'établissement des relations diplomatiques Chine-Maroc: huit grands moments," *Le Matin*, February 7, 2018, https://lematin.ma/journal/2018/soixantieme-anniversaire-letablissement-relations-diplomatiques-chine-maroc-huit-grands-moments/286794.html

Soliman, Mahmoud and Jun Zhao. "The Multiple Roles of Egypt in China's 'Belt and Road' Initiative," *Asian Journal of Middle Eastern and Islamic Studies* 13, 3 (2019): 428–44.

Sotloff, Steve. "*China's Libya Problem*," *The Diplomat*, March 14, 2012, https://thediplomat.com/2012/03/chinas-libya-problem/

Soual, M. "L'Afrique a le potentiel pour nourrir le monde," *Jeune Afrique* (2017). http://www.jeuneafrique.com/mag/485064/economie/lafrique-a-le-potentiel-pour-nourrir-le-monde/

Souiah, Farida. "La société algérienne au miroir des migrations chinoises," *Moyen Orient* 7, August–September: 15–52, https://www.pairault.fr/sinaf/doc_importes/fs2010.pdf

Souli, Sarah. "Tunisia Hopes Boost in Chinese Investment Can Ease Economic Woes," *Al-Monitor*, March 19, 2018, https://www.al-monitor.com/pulse/originals/2018/03/boost-china-investment-tunisia-europe-trade.html

Starting Africa's Agricultural Revolution. https://africanbusinessmagazine.com/company-profile/african-green-revolution-forum-agrf/starting-africas-agricultural-revolution/

Statista. "China: Growth Rate of Real Gross Domestic Product (GDP) from 2011 to 2024." February 21, 2019, https://www.statista.com/statistics/263616/gross-domestic-product-gdp-growth-rate-in-china/

Stevis-Gridneff, Matina. "More of Africa Finds Itself in China's Debt," *The Wall Street Journal*, July 25, 2018, https://www.wsj.com/articles/more-of-africa-finds-itself-in-chinas-debt-1532549741

Story, Jonathan. "China: Workshop of the World?" *Journal of Chinese Economic and Business Studies* 3, 2 (2005): 95–109.

Strüver, George. "China's Partnership Diplomacy: International Alignment Based on Interests or Ideology," *The Chinese Journal of International Politics* 10, 1 (Spring 2017): 33, DOI: https://doi.org/10.1093/cjip/pow015

Sun, Degang. "China's Partnership Diplomacy in the Middle East," unpublished paper, March 10, 2020 (personal documents).

Sun, Degang and Yahia Zoubir. "China's Response to the Revolts in the Arab World: A Case of Pragmatic Diplomacy," *Mediterranean Politics* 19 (January 2, 2014). DOI: https://doi.org/10.1080/13629395.2013.809257

Sun, Degang and Yahia H. Zoubir. "Development First: China's Investment in Seaport Constructions and Operations along the Maritime Silk Road," *Asian Journal of Middle Eastern and Islamic Studies*, 11.3 (2017): 35–47.

Sun, Degang and Yahia H. Zoubir. "China's Participation in Conflict Resolution in the Middle East and North Africa: A Case of Quasi-Mediation Diplomacy?" *Journal of Contemporary China*, 27, 110 (2017): 224–43.

Sun, Yun. "Syria: What China Has Learned from Its Libya Experience," *East-West Center Asia Pacific Bulletin* 152, February 27, 2012, https://www.eastwestcenter.org/system/tdf/private/apb152_1.pdf?file=1&type=node&id=33315

Sun, Yun. "China's 2018 Financial Commitments to Africa: Adjustment and Recalibration," *Brookings Institution*, Africa in Focus, September 5, 2018, https://www.brookings.edu/blog/africa-in-focus/2018/09/05/chinas-2018-financial-commitments-to-africa-adjustment-and-recalibration/

Sylla, Adama. "Au cœur du business avec la Chine," *Challenge*, December 2, 2014, https://www.challenge.ma/au-coeur-du-business-avec-la-chine-40786/

Tadjer, Rafik. "Chine-Algérie, khawa khawa: quand l'ambassade de Chine à Alger reprend un slogan du hirak" ["China-Algeria, khawa khawa": When the Chinese Embassy in Algiers Takes Up a Slogan from the Hirak], *TSA*, April 22, 2020, https://www.tsa-algerie.com/chine-algerie-khawa-khawa-quand-lambassade-de-chine-a-alger-reprend-un-slogan-du-hirak/

Taing, J. P. (2015). "L'immigration chinoise à Alger: l'émergence d'une place marchande à Bab Ezzouar?" [The Chinese Immigration in Algeria: The Emergency of a Marketplace in Bab Ezzouar?], *Les Cahiers d'EMAM. Études sur le Monde Arabe et la Méditerranée*, (26).

Tallantyre, Steve. "Javier Bardem Gaffe Sparks Diplomatic Row," *The Local*, February 26, 2014, https://www.thelocal.es/20140226/spanish-stars-joke-starts-france-morocco-diplomatic-row

"Tangier: King Mohammed VI Launches $1 Billion Chinese Investment Project," *Morocco World News*, March 20, 2017, https://www.moroccoworldnews.com/2017/03/211612/tangier-king-mohammed-vi-launch-largest-chinese-investment-project-north-africa/

TEDA Suez. "Current Development Situation," April 27, 2017, http://www.setc-zone.com/system/2017/04/27/011260662.shtml

TEDA Suez. "Launch of Expansion Area of China-Egypt TEDA Suez Economic and Trade Cooperation Zone," April 27, 2017, http://www.setc-zone.com/system/2017/04/27/011260701.shtml

The Diplomat. "China's prickly Gaddafi ties," 2011, https://thediplomat.com/2011/03/chinas-prickly-gaddafi-ties/

The Economist. "Gateway to the Globe: China Has a Vastly Ambitious Plan to Connect the World," July 26, 2018, https://www.economist.com/briefing/2018/07/26/china-has-a-vastly-ambitious-plan-to-connect-the-world

"The New Mohammed VI Bridge Brightens Morocco with Dazzling Light Display," *AFP*, July 21, 2016, https://www.yahoo.com/news/mohammed-vi-bridge-brightens-morocco-dazzling-light-display-200415184.html

The North Africa Post. "China Sends Morocco Medical Aid to Fight Coronavirus," March 23, 2020, https://northafricapost.com/39269-china-sends-morocco-medical-aid-to-fight-coronavirus.html

The Telegraph. "Minister: China World's Largest Source of Tourists," *The Telegraph*, March 28, 2019, https://www.telegraph.co.uk/china-watch/travel/china-world-tourist-numbers/.

The Yearbook of the United Nations—1971, "Questions Relating to Asia and the Far East," https://www.unmultimedia.org/searchers/yearbook/page.jsp?volume=1971

&page=139&srq=china%20resolution%202758&srstart=0&srvolumeFacet=1971&sroutline=false&searchType=advanced

TIMEP Brief. "China's Role in Egypt's Economy," *The Tahrir Institute for Middle East Policy*, November 21, 2019, https://timep.org/reports-briefings/timep-brief-chinas-role-in-egypts-economy/

Tlemçani, Rachid. "Policing Algeria under Bouteflika: From Police State to Civil State," in *The Politics of Algeria: Domestic Issues and International Relations*, edited by Yahia H. Zoubir. London & New York: Routledge, 2020.

"Trade Exchange between Egypt, China Hits $13.2 Bn in 2019," *Egypt Today*, May 8, 2020, https://www.egypttoday.com/Article/3/86546/Trade-exchange-between-Egypt-China-hits-13-2bn-in–2019

Trading Economics. "Ease of Doing Business in Egypt," https://tradingeconomics.com/egypt/ease-of-doing-business

"Tunisia Imports from China, 2019," *Trading Economics*, November 2020, https://tradingeconomics.com/tunisia/imports/china

United Nations Security Council. "Resolution 2468 (2019)," April 30, 2019, https://www.securitycouncilreport.org/atf/cf/%7B65BFCF9B-6D27-4E9C-8CD3-CF6E4FF96FF9%7D/S_res_2468.pdf

UNSMIL, "SRSG Ghassan Salamé Briefing to the Security Council," November 18, 2019, https://unsmil.unmissions.org/srsg-ghassan-salame-briefing-security-council-November-18,-2019

US Energy Information Administration, Algeria's Key Energy Statistics 2018, https://www.eia.gov/beta/international/country.php?iso=DZA

Vallejo, María Cristina et al. "Evading Sustainable Development Standards: Case Studies on Hydroelectric Projects in Ecuador," *Boston University Global Development Policy Center*, Working Paper, October 19, 2018, http://www.bu.edu/gdp/files/2018/10/GEGI_GDP-Ecuador-WP.pdf

"Visiting Chinese Prime Minister Zhao Ziyang and Moroccan Prime," *United Press International*, December 27, 1982, https://www.upi.com/Archives/1982/12/27/Visiting-Chinese-Prime-Minister-Zhao-Ziyang-and-Moroccan-Prime/5101400898239/

Volkmann, Eliza. "Tunisia: An Economy Drowning in Debt," *Arab News*, January 31, 2018, http://www.arabnews.com/node/1237021/middle-east

Wagner, Julien. "Engrais: OCP, quelle stratégie en Afrique ?" *Jeune Afrique*, April 17, 2018, https://www.jeuneafrique.com/mag/549143/economie/engrais-ocp-quelle-strategie-en-afrique/

Wagner, Julien. "Morocco's OCP—A Big, Green Mining Machine," *The Africa Report*, January 18, 2019, https://www.theafricareport.com/413/mining-a-big-green-mining-machine/

Waldron, Arthur N. (Ed.). *China in Africa*. 1st Edition. Washington, DC: The Jamestown Foundation, 2009.

Wang, Betty. "China's Economic Growth Hits a 30 Year Low," *Australian Broadcasting Company*, January 21, 2019, https://www.abc.net.au/radionational/programs/drive/chinas-economic-growth-hits-a-30-year-low/10733492

Wanjun, Wu and Pedro Sobral. "China's Non-interference Policy towards Western Sahara Conflict," *Africana Studia*, 29 (2018): 131–43.

Weatherley, Dan. "China-Led Consortium Wins High-Speed Rail Project in Egypt," *Construction Global*, September 16, 2020, https://www.constructionglobal.com/construction-projects/china-led-consortium-wins-high-speed-rail-project-egypt

Wehry, Fredric and Sandy Alkoutami. "China's Balancing Act in Libya," *Carnegie Endowment for International Peace*, May 10, 2020, https://carnegieendowment.org/2020/05/10/china-s-balancing-act-in-libya-pub-81757

Weymouth, Lally. "Rare Interview with Egyptian Gen. Abdel Fatah al-Sissi," *The Washington Post*, August 3, 2013, https://www.washingtonpost.com/world/middle_east/rare-interview-with-egyptian-gen-abdel-fatah-al-sissi/2013/08/03/a77eb37c-fbc4-11e2-a369-d1954abcb7e3_story.html

Wong, John. "China's Rising Economic Soft Power," *Asia Dialogue*, March 25, 2016, https://theasiadialogue.com/2016/03/25/chinas-rising-economic-soft-power/

Wood, David. "Egypt Loves China's Deep Pockets," *Foreign Policy*, August 28, 2018, https://foreignpolicy.com/2018/08/28/egypt-loves-chinas-deep-pockets/

World Bank Group. "Doing Business 2019: Training for Reform," *Flagship Report*, May 2019, http://www.worldbank.org/content/dam/doingBusiness/media/Annual-Reports/English/DB2019-report_web-version.pdf

Xi, J. (2014). "Promoting the Silk Road Spirit and Deepening China-Arab Cooperation," speech at the opening ceremony of the 6th Ministerial Meeting of the China–Arab States Cooperation Forum. December 9, 2019, http://www.china.org.cn/report/2014-07/14/content_32941818.htm

"Xi Meets Morocco's Prime Minister," Ministry of Foreign Affairs of the PRC. August 15, 2019, https://www.fmprc.gov.cn/mfa_eng/zxxx_662805/t1592950.shtml

Xinhua. "Morocco, China Give New Impetus to Bilateral Partnership in 2017," *Global Times*, December 31, 2017, http://www.globaltimes.cn/content/1082762.shtml

Xinhua. "China's Agribusiness Giant New Hope Expands in Egypt amid Growing Sino-Egyptian Ties," March 19, 2018, https://tribune.com.pk/story/1663137/3-

chinas-agribusiness-giant-new-hope-expands-egypt-amid-growing-sinoegyptian-ties/

Xinhua. "China and Another Two Arab Countries Sign MOUs on the Belt and Road Initiative," *Belt and Road Portal*, July 12, 2018, https://eng.yidaiyilu.gov.cn/home/rolling/59886.htm

Xinhua. "China's Jushi Firm Celebrates Largest Fiberglass Production in Egypt," *Xinhuanet*, August 29, 2018, http://www.xinhuanet.com/english/2018-08/29/c_137426120.htm

Xinhua. "Interview: Libya Welcomes Return of Chinese Companies, PM Says Ahead of FOCAC Beijing Summit," August 31, 2018, http://www.xinhuanet.com/english/2018-08/31/c_137434072.htm

Xinhua. "Libya Welcomes Return of Chinese Companies, PM Says Ahead of FOCAC Beijing Summit," *China Daily*, September 1, 2018, http://www.chinadaily.com.cn/a/201809/01/WS5b8a2b1aa310add14f389061.html

Xinhua. "Xi Meets Algerian Prime Minister," *Xinhuanet*, September 5, 2018, http://www.xinhuanet.com/english/2018-09/05/c_137447518.htm

Xinhua. "Xi Meets Tunisian Prime Minister," *Xinhuanet*, September 5, 2018, http://www.xinhuanet.com/english/2018-09/05/c_137447045.htm

Xinhua. "Confucius Institute Opens Classroom in Tunisia," *Xinhuanet*, November 13, 2018, http://www.xinhuanet.com/english/2018-11/13/c_129992290_2.htm

Xinhua. "Feature: China Cultural Center in Morocco's Rabat launched," *Xinhuanet*, December 18, 2018, http://www.xinhuanet.com/english/2018-12/18/c_137682999.htm

Xinhua. "Chinese Tourists to Tunisia Witness Boom in 2018," October 28, 2018, http://www.xinhuanet.com/english/2018-10/28/c_137562912.htm

Xinhua. "Confucius Institute Opens Classroom in Tunisia," November 13, 2018, http://www.xinhuanet.com/english/2018-11/13/c_129992290.htm

Xinhua. "Xi Pledges Further Development of China-Algeria Strategic Partnership," December 20, 2018, http://www.xinhuanet.com/english/2018-12/20/c_137687090.htm

Xinhua. "Feature: China, Egypt Join Hands to Build CBD Project in Egypt's New Capital City," March 19, 2019, http://www.xinhuanet.com/english/2019-03/19/c_137907912.htm

Xinhua. "1st Confucius Institute in Tunisia Inaugurated," April 11, 2019, http://www.xinhuanet.com/english/2019-04/11/c_137966337.htm

Xinhua. "Xi Meets Egyptian President," *Xinhuanet*, April 25, 2019, http://www.xinhuanet.com/english/2019-04/25/c_138009830.htm

Xinhua. "Chinese Tourists in Tunisia up by 10.1 Pct by Aug. 10," August 21, 2019 http://www.xinhuanet.com/english/2019-08/21/c_138324265.htm

Xinhua. "Egyptian-Chinese University Adds New Aspect to Growing Egypt-China Cooperation," September 9, 2019, http://www.xinhuanet.com/english/2019-09/09/c_138378202.htm

Xinhua. "Chinese Embassy in Tunisia Welcomes New Batch of Chinese Medical Team," November 4, 2019, http://www.xinhuanet.com/english/2019-11/04/c_138525855.htm.

Xinhua. "Chinese Firm Supports Construction of Trans-Saharan Highway Project in Nigeria," November 12, 2019, http://www.china.org.cn/business/2019-11/12/content_75398522.htm

Xinhua. "Huawei Awards Prizes to Tunisian ICT Students, Instructors," December 21, 2019, http://www.xinhuanet.com/english/2019-12/21/c_138647189_4.htm

Xinhua. "China-Sponsored Training Courses Help Enhance China-Tunisia Cooperation: Embassy," January 11, 2020, http://www.xinhuanet.com/english/2020-01/11/c_138695151.htm

Xinhua. "China Asks for Earnest Implementation of Outcome of Berlin Conference on Libya," February 13, 2020, http://www.xinhuanet.com/english/2020-02/13/c_138778669.htm

Xinhua. "Interview: Tunisia Satisfied with Tunisia-China Cooperation in Fighting COVID-19: Health Minister," May 8, 2020, http://www.xinhuanet.com/english/2020-05/08/c_139038916.htm

Xinhua. "COVID-19 Has 'Little Impact' on Egypt-China Bilateral Trade: Chinese Ambassador," June 19, 2020, http://www.xinhuanet.com/english/2020-06/19/c_139149954.htm

Xinhuanet. "Algerian PM Lauds Efficiency of Chinese Company in Highway Construction Project," April 30, 2017, http://www.xinhuanet.com//english/2017-04/30/c_136246926.htm

Xinhuanet (In Arabic). الجزائر والصين مثال يحتذى به في التعاون والصداقة الدائمة [Algeria and China are Models of Cooperation and Lasting Friendship], February 26, 2014, http://arabic.people.com.cn/31660/8547268.html

Xinhuanet (In French). "Les pays en développement doivent renforcer leur solidarité pour mieux défendre leurs intérêts, déclare le président chinois" [Developing countries must strengthen their solidarity to better defend their interests, says Chinese president], February 4, 2004. Retrieved from http://french.china.org.cn/french/100564.htm

Yahya, Marwa. "Chinese Investments in Egypt's Electricity Sector in Continuous Increase: Official," *Xinhuanet*, September 8, 2018, https://mail.yahoo.com/d/folders/1?.src=fp&guce_referrer=ahr0chm6ly9sb2dpbi55ywhvby5jb20v

&guce_referrer_sig=aqaaagunarvcaorcnpblq8hb_fe_ffeo0ef2emysdcqa6k2uqjr9pj1nr0apzhtn8sgc8lcucd3l7hgrjbv2vjiz1scug33elvsf1bshntn8n1tktxc_qg16icq8bxqclpabxjfx-i_ro3g0_-1epdofol8o1cp33ix3yuoh1hoc3of-

Ybarra, Maggie. "The Politics of Selling Weapons to Algeria-Algiers Looks to Shift Away from Its Dependence on Moscow," *The National Interest*, March 7, 2019, https://nationalinterest.org/feature/politics-selling-weapons-algeria–46362

Yerkes, Sarah and Marwan Muasher. "Decentralization in Tunisia: Empowering Towns, Engaging People," *Carnegie Endowment for International Peace*, May 17, 2018 https://carnegieendowment.org/2018/05/17/decentralization-in-tunisia-empowering-towns-engaging-people-pub–76376

Yi Lu, Yi. "U.S. Ambassadors Death Draws Cheers and an Ugly Rumour on China's Web," *The Atlantic*, September 18, 2012, https://www.theatlantic.com/international/archive/2012/09/us-ambassadors-death-draws-cheers-and-an-ugly-rumor-on-chinas-web/262514/

Ying, Ding. "Out of Libya," March 6, 2011, http://www.bjreview.com/print/txt/2011-03/06/content_338897.htm

Ying Xin Wang, Tang. "Algeria, China Strengthen Strategic Partnership," *China Daily*, December 19, 2008, http://www.chinadaily.com.cn/cndy/2008-12/19/content_7320543.htm (access no longer available).

Youssef, Nour. "Egyptian Police Detain Uighurs and Deport Them to China," *New York Times*, July 6, 2017, https://www.nytimes.com/2017/07/06/world/asia/egypt-muslims-uighurs-deportations-xinjiang-china.html

Yuan, Dang. "Malaysia's Mahathir Dumps Chinese Projects Amid 'New Colonialism' Fear," *DW*, August 21, 2018, https://www.dw.com/en/malaysias-mahathir-dumps-chinese-projects-amid-new-colonialism-fear/a–45160594

Zambelis, Chris. "China's Inroads into North Africa: An Assessment of Sino-Algerian Relations, *China Brief* 10, 1 (January 7, 2010), https://jamestown.org/program/chinas-inroads-into-north-africa-an-assessment-of-sino-algerian-relations/

Zerrouki, Nasser. "Boudouaou: Bagarre dans un chantier chinois" [Boudouaou: Fight in a Chinese Construction Site], *Liberté*, February 10, 2016, https://www.liberte-algerie.com/actualite/bagarre-dans-un-chantier-chinois–241866

Zhang, Juan and William X. Wei. "Managing Political Risks of Chinese Contracted Projects in Libya," *Project Management Journal* 43, 4 (2012).

Zhao, Suisheng. "The China Model and the Authoritarian State," *East Asia Forum*, August 31, 2011, https://www.eastasiaforum.org/2011/08/31/the-china-model-and-the-authoritarian-state/

Zhou, Hang. "China's Balancing Act in the Western Sahara Conflict," *Africana Studia* 29 (2018): 145–56, https://www.aljazeera.com/news/2020/12/11/us-recognised-moroccos-claim-to-western-sahara-now-what

Zongze, Ruan and Zeng Aiping. Senior Fellows at China Institute for International Studies (interviews with the authors, September 2019), Beijing, China.

Zoubir, Yahia H. "US and Soviet Policies toward France's Struggle with Anti-colonial Nationalism in North Africa," *Canadian Journal of History/Annales d'Histoire Canadiennes* 30, 3 (1995): 439–66.

Zoubir, Yahia H. "The Dialectics of Algeria's Foreign Relations from 1990 to the Present," in *Algeria in Transition-Reforms and Development Prospects*, edited by Ahmed Aghrout. London & New York: Routledge, 2004, 151–82.

Zoubir, Yahia H. "The Welcome Multilateralization of Global Power," in Belt and Road Initiative: Toward Greater Cooperation Between China and the Middle East, *Brookings Doha Center*, Event Proceedings, January 13–14, 2018, 4, https://www.brookings.edu/wp-content/uploads/2018/01/English_BDC_SASS_Event_Proceedings.pdf

Zoubir, Yahia H. "China's 'Health Silk Road' Diplomacy in the MENA, Konrad Adenauer Stiftung," *Mediterranean Dialogue Series*, July 2020.

Zoubir, Yahia H. "Les relations de la Chine avec les pays du Maghreb: la place prépondérante de l'Algérie" [China's Relations with the Maghreb Countries: The Predominance of Algeria], *Confluences Méditerranée*, 109, 2 (2019): 91–103.

Zoubir, Yahia H. "The Algerian-Moroccan Rivalry: Constructing the Imagined Enemy," in *Shocks and Rivalries in the Middle East and North Africa*, edited by Imad Mansour and William R. Thompson. Washington, DC: Georgetown University Press, 2020.

Zoubir, Yahia H. "'The Giant Afraid of Its Shadow': Algeria, the Reluctant Middle Power," in *Unfulfilled Aspirations: Middle Power Politics in the Middle East*, edited by Adham Saouli. Oxford: Oxford University Press/Hurst, 2020, 67–90.

Zoubir, Yahia H. "Expanding Sino-Maghreb Relations: Morocco and Tunisia," *Research Paper, Chatham House*, February 20, 2020, https://www.chathamhouse.org/search/site/zoubir

Zoubir, Yahia H. "Can Algeria Overcome Its Long-lasting Political Crisis?" *Brookings*, January 15, 2020, https://www.brookings.edu/blog/order-from-chaos/2020/01/15/can-algeria-overcome-its-long-lasting-political-crisis/

Zoubir, Yahia H. "Algeria and the Sahelian Quandary: The Limits of Containment Security Policy," The Sahel: Europe's African Borders, Dalia Ghanem-Yazbeck edited by, R. Barras Tejudo, G. Faleg, Y. Zoubir, *Euromesco Joint-Policy Paper*, 70–95, https://www.euromesco.net/wp-content/uploads/2018/03/EuroMeSCo-Joint-Policy-Study-8_The_Sahel_Europe_African_Border.pdf

Zoubir, Yahia H. "Russia and Algeria: Reconciling Contrasting Interests," *The Maghreb Review*, 36, 3 (2011): 99–126.

Index

African Agriculture (AAA) initiative 177
African Development Bank (AFDB) 182–3
Afro-Asian People's Solidarity Organization 94
Afro Barometer 114
Ajijti, Jihane 178, 179
Akhannouch, Aziz 172
Alcomsat-1 144–5
Algeria 8–11, 14, 17–18, 125, 149–51, 202–4
    BRI 134–6
    culture 146, 147
    economic relations 137–41
    Energy relations 142–3
    health 147, 148
    military cooperation 143–6
    war of independence 126–34
    war of liberation 126–7
Alkoutami, Sandy 6, 12–13
Al-Naggar, Ahmed 31
Alterman, Jon 100
Arab Barometer 114–15
Arab Spring 8, 9, 15, 43, 46, 65, 71, 77, 93–101
Attijariwafa Bank (AWB) 168, 170, 175, 184
Aviation Corporation of China (AVIC) 38

Bandung Conference 2, 28, 126
Banque Marocaine du Commerce Exterieur (BMCE) 10, 168, 170, 175, 182, 185, 190
Baru, aikanti Kacalla 180
Beijing Consensus 46
Beijing Summit 12, 80
Belt and Road Initiative (BRI) 1, 3–5, 7–12, 14, 18, 19, 22, 31–4, 50, 66, 80, 82–4, 86, 87, 93, 99, 107–8, 116, 131, 134–6, 149, 150, 167, 185, 186, 200, 201, 203

Ben Ali, Zine el Abidine 93, 97, 98, 112
Benjelloun, Othman 182
Bensalah, Abdelkader 136
Bensalah, Meriem 174
Bouabid, Maati 170
Bouhdoud, Mamoune 182
Bourguiba, Habib 93–5
Bouteflika, Abdelaziz 130, 132, 133, 137, 138, 157 n.70
Brautigam, Deborah 95

Casablanca Finance City (CFC) 9, 175, 182
Chahed, Youssef 12, 93, 99, 101
Cherifian Company of Industrial and Railway Equipment (SCIF) 183–4
China Aerospace Science and Technology Corporation (CASC) 144
China-Arab States Cooperation Forum (CASCF) 2, 13, 100, 104, 107, 134–6
China Automobile Manufacturers Association (CAAM) 141
China Communications Construction Company (CCCC) 9, 168
China Development Bank 39, 184, 185
China First Highway Engineering Co. (CFHEC) 187
China Fortune Land Development Company (CFLD) 10
China Harbor Engineering Company (CHEC) 140
China National Petroleum Corporation (CNPC) 68–71, 83, 107
China Railway Construction Corporation (CRCC) 10, 204
China Road and Bridge Corporation (CRBC) 10, 168
Chinese Civil Engineering Construction Corporation (CCECC) 138, 139

Chinese Communist Party (CCP) 6, 7, 14, 17, 94, 101
Chinese community 40, 140, 147
Chinese language 11, 41, 102, 103, 146, 151
Chinese Ministry of Commerce 8
Chinese State Construction Engineering Corporation (CSCEC) 39, 139, 140, 202
Chongqing Regal Automotive Parts 187
comprehensive strategic partnerships (CSPs) 3–5, 18, 130–1, 136, 145, 149, 150
Confucius Institutes and Confucius Classrooms 103
COVID-19 40, 84, 117, 132, 147–8, 150, 151, 188–9
   and pandemic diplomacy 201–3
   Sino-Moroccan relations 188–9
   on Sino-Tunisian relationship 110–11
cultural power 7–11
Cultural Revolution 29

Declaration on Strategic Partnership and Cooperation 130
Dejiang, Zhang 72
Djerad, Abdelaziz 136

East-West Highway 9, 10, 204
Economic power 7–11
Economic relations 37, 146, 167–8
   Chinese-Tunisian 96–7, 104–7, 114
   Egyptian-Chinese 40, 48–9
   Sino-Algerian 137–41
   Sino-Egyptian 31–4
   Sino-Moroccan 167, 185, 190
Education and cultural exchanges 102–3
Egypt 5–6, 8–12, 14–16, 201, 203–4. *see also* Sino-Egyptian relations
   Chinese tourism to 39–40
   medical supplies to 202
Egyptian-Chinese Applied Technology College 41
Egyptian-Chinese University (ECU) 41
Ekman, Alice 13
Elalamy, Moulay Hafid 181–2
Elloumi Rekik, Salma 102
El-Sisi, Abdel-Fattah 27–8, 30, 34, 37, 38, 43–5. *see also* Sino-Egyptian relations

Energy relations 142–3
Enlai, Zhou 28–9, 66, 95, 126, 169, 170
Esper, Mark 148
Essebsi, Beji Caid 93, 99
Europe 87, 104, 108, 116–18, 125, 149, 168, 172, 182, 186
European Commission 116–17
European Union 8, 11–12, 104, 114–17, 125, 128, 131, 133, 150
   EU–Morocco relations 172

Five Principles of Peaceful Coexistence 112–13, 126
Food and Agriculture Organization (FAO) 177
Foreign Direct Investment (FDI) 15, 49, 109, 129, 143, 175, 189
Foreign policy 73–7
Forum on China-Africa Cooperation (FOCAC) 12, 13, 128, 130, 135–7, 181
Franco-Moroccan partnership 182

Gaddafi, Muammar 6, 12, 65–71, 76, 78, 80, 88
German Goethe Institute model 103
Going East strategy 43–8
Going Global strategy 18, 68, 72, 170
Goldstein 3
Going West Strategy 33
Government of National Accord (GNA) 6, 9, 12, 79, 80, 82, 83
Great Rejuvenation of the Chinese Nation Strategy 135, 136
Groupe Banque Centrale Populaire (BCP) 175

Haftar, Khalifa 6, 79–83
Hammouchi, Abdellatif 173
Hassan II, King 169–70
Health Silk Road Diplomacy 202
Hollande, François 173
Huawei 9, 14, 17, 110, 113, 118, 139, 170, 187
Hutchison Port Holdings (HPH) 38

Industrial and Commercial Bank of China (ICBC) 184
International Monetary Fund 33

Investment 3–5, 8–11, 14–18, 27, 32–5, 37–40, 48–50, 93, 104–12, 116, 118, 136–9, 168, 175, 186–90, 204

Jalloud, Abdulsalam 66, 67
Jhinaoui, Khemais 101, 108
Jiabao, Wen 72
Jiechi, Yang 74, 98, 148
Jinping, Xi 1, 3, 12, 18, 30, 34, 73, 101, 131, 135, 136
Jintao, Hu 2, 72, 130
Joint Comprehensive Plan of Action 13
Jun, Zhai 99

Keqiang, Li 131, 136
Kozlowski, Nina 189

Lahlou-Filali, Myriam 189
Laraki, Ahmed 170
Le Corre, Philippe 116
Libya and China 6, 9, 10, 12–16, 65–6, 85–8, 99, 142, 199
  evacuation 71–3
  foreign policy 73–7
  Gaddafi 66–71
  Government of National Accord 79–81
  Haftar attack 79–83
  oil imports 68–71
  trading 78–9
Lihan, Zhu 6–7, 13, 14
Long March-3B launch vehicle 144

Mahathir Mohamad 50
Maritime Silk Road 104, 107–8, 140, 141
Medjerdah-Cap Bon Canal 96
memorandums of understanding (MoUs) 1, 4, 9, 10, 131, 136, 143, 167, 168, 181, 186
Middle East and North Africa (MENA) 1, 3–5, 8, 12, 15, 17, 18, 33, 84, 86, 112, 115, 125, 127, 134, 135, 142, 146–8, 199, 204
Ministry of Commerce (MOFCOM) 71
Mohammed VI Bridge 183
Mohammed VI, King 9, 167, 170, 185
Moroccan Bank for Commerce and Industry (BMCI) 184

Moroccan National Tourist Office (ONMT) 183
Morocco 9, 11–13, 18–19, 132–5, 143–4, 203. *see also* Sino-Moroccan relations
  AWB 168, 170, 175, 184
  OCP 167–9, 171, 178–80, 187
Morsi, Mohamed 44
Mubarak, Hosni 29–30, 34–5, 38, 44, 46–8
Muslims 47–8, 51, 104, 134, 201

Nasser, Gamal Abdel 2, 28–30, 43, 47, 52 n.8
National Bank of Egypt 35
National Liberation Front (FLN) 126
National Oil Corporation (NOC) 69, 78, 80
National Popular Army (ANP) 144, 145
National Transitional Council (NTC) 71, 74, 76, 78
NATO 6, 14, 74, 76, 78, 93, 200
Noninterference 6, 7, 9, 12–14, 18, 45, 74, 81–3, 112, 126, 128, 132, 133
Nye, Joseph 22

Obama, Barack 33, 44, 45, 51
Office Cherifien des Phosphate (OCP) 167–9, 171, 178–80, 187
Oil
  companies 128–9, 142–3, 145
  diplomacy 129
  imports 68–71, 80
One Belt One Road (OBOR) 73, 74, 134
One China policy 95, 96, 98, 100, 113, 115

Paal, Douglas H. 107, 112
Palestine Liberation Organization (PLO) 2, 96, 127
Partnership diplomacy 3
Peiding, Ji 101
People-first diplomacy 73
People's Liberation Army (PLA) 73
People's Liberation Army Navy (PLAN) 14
People's Republic of China (PRC) 2, 28–31, 66, 67, 84, 85, 125–33, 142, 144, 169
people-to-people exchanges 10–11, 19
Pharmaceuticals 188–9
Polisario Front 132, 169

Pompeo, Mike 112
Provisional Government of the Algerian Republic (GPRA) 126

Right to Protect (R2P) 75, 76, 81, 84, 85
Ritter, Daniel 43–4
Russian P-800 145

Sadat, Anwar 29–30
Sahrawi Arab Democratic Republic (SADR) 133, 169
Saied, Kais 99
El-Sarraj, Fayez 80
Saudi Arabia 2
Security and Defense cooperation 14–15
Sellal, Abdelmalek 131
Serraj, Fayez 6, 83
Shalgam, Abdulrahman 69
Shangkun, Yang 97
Shambaugh, David 113–15
Silk Road 2, 11, 31, 41, 186
Singh, Michael 104–5
Sino-African Entrepreneurs Summit (SAES) 181–2
Sino-Algerian cooperation 147
Sino-Algerian relations. *see also* Algeria
  economic relations 137–41
  military cooperation 143–6
  war of independence 126–34
Sino-Arab Chemical Fertilizers Company (SACF) 106
Sino-Arab relations 1–4
Sinochem 169, 171
Sino-Egyptian relations 27–8, 48–51
  cultural relations 41
  economic relations 31–41, 48–9
  Going East strategy 43–8
  history 28–30
  investment 35
  military relations 42–3
  political relations 30–1
  trading 34–6
Sino-Moroccan relations 167–8, 189–90
  banking relations 184–5
  car manufacturers 176–7
  Covid-19 188–9
  fertilizer and agricultural development 177–80

  history 168–71
  infrastructure 175–6
  MINURSO 172–4
  strategic partnership 185–8
Sino-Soviet 67, 169
Al-Sissi, Abdel-Fattah 12, 204
Siyala, Mohammed 80
Special Economic Zone (SEZ) 37
Stephens, Christopher 77
Strategic Cooperation Agreement 30, 35
strategic partnerships (SPs) 3, 4, 185–8
Strüver, George 3
Suez Canal Economic Zone 10, 38
Suez Canal Project 33

Taiwan 31, 66, 67, 69, 72, 95, 98, 127, 133, 134
Tajani, Antonio 149–50
Tang Jiaxuan 97
Tebboune, Abdelmadjid 143, 148
Tech City 9, 10
Al-Thinni, Abdullah 6
Tianjin Economic-Technological Development Area (TEDA) 37–8
Tourism 5, 7, 11, 17–19, 35, 39–40, 49, 94, 101–2, 104, 106–7, 117, 151, 174, 188, 190
Trading 8–9, 34–6
Trans-Saharan highway project 138–9
Transtech Engineering Corporation (TEC) 170–1
Trump, Donald 14, 45, 111, 172, 203
Tunisia and China 17, 93–4, 99–100, 117–18
  Arab Spring 94–9
  BRI 107–8
  COVID-19 pandemic 110–11
  diplomatic relations 101–2
  economic relations 104–7
  education and exchanges 102–3
  Europe 116–17
  infrastructure investment 109–10
  United States 113–15
Turkey 82–4, 87

UN Human Rights Council (UNHCR) 48
United Arab Emirates (UAE) 2, 14, 45, 82, 86, 87, 151

United Nations Framework Convention on Climate Change (UNFCCC) 177
United Nations Mission for the Referendum in the Western Sahara (MINURSO) 172–4
United Nations Security Council (UNSC) 74–8, 81, 82, 128
United States 1, 14, 16, 18, 19, 45, 67, 93, 101, 108, 109, 112–16, 203, 204
and Morocco 172–4
UN Security Council 46, 85, 108, 127, 132, 133
USSR 67, 126, 127

Weapons of Mass Destruction (WMD) program 67
Wehry, Frederic 6, 12–13
WiMAX network 71

Win-win strategy 127–8, 149, 150, 185
World Tourism Cities Federation (WTCF) 183

Xiannian, Li 29–30
Xiaoping, Deng 2, 29, 127
Xichang Satellite Launch Center (XSLC) 144

Yi, Wang 85, 101, 134
Youssoufi, Abderrahmane 170

Zemin, Jiang 97, 170
Zeng, Aiping 5, 7
Zhongyang, Peng 187
Ziyang, Zhao 170
Zongze, Ruan 5, 7, 8

www.ingramcontent.com/pod-product-compliance
Lightning Source LLC
Chambersburg PA
CBHW062130300426
44115CB00012BA/1874